Nelson Thornes Shakespeare

Antony and Cleopatra

Volume editor: **Tony Farrell**

Series editors: **Duncan Beal and Dinah Jurksaitis**

Series consultant: **Peter Thomas**

Published in 2004 by:
Nelson Thornes Ltd
Delta Place
27 Bath Road
CHELTENHAM
GL53 7TH
United Kingdom

04 05 06 07 08 / 10 9 8 7 6 5 4 3 2 1

A catalogue record for this book is available from the British Library

ISBN 0-7487-8602-3

Illustration by Peters and Zabransky

Page make-up by Tech-Set

Printed and bound in Spain by GraphyCems

Acknowledgements

Mary Evans Picture Library, pp. 2, 10, 46, 86, 90, 118, 148, 204; Mary Evans Picture Library/Douglas Dickins, p. 9; Mary Evans Picture Library/Thomas Gilmore Collection, p. 36; Mary Evans Picture Library/Edwin Wallace, p. 60

Contents

Preface

The very name *Shakespeare* can overwhelm: so many associations with culture and history. We hope you will approach the plays with curiosity and a willingness to embrace the strangeness of Shakespeare's world: those quaint ways, weapons and words!

Our aim in the **Nelson Thornes Shakespeare** series is to provide a bridge between Shakespeare's world and our own. For all the differences between the two worlds it is intriguing to find so many similarities: parents and children; power games; loyalty and treachery; prejudice; love and hate; fantasy and reality; comedy and horror; the extremes of human behaviour. It is oddly moving to find that the concerns of the human race have not changed so much over the centuries, and that Shakespeare's themes are modern and recognisable.

The unfamiliarity of the language is best regarded not as a barrier, but as a source of interest. On the left-hand pages we have not only explained unfamiliar words, but have also drawn attention to aspects of wordplay, imagery and verse. The left-hand pages also have reminders that this is a piece of theatre, written to be performed and experienced visually. The **performance feature** boxes invite you to consider such questions as: *How might this character react? What actions might be appropriate here? Try reading/acting this section in this way...* You are not fed one interpretation; you make the decisions.

To help you place individual scenes in the context of the whole play there is a **comparison feature** at the end of each scene: *Where else have we seen characters behaving like this? How do events in this scene parallel events two scenes back?* A brief **scene summary** brings together the main developments within that scene.

At the beginning of the play there are some **introductory essays** on background topics. They highlight aspects of Shakespeare's world which show a different outlook to our own: *How did they conduct courtship in his day? How has the status of the monarchy changed? What about their view of magic and the supernatural?*

A separate **Teacher Resource Book** contains material which will help deepen your understanding of the play. There are **worksheets** on individual scenes – valuable if you have missed any of the class study. They will also provide a good background which will help you demonstrate your knowledge in coursework essays. To this end, the book also contains some **Coursework Assignment essay titles** and hints on how to tackle them. The play and resource book together provide enough support to allow you to study independently, and to select the assignment you want to do, rather than all working together as a class.

Our aim is that you finish the play enthused and intrigued, and eager to explore more of Shakespeare's works. We hope you will begin to see that, although ideally the plays are experienced in performance, there is also a place for reading together and discussing as a class, or for simply reading them privately to yourself.

Foreword

Who bothers to read introductions, especially introductions to plays by Shakespeare?

Well, you do, obviously, and that's a good start if you want to get more from your literature study. Reading this Foreword will help you to get more from Shakespeare's writing and from the accompanying material provided with the play.

Shakespeare – the great adapter

Shakespeare is regarded as a great writer, but not because he was an original inventor of stories. His plays are nearly all adaptations of stories he found in books, or in history – or in somebody else's play. His originality came from the way he used this material. He changed his sources to suit himself and his audiences and was never afraid to change the facts if they didn't suit him.

The best way of understanding what Shakespeare thought valuable in a story is to look at the way he altered what he found.

The **Introductory essays** show how he changed characters or time-scales to enhance the dramatic effect or to suit a small cast of actors.

Shakespeare – the great realist

What Shakespeare added to his source material was his insight into people and society. He understood what makes people tick and what makes society hold together or fall apart. He showed how people behave – and why – by showing their motives and their reactions to experiences such as love, loss, dreams, fears, threats and doubts. These have not changed, even if we think science and technology make us different from people in Shakespeare's day. He was also realistic. He avoided stereotypes, preferring to show people as a complex mixture of changing emotions.

When you use the character sheets provided by your teacher, you will see this realism in action. His characters behave differently in different circumstances, and they change over time – just as we do in real life.

Shakespeare – the language magician

Shakespeare's cleverness with language is not just his ability to write beautiful poetry. He also wrote amusing dialogue, common slang, rude insults and the thoughts of people under pressure. He wrote script that uses the sounds of words to convey emotion, and the associations of words to create vivid images in our heads.

When you use the glossary notes you will see how his language expresses ugliness, hatred, suspicion, doubt and fear as well as happiness, beauty and joy.

Shakespeare – the theatrical innovator

Theatre before Shakespeare was different from today. Ordinary people enjoyed songs and simple shows, and educated people – the minority – enjoyed stories from Latin and Greek. Moral and religious drama taught right and wrong and there were spectacular masques full of music and dance for the audience to join in. Shakespeare put many of these elements together, so most people could expect something to appeal to them. He was a comprehensive writer for a comprehensive audience, writing to please the educated and the uneducated. He was the first to put realistic people from every walk of life on stage – not just kings and generals, but characters who talked and behaved like the ordinary folk in the audience. He was less interested in right and wrong than in the comedy or tragedy of what people actually do. *Only Fools and Horses* and *EastEnders* are dramas which follow a trend started by Shakespeare over four hundred years ago. He managed this in theatres which lacked lighting, sound amplification, scene changes, curtains or a large cast of actors.

The performance features accompanying the play text will help to show you how Shakespeare's stagecraft is used to best dramatic effect.

Whether you are studying for GCSE or AS, the examination is designed to test your ability to respond to the following:

1 Shakespeare's ideas and themes
2 Shakespeare's use of language
3 Shakespeare's skill in writing for stage performance
4 The social, cultural and historical aspects of his plays
5 Different interpretations of the plays.

1a. Showing personalities (ideas and themes)

Shakespeare thought drama should do more than preach simple moral lessons. He thought it should show life as it was, daft and serious, joyful and painful. He didn't believe in simple versions of good and evil, heroes and villains. He thought most heroes had unpleasant parts to their nature, just as most villains had good parts. This is why he showed people as a mixture. In *Hamlet*, he wrote that the dramatist should **hold a mirror up to nature**, so that all of us can see ourselves reflected. As he picks on the parts of human behaviour that don't change (fear, jealousy, doubt, self-pity), his characters remind us of people we know today – and of ourselves – not just people who lived a long time ago. This is because Shakespeare shows us more than his characters' status in life. He knew that beneath the robes or the crown there is a heart the same as any tradesman's or poor person's. He knew that nobody in real life is perfect – so he didn't put perfect characters on his stage.

In *Antony and Cleopatra* Shakespeare shows how the private person under the famous public face was just like anybody else in showing moods, doubts, doing the wrong thing and misjudging others. Where love, honour, pride or ambition are concerned, people are not always good at doing what's best, even if they are generals, queens or rulers of empires. Shakespeare's understanding is that human beings, whatever their wealth, rank or status, are all flawed: **The gods do give us faults – 'tis that that makes us human**.

1b. Showing what society was/is like (ideas and themes)

In *Hamlet*, Shakespeare declared that drama should show the **form and pressure of the age**, meaning the structure of the times we live in and the pressures and influences it creates.

Elizabethan England had known great conflict and turmoil through civil unrest and was also always under threat from other countries (Shakespeare was 20 at the time of the Spanish Armada). It was also a nation changing from the old ways of country living. London and other cities were growing, and voyagers were exploring other lands. New trades were developing, and plague and disease spread quickly in crowded parts of the cities. Most people were superstitious, but science was beginning to make its mark. People still generally believed in the Divine Right of Kings, but they were beginning to think that bad kings may be removed for the country's good. One such example was Charles I who was executed only 33 years after Shakespeare's death.

In *Antony and Cleopatra* individuals are shown trying to do what they want, but being forced into other choices by social pressures – by duty and responsibility in Antony's case. Also, even in a society with different social classes, it's not just the powerful who have the best understanding of things. Both Antony and Cleopatra receive good advice from their social inferiors, but think they can ignore it because they are socially superior. Notice the way Cleopatra ignores the advice of Charmian, and Antony ignores the advice of Enobarbus, Canidius and a soldier not to fight at sea. The insights into politics (manoeuvres on Pompey's barge and the excellent scene in which Sossius is recalled) are examples of how it is possible to be too successful a subordinate for your own good.

2. Shakespeare's use of the English language (sound and image)

Shakespeare wrote the speech of uneducated servants and traders but he could also write great speeches using rhetoric. Whether it is a dim-witted inn-servant called Francis in *Henry IV Part One*, or a subtle political operator like Mark Antony in *Julius Caesar*, Shakespeare finds words to make them sound and seem convincing.

Metaphors conveying key elements of the play's themes are abundant in *Antony and Cleopatra*. Appetite and relish are suggested when Cleopatra is described as a **morsel for a monarch** when she was young, in her **salad days**. Heroic excellence is conveyed in an image of rising above the environment:

> **his delights**
> **Were dolphin-like; they show'd his back above**
> **The element they lived in**.

The play is also rich in metaphors expressive of tragic change and decay, as when Cleopatra laments the fate of those who lose their youthful charms:

> Against the blown rose may they stop their nose
> That kneel'd unto the buds.

3a. Writing for a mixed audience (writing for stage performance)

As a popular dramatist who made his money by appealing to the widest range of people, Shakespeare knew that some of his audience would be literate, and some not. So he made sure that there was something for everybody – something clever and something vulgar, something comic and something tragic.

There is plenty in *Antony and Cleopatra* to please those who want to see great historical events enacted, or who appreciate insights into the workings of conscience, duty, loyalty and love. It also has battle scenes, comic scenes involving risqué jokes about where you would like to have an extra inch in a husband, and knockabout comedy of messenger abuse. It has insight into the way world-shaking events are influenced by great political and military leaders. There are some comic moments in which Shakespeare shows a playful side to these great historical figures: for example, Cleopatra getting a slave to dive under water to put a dried salt cod onto the sleeping Antony's fishing line so that he thinks he has caught something. There is a mixture of tragedy and comedy at the end when the Clown brings in a comic practicality to remind us that when the great depart, life goes on.

3b. Shakespeare's craft (writing for stage performance)

Shakespeare worked with very basic stage technology but, as a former actor, he knew how to give his actors the guidance they needed. His scripts use embedded prompts, either to actors, or to the audience, so that he did not have to write stage directions for his actors. If an actor says, **Put your cap to its proper purpose**, it is a cue to another actor to be using his hat for fancy gestures, rather than wearing it on his head. If an actor comes on stage and says, **So this is the forest of Arden**, we know where the scene is set, without expensive props and scenery.

4. Social, cultural and historical aspects

There are two ways of approaching this. One way is to look at what the plays reveal for us about life in Shakespeare's time – and how it is different from today. The other is to look at what the plays reveal for us about life in Shakespeare's time – and how it is the same today.

In *Antony and Cleopatra* Shakespeare gives us an insight into two kinds of culture – the efficient, militaristic society of Rome whose river (the Tiber) provided access to trade and sea power, and the more relaxed and self-indulgent Egypt, whose river (the Nile) provided fertile agricultural land. Both societies have their own cultures and values: **a Roman thought hath struck him** suggests duty and seriousness, compared with **in the East my pleasure lies**.

Peter Thomas

Introductory essays

1 The staging of *Antony and Cleopatra*

The opening of Shakespeare's Globe Theatre in 1996 close to the site of the original Globe gave modern audiences a chance to experience what it might have been like to see a play performed on an Elizabethan/Jacobean stage. The reconstruction of the new Globe was based on designs of existing buildings of the period and practical advice from actors about working on such a stage. The outcome of all this is a stage similar to the one Shakespeare wrote for.

Shakespeare's stage

The stage used by Shakespeare and his contemporaries was a bare space about 15 metres wide by 10 metres deep that thrust out into the audience's standing area. Hence this style of stage is sometimes called the 'thrust stage'. The stage was built up about a metre above the floor of the theatre and the audience would stand close to the actors at the side and in front. The closeness created intimacy and the raised platform had several advantages. It allowed the audience both at the back and in the lower seats to see the action; secondly it had built into it a trapdoor, accessed from the back of the stage, that was used for the entrances of ghosts or spirits, such as Hamlet's father's ghost in Act 1 of *Hamlet*. The space below could also allow musicians to play beneath the stage, as they do in Act 4 Scene 3 of *Antony and Cleopatra*, where the stage direction reads **Music of the hautboys is under the stage**. The intention of having the musicians playing oboes beneath the stage is to create an eerie, mysterious and supernatural atmosphere, in the same way that modern films use music to create an appropriate mood in the audience. The sound of the oboe was associated in the audience's mind with bad omens. In Act 4 Scene 1 of *Macbeth* Shakespeare used hautboys to create an unworldly atmosphere when the witches' cauldron 'disappears' via the trapdoor in front of Macbeth's eyes.

There was no space above the stage that would accommodate scenery being lowered or raised. At the back of the stage was a wall with at least two side entrances. This allowed one group of actors to leave as another entered, or for two groups to enter from different sides, such as in Act 3 Scene 2: **Enter Agrippa at one door, Enobarbus at another**. There may also have been a central door for grand entrances such as Antony and Cleopatra's in the play's first scene.

Behind the stage wall was the backstage area known as the 'tiring house' where the actors changed and stage furniture and props were kept ready. Above the tiring house and in view of the audience there would have been an upper gallery area or balcony. This would have been used most memorably for Juliet's famous query about Romeo and, in *The Merchant of Venice*, for Shylock's daughter Jessica to throw down her father's gold and jewels to the waiting Christians below. In Act 4 Scene 15 of *Antony and Cleopatra* the area might have been used as part of the operation of raising the dying Antony into Cleopatra's arms. There has been much conjecture about how this effect was achieved, but there is no clear evidence to point out conclusively how the stage direction **They heave Antony aloft to Cleopatra** was carried out.

Setting a scene

For Shakespeare's audience the stage was a fluid place with action moving swiftly from one 'setting' to another. When characters entered it was a new scene, and when the stage was cleared it was the end of a scene. There might be a pause of only a few seconds between a character walking into a new scene after the stage had been emptied from the previous scene, but the audience would accept that this new scene was a different time or place. In Shakespeare's plays there was no artificial division between scenes; it was later editors who added the scene divisions that modern texts use.

For some scenes items of stage furniture might be brought on to indicate 'place', such as a throne or a bed. But because the stage was a fast-changing, non-specific place, there was very little stage furniture. The setting of Shakespeare's stage was created by what the characters brought to that stage in terms of their lines, their garments and the occasional prop, such as a sword or food and drink. This kind of information told the audience where in their own imagination they had to set the scene. Often props would be brought on to indicate time and place, such as actors with lanterns to indicate a scene at night. In the open-air theatres, such as the Globe, Rose and Swan, plays were performed in the afternoon, with only natural light. It was only in some indoor venues, such as the halls of great houses, Inns of Temple or guilds, that candles were used for the first 'footlights'.

The Globe theatre (right), as shown in a contemporary drawing.

Because of the limited visual clues to help the audience identify a setting, the characters had to give further indications of time and place, if these were important, in their lines. In *The Merchant of Venice*, for example, the character Gratiano begins Act 2 Scene 6, **This is the penthouse**. If Shakespeare wanted the audience to know that there was a storm, such as at the start of *The Tempest*, he would tell the audience in the words and actions of the characters. At the start of Act 3 of *King Lear* the actors speak frequently of the foul weather that is **blowing the earth into the sea**, indicating the violent storm raging on the heath.

Similarly at the start of *Macbeth* the witches and Macbeth both make references to the foul weather. At the start of Act 2 Scene 4 of *As You Like It* Rosalind announces, **Well, this is the forest of Arden**. This is after actors dressed **like foresters** have already come on to the stage.

Some of Shakespeare's plays were performed indoors. There are contemporary records of plays being requested by the rich and powerful, including the monarchs of the time, and of being played in large halls. In 1602 the first performance of *Twelfth Night* took place at the Middle Temple Hall. At these performances the shape of the halls allowed the audience to sit on three sides of the acting area. One of the shorter ends of the hall would serve as the tiring house, with doors for exits and entrances. There was often a minstrel's gallery that could be used not only for the musicians but also for the balcony area.

The technical resources of an Elizabethan/Jacobean stage were limited. Alexandria and Rome would have looked very similar, for example, as would internal or external scenes. For all its apparent disadvantages, however, the bareness of the stage allowed Shakespeare to make it anywhere he wished: he could switch from a battlefield to Cleopatra's court in seconds. And Shakespeare created variety and interest by the language and movement of his plots. But this concept of the bare stage was not to last.

Changes in theatrical style after Shakespeare

Over the centuries Shakespeare's concept of a stage that allowed quick changes in time and place was overtaken by productions that concentrated more on the separation of the scenes into the realism of different times and places. In 1759 the first revival of the play reduced its original quick-changing locations of forty-two scenes down to twenty-seven with more fixed locations. Much of the bawdy language was cut too. The play became a simple love story, rather than a mix of love and politics.

Nineteenth-century productions of the play became obsessed with representing each scene as naturalistically as possible. Sticking faithfully to the original forty-two scenes would have caused them huge problems in this respect. Productions involved building massive complicated sets that had to be moved into place for each different setting. Sometimes the actors' words were drowned out by the sound of the heavy scenery being prepared back stage for the next scene. As with David Garrick's production in 1759, the solution to the problem of needing quick set changes brought about by a succession of short scenes was to amalgamate several scenes or cut them out altogether. The emphasis was on creating 'place' not through the actors' words and movement, but by realistic stage scenery. One famous nineteenth-century production staged a full-scale sea battle with galleys and a large cast. The play suffered in these extravagant productions, obsessed with realistic scene settings, which were little more than spectacles to amaze the audience. *Antony and Cleopatra*, even with several scenes cut, became an 'Oriental pantomime' lasting over four hours, according to one critic, who complained about the time needed to switch elaborate sets and provide lavish spectacle in every scene.

Film, the new art form of the early twentieth century, was better than the theatre at providing epic productions of plays such as *Antony and Cleopatra*. Using sophisticated indoor and outdoor 'sets', along with the famous Hollywood banner of a 'cast of thousands', film could achieve the realistic settings of palaces, solemn temples and pageants, such stuff that theatre productions could only dream of. The nineteenth-century productions lost sight of the truth about drama – that although the play deals with big themes and big ideas covering time and space, it is on the small stage using the actors' words and actions that these big ideas and themes are best presented.

During the twentieth century some theatre directors began to move back to Shakespeare's concept of the non-illusional bare 'scaffold', a stage that asks the audience to use their imagination and that does not rely on spectacle. At the start of Act 2 of *As You Like It*, for example, the Duke reflects that in **these woods** he finds **tongues in trees, books in the running brooks/sermons in stones, and good in everything**. In the opening of *Henry V* Shakespeare urges his contemporary audience in the Globe: **On your imaginary forces work** and **Think when we talk of horses that you see them**. Directors are now urging modern audiences to do the same: use the imagination, listen to the words and watch the actors.

Critics, however, still find fault with the attempts of some modern productions to stage *Antony and Cleopatra*. One review of the RSC's 2002 production complained about the director's cutting of scenes in order to impose order on the play. Michael Billington felt that losing Scene 7 of Act 2 aboard Pompey's galley **sacrifices a vital political cynicism** and chopping Cleopatra's treasurer Seleucus in Act 5 **loses the queen's element of contradictory calculation**.

But you have to make your own mind up about how Shakespeare intended *Antony and Cleopatra* to be enjoyed and understood. The best way for you to do that is to go and see it performed, preferably a performance in a venue like the new Globe, and then judge for yourself. When you do, remember the question Shakespeare asked his audience at the start of *Henry V*: **Can this cockpit hold/The vasty fields of France**? Ask yourself a similar question: Can you use your imagination, and let your eyes look on that cockpit of a stage and see the ancient worlds of Rome and Egypt inhabited by those two legendary lovers, Cleopatra and Antony?

2 A timeline of key events in the history of *Antony and Cleopatra*

At around three hours, *Antony and Cleopatra* is one of Shakespeare's longest plays. Its forty-two scenes cover ten years of historical action from 40 to 30 BC. The play's varied settings are spread across Western Europe, from Italy to Egypt and Greece.

- Act 1 is set mainly in Alexandria, with one scene in Rome.
- Act 2 deals with Roman matters, with one scene in Egypt.
- Act 3 switches between at least six settings, including Rome, Athens and Alexandria.

- Act 4's fifteen scenes switch from battles to palaces.
- Act 5 has only two scenes, one in Caesar's camp outside Alexandria, the final one inside Cleopatra's palace.

Several key historical events that predate *Antony and Cleopatra* are material for Shakespeare's play *Julius Caesar*:

48 BC: Julius Caesar defeats Pompey the Great at the Battle of Pharsalus. Cleopatra begins her relationship with Julius Caesar.

47 BC: Birth of their child Caesarion.

c.46 BC: Cleopatra takes their son with her to visit Caesar in Rome.

44 BC: Julius Caesar adopts Octavius as Caesar Octavius, his son and heir. Caesar is assassinated. Antony and Lepidus become heads of the Roman state.

43 BC: Caesar Octavius joins with Antony and Lepidus: these are the Triumvirs who rule the Roman state.

42 BC: Brutus and Cassius, who assassinated Julius Caesar, are killed at Philippi by Antony and Caesar Octavius. The Triumvirs divide the Empire between them: Antony is to rule the Eastern section.

41 BC: Antony meets Cleopatra at Tarsus on the river Cydnus. Civil war in Rome: Antony's wife and brother, Fulvia and Lucius, fight against Caesar Octavius.

Antony and Cleopatra opens in 40 BC with the death of Fulvia, Antony's wife, in Greece where she had fled after the campaign against Caesar Octavius. These are the key historical events that form the background to the play:

40 BC: Cleopatra gives birth to twins by Antony. Antony leaves her for four years as he returns home to sort out problems in Rome. A peace treaty between Antony and Caesar Octavius is sealed by his marriage to Octavia, half-sister of Caesar Octavius. The Triumvirs re-divide the Empire: Antony still controls the East.

39 BC: The Triumvirs meet with Sextus Pompey (son of Pompey the Great) and, as part of a peace treaty, give him control of a small part of the Empire. Antony lives in Athens with his wife Octavia. (They have two daughters, both named Antonia.)

38 BC: Ceasar Octavius loses half his fleet in a battle with Pompey. Antony leaves off fighting the Parthians in the East to support Caesar Octavius. A misunderstanding almost brings a war between the two, but Octavia pacifies the situation. Antony returns East to Cleopatra.

37 BC: Caesar Octavius, and his great general Agrippa, defeat Pompey's army. Pompey escapes East, but on Antony's orders is killed. Octavia goes to Athens to meet Antony, but Antony cancels his visit and Octavia returns to Rome. Antony acknowledges paternity of the twins Cleopatra gave birth to and names them after the Sun and the Moon, Alexander Helios (Sun) and Cleopatra Selene (Moon).

36 BC: Lepidus tries to take Sicily from Caesar Octavius, but is defeated and banished from power. The Roman Empire is now split between Antony

5

in the East and Caesar Octavius in the West. Antony renews his campaign against the Parthians, which lasts for two years. Antony marries Cleopatra and she gives birth to another son, Ptolemy Philadelphus.

34 BC: Antony makes the Donations of Alexandria: he enthrones Cleopatra as Queen of Kings and Caesarion as King of Kings and distributes the kingdoms of the Middle East among their own children.

33 BC: News of Antony's Donations of Alexandria reaches Rome. Fruitless diplomatic discussions take place and preparation for war begins.

32 BC: Antony divorces Octavia. Caesar Octavius discovers that Antony has acknowledged the birthright of Caesarion in his will (thereby making him a threat to Caesar Octavius), where he also expresses his wish to be buried by Cleopatra's side. Caesar Octavius spreads the rumour that Antony wants to relocate the capital of the Empire to Alexandria. The West of the Empire supports Caesar Octavius.

31 BC: Antony and Cleopatra advance to Greece as part of their preparations for war. Caesar Octavius declares war on Cleopatra but, for political reasons, not on Antony. Caesar Octavius defeats Antony and Cleopatra at Actium and they retreat to Egypt.

30 BC: After the battle of Alexandria, when Antony's forces refuse to fight against the Romans, Antony commits suicide, believing Cleopatra has died. Nine days later on 10 August, Cleopatra, the last pharaoh, takes her own life. Caesar Octavius has Caesarion murdered, but lets Cleopatra's other children live, to be brought up by Octavia. On 30 August, Caesar Octavius proclaims himself Pharaoh of Egypt and becomes sole ruler of the Roman Empire.

29 BC: Caesar Octavius finally subdues the East and celebrates with a triumphant procession through Rome.

27 BC: Caesar Octavius renames himself Caesar Augustus.

Map showing important locations in the play.

3 Who was the real Cleopatra?

The story of Cleopatra and her lover Antony was famous even in Roman times, and although she died over two thousand years ago, her life and death still have a fascination for us. Why is it that of the two famous lovers it is Cleopatra who attracts by far the more interest? Is it simply because she is thought to be one of the most seductive women in history? An enigmatic figure, she lived her life and death in such a way that she continues to arouse our curiosity.

The myth and the facts

It is not easy to extract the real Cleopatra from Roman and later myths. The myth of Cleopatra, begun already by 40 BC, centres around the themes of sexual passion, desire, forbidden love, moral transgression and female emancipation. The Roman myth makers saw her as a dangerous figure: she was a woman who had power and influence, who knew what to do and how to do it in order to achieve her goals. She was a clear threat to the male-dominated belief system on which Rome was built. Instead of being accepted as a powerful female monarch who could contest the Roman world as an equal to men, her image was turned into that of a scheming immoral woman who used her feminine wiles and devouring sexual appetite to undermine the men of power with whom she had relationships.

For such a famous historical figure we know relatively few hard facts about her, and many of these come from the historian Plutarch, who was writing over 150 years later. We know less about Cleopatra than we do about pharaohs who lived a thousand years before her. And although Egypt is full of monuments to death – sphinxes, pyramids and great tombs – nobody knows the place of her burial.

By reputation Cleopatra was intelligent, speaking ten languages, including her native Egyptian, which previous rulers had not bothered to learn. Gifted in mathematics, philosophy and astronomy, she was also politically shrewd. Yet, amazingly for a woman with such a reputation for attracting powerful men, very little evidence survives of her physical appearance or facial features, apart from a handful of coins and some sculptures of doubtful provenance. It is significant that on the reverse of the Roman-issued coins depicting Cleopatra with the image of Antony she appears more Roman in appearance than on the coins with her head that were issued in Egypt. Manipulating one's public image was important even two thousand years ago.

Reputedly Cleopatra was not a great beauty, but took great care of her appearance and practised her seductive arts, making herself intensely attractive to men. Plutarch wrote that her actual beauty was not so remarkable but it was **the charm of her presence that was irresistible**. One question that has fascinated historians is whether Cleopatra was black. Her ancestry was Macedonian, but there is no clear evidence of the ancestry of her mother or paternal grandmother. Critics argue that if Cleopatra were black surely Roman historians would have seized on this as another means of inflicting damage on her reputation. But there are no surviving contemporary written descriptions of her, and without images or written descriptions she remains, enigmatically, a queen without a face.

Antony and Cleopatra

Early years

The Cleopatra of the play was only one of many Egyptian queens so named. She was Cleopatra VII, born in Alexandria, Egypt's capital, in 69 BC. But even the year of her birth depends on trusting Plutarch's assertion that she was thirty-nine when she died. Her family, the Ptolemies, had ruled Egypt for over 250 years with increasing terror and ruthlessness. Her father, the weak, cruel and unpopular ruler Ptolemy XII, was probably married to his own sister, Cleopatra V. During the time of the Ptolemies incestuous marriages were common and had political advantages, such as keeping power in the family. It was also advantageous to women of the Ptolemy dynasty who wanted a share of political power. Cleopatra had an elder sister, Cleopatra VI, who died of unknown causes around 56 BC.

In 58 BC the people of Alexandria rebelled and overthrew Ptolemy XII. He fled to Rome and his eldest daughter, Berenice, took the throne. In 55 BC he reclaimed his throne with the help of the Roman general Pompey. Berenice, Cleopatra's sister, was beheaded, leaving Cleopatra VII the pharaoh's oldest child. When her father died in 51 BC, leaving his children in Pompey's care, Cleopatra and her brother Ptolemy XIII inherited the throne.

So Cleopatra, at about eighteen years of age, began her rule of Egypt. She married her brother Ptolemy XIII, aged about twelve, but it was a marriage of convenience only, and Ptolemy XIII was pharaoh in name only. For three years he remained in the background while Cleopatra ruled alone. She ruled well and identified herself closely with the ordinary people of Egypt, giving them protection and easing their tax burdens. She also built up the wealth of the temples. She saw herself intimately bound up in the country of Egypt and its future. After three years Ptolemy's advisors, led by Pothinus, a eunuch, conspired against her. They resented Cleopatra's independence and overthrew her, leaving Ptolemy the sole ruler of Egypt. Cleopatra fled to Syria with her younger sister, Arsinoe.

In 48 BC, determined to regain her throne, Cleopatra amassed an army on Egypt's border. Pompey at that time was fighting against Julius Caesar for control of the Roman Empire. Pursued by Caesar after losing a battle, Pompey sailed to Alexandria to seek Ptolemy's protection. Ptolemy's advisors thought it would be safer to side with Caesar, and had Pompey murdered.

Cleopatra and Julius Caesar

Before Caesar reached Alexandria Ptolemy's supporters brought him the gift of Pompey's head. But Caesar was horrified by this brutal murder of his one-time friend. He seized control of the city and ordered both Ptolemy and Cleopatra to dismiss their armies and meet with him. Cleopatra knew that if she entered Alexandria openly, Ptolemy would have her killed. So she arranged to be smuggled to Caesar inside a rug. Caesar, thirty years older than Cleopatra, was captivated by her and they became lovers. Ptolemy was furious when he found out and Caesar had him arrested. Ptolemy's army besieged the palace. Eventually, after almost six months of fighting, Caesar's forces were victorious and he restored Cleopatra to the throne. Her sister, Arsinoe, was taken to Rome in chains and the body of her brother was found floating in the Nile.

8

By 47 BC Cleopatra was ruling Egypt alongside her remaining brother, the eleven-year-old Ptolemy XIV. She gave birth to a son named Caesarion and around 46 BC went to Rome with him. Caesar celebrated his relationship with Cleopatra by erecting a statue of her covered in gold in the Temple of Venus Genetrix, goddess of motherhood, love and life. Roman myth makers chose to ignore the motherly aspect of Cleopatra's symbolic association with Venus, and instead focused entirely on the sexual aspect. Remarkably the gold statue of Cleopatra stood for over three hundred years.

One aspect of Egyptian life that scandalised Rome was the freedom that Egyptian women had in choosing their husbands. In Rome, women were much more severely restricted and their freedoms limited, as exemplified in the character of Octavia, Caesar Octavius' sister in *Antony and Cleopatra*. Was the fear of Cleopatra becoming Empress of Rome, ruling alongside Julius Caesar, one of the reasons that led to his assassination? After Caesar's murder in 44 BC she returned to Egypt and her younger brother mysteriously disappeared. Did Cleopatra remove him as a threat? In the turbulent history of the Ptolemies mothers had killed sons, uncles had raped nieces, sisters had been beheaded or sent into slavery. Ptolemy XIV's death would have been a routine act in a long history of Ptolemaic political ruthlessness. Cleopatra saw herself as a power player on the world stage.

One representation of Cleopatra on the wall of the temple of Hathor shows her standing behind her son, Caesarion.

Cleopatra and Antony

In 41 BC the famous first meeting between Antony and Cleopatra took place at Tarsus. Antony ruled the Eastern third of the Roman world, Caesar Octavius and Lepidus the others. Plutarch describes how, in order to meet Antony, Cleopatra arrived on a barge, lavishly decorated with purple sails, silver oars and a gilded stern. She intended to impress Antony because she saw how he could benefit her. Antony undoubtedly had similar intentions.

Their liaison strengthened Cleopatra's position on the throne, but the alliance quickly moved beyond politics and was strengthened by the birth of their twins. Her relationship with Antony fuelled the Roman myth that she was a scheming oriental courtesan intent on seducing noble Romans for her own sexual pleasure and political gain. To elaborate the myth, stories were also told about excesses in eating and drinking. Antony's political ambitions were to seize power in Rome after the predicted civil war. With Cleopatra's wealth he could pay his legions better than those in Rome could.

Antony showered Cleopatra with gifts including Cyprus, parts of Syria and Jericho. Cleopatra's influence over Antony can be gauged by what Plutarch wrote about her:

> **Were Antony serious or disposed to mirth, she had at any**
> **moment some new delight or charm to meet his wishes: at every**
> **turn she was upon him, and let him escape her neither by day nor**
> **by night. She played at dice with him, drank with him, hunted**
> **with him: and when he exercised in arms, she was there to see.**

In Rome, Caesar Octavius tried to exploit Cleopatra's influence over Antony. He portrayed Antony as becoming effeminate and weak and accused him of all sorts of immorality, debauchery and drunkenness with Cleopatra. Called 'Meretrix Regina', the 'Whore Queen', she became a symbol of the Oriental excess that threatened, by her relationship with Antony, to unman the very centre of Roman political and military authority. Antony replied to Caesar Octavius in a public letter of 33 BC, accusing him of being a hypocrite and, in unambiguous words, of enjoying sex with women other than his wife!

Though Antony and Cleopatra were close, they were not inseparable, and Cleopatra lived without him for years at a time, ruling Egypt alone. Under her Egypt had grown rich and she used her country's wealth to build up a fleet of war galleys to support their joint ambitions.

Cleopatra's suicide has fascinated artists down the centuries. In this nineteenth-century painting she is depicted dying on a couch or daybed.

Caesar Octavius quickly moved to challenge the growing threat of Antony and Cleopatra. Finally in 31 BC Cleopatra's fleet met Caesar's. During the long hot summer her fleet of war galleys was blockaded in a bay on the west coast of Greece by Roman ships. The only escape route was through the narrow straits of Actium. It is difficult to know what happened during the decisive battle, but it appears that Cleopatra's fleet tried to break out through a gap in Caesar Octavius' line of ships. Antony changed to a lighter, more manoeuvrable ship and followed her. Shakespeare's version of events supports the myth that Cleopatra was a weak woman deserting the battle, but it seems that her attempted break-out in numbers was a planned strategy. The evidence for this is that Cleopatra's war galleys had set out with sails, which were normally carried only on long journeys. (Usually battles were fought under the power of oars rather than sail.) However, her attempt to break her fleet out of the blockade and sail home was unsuccessful, and though she and Antony escaped their forces were defeated.

Final days

On their return to Egypt, Cleopatra went to Alexandria while Antony, hearing his troops had deserted to Caesar Octavius, tried to commit suicide. He was stopped by friends who took him to Cleopatra. Although Antony was distraught at the defeat and the desertion of his soldiers, Cleopatra was much more optimistic; she thought that the defeat was only a minor setback and that ultimate victory over Caesar Octavius was still possible. Caesar Octavius, however, pressing home his military advantage, invaded Egypt and advanced on the capital Alexandria, where Cleopatra and Antony awaited them. Plutarch gives an account that at midnight on the night before the battle marvellous strange music was heard as though revellers were leaving the city. Those listening thought it meant that the gods were deserting Antony. Shakespeare uses this incident in Act 4 Scene 3.

As Alexandria fell to the Romans, Antony killed himself. Cleopatra feared her fate was to be that of her sister Arsinoe, remembering how Arsinoe was humiliated, an exotic princess dragged in chains through the streets of Rome. She also had presumably witnessed Roman triumphs during her stay in Rome with Julius Caesar and would have known that the most distinguished and dangerous of Rome's captured enemies never reached the end of the victory procession – they were put to death in the Forum.

Shakespeare describes Cleopatra's fears vividly in the play's final scene. Whatever her motives for suicide, it seems that Cleopatra did not trust Caesar Octavius' intentions for her. On 10 August 30 BC, nine days after Antony's death, Cleopatra took her life. In the same way that Antony's death was a 'Roman death', as he fell on his own sword, so Cleopatra's death was an 'Egyptian death', as she, the last in a long line of pharaohs to rule Egypt, achieved immortality. She poisoned herself with the bite of the deadly cobra, or asp, the royal snake of Egypt. Plutarch's account is that a snake expert brought her a cobra hidden in a basket of figs. The cobra's deadly venom killed within moments of it entering the victim's bloodstream.

Most historians take the view that in ending her life at the moment of her choosing, she remained in control until the end. They go on to argue that her death cheated Caesar Octavius of his chance to display her as a trophy of his successes in the East, his acquisition of the vast wealth of Egypt, his defeat of Antony and his total supremacy over the Roman world. Others argue that Caesar Octavius could have prevented her suicide if he wished. According to this argument he allowed her to take her own life because of his fear that Cleopatra, and her son Caesarion, had stronger claims than he did to rule Rome. Caesar Octavius was the great-nephew of Julius Caesar and had been adopted by Caesar in his will. However, Cleopatra claimed that her child, Caesarion, was Julius Caesar's natural heir. Alive, mother and son would always pose a threat to Caesar Octavius' claims to rule. It was a threat that was finally removed when, after Cleopatra's death, the sixteen-year-old Caesarion was murdered. It is interesting to note that her three remaining children were unharmed and were allowed to live in peace after her death.

Whatever was in Caesar Octavius' mind, a 'Cleopatra' did take part in his three days of triumphal procession in 29 BC, as a wax figure of her, complete with model asp, paraded through Rome. Was this wax figure just poor compensation for what Caesar Octavius had intended, the real Cleopatra walking in chains in front of his chariot? An opposing view is that Caesar Octavius feared what might happen if he brought Cleopatra to Rome: would the Roman crowds accept the public execution of a royal woman? And if not, what was to happen to her when the procession was over? Could he keep Cleopatra safely under control, or would she become a permanent magnet for political dissidents? A careful planner, Caesar Octavius would have weighed up the advantages and disadvantages of staging a major triumphal display that included Cleopatra. No matter how carefully it may have been staged, her appearance always risked giving the wrong message and creating the wrong outcome.

Whatever his motives, Caesar Octavius' victory parade drew a line under the civil war and marked the start of a new peaceful regime. He changed his name from Caesar Octavius to become the Emperor Caesar Augustus. Later, when he was honoured by having a month named after him, he chose the month in which Cleopatra died, the eighth month, to become Augustus, rather than the ninth month, the month of his birth.

It may be said that in one way Cleopatra cheated death itself, because she achieved what all the Egyptians monarchs wanted – immortality. More than two thousand years later the story of this enigmatic woman continues to fascinate and in every play, painting, poem, book and film in which she appears she once again comes alive. She has become more than an icon of female sexuality, but has also been adopted by women who seek emancipation and equality.

4 Is *Antony and Cleopatra* a tragedy?

Classical tragedy and comedy

A tragedy usually involves the relentless destruction of the main character or characters. In Shakespeare's time ideas about tragic drama came from classical Greek and Roman dramatists, such as Aeschylus and Seneca. The bloodthirsty 'revenge tragedies' most popular in Shakespeare's time were loosely based on the style of Seneca. The Greek philosopher Aristotle described tragedy as a process where the audience is 'cleansed' after experiencing pity and fear while watching a central character who, despite admirable qualities, suffers a disastrous downfall due to pride or an error of judgement.

In Athens there were two types of drama in addition to tragedy – comedy and satyr plays. Satyr plays were humorous, pantomime-like dramas performed at the end of a cycle of three tragedies. The comedy in the satyr plays complemented the tragedies, making the experience an imitation of real life by allowing the theatre to offer not only death, but also the power of regeneration. Tragedy, it seems, is not always to be watched with deadly seriousness, as Shakespeare's episode with the Clown in Act 5 of *Antony and Cleopatra* shows by mixing comedy and tragedy to great effect. The close relationship between these types of drama can be seen in the Greek dramatic masks of comedy and tragedy, often depicted as hanging together.

Classifying Antony and Cleopatra

Antony and Cleopatra, written in 1606/7, came after a distinguished sequence of great tragedies: *Othello* in 1604, *King Lear* in 1605 and *Macbeth* in 1606. However, critics down the centuries have never ranked *Antony and Cleopatra* alongside these tragedies. Hazlitt viewed the play as the finest of Shakespeare's histories, and did not put it in the class of his great tragedies. So classifying *Antony and Cleopatra* has always been a problem. Some critics see it linked to *Troilus and Cressida*, a long-ignored play that was also hard to classify, as it fell between tragedy, comedy and history. Other critics argue that *Antony and Cleopatra* was part of the bridge between his middle plays and his last period of experimental romances, *Cymbeline* (1609), *The Winter's Tale* (1611) and *The Tempest* (1611). They see in *Antony and Cleopatra* a mood of wonder, celebration and delight that anticipates Shakespeare's later 'romances'.

As the play ends with its two heroes dead by their own hands, you may think that it is surely a tragedy. There are several problems with this interpretation, however.

The plot

The first problem is the plot. Shakespeare must have known what he was doing with his plot at this period in his playwriting career. His plot follows closely the historical events in North's translation of Plutarch, and presents the death of Antony with a full final act remaining. The focus of the play then switches to Cleopatra, who survives the two scenes of Act 5 before making a better death at the end of it all than did Antony.

Although this unusual climax does not follow the classical conventions for a tragic ending, Shakespeare was working under the constraints of familiar historical events. He was aware that his audience would know the story of these famous lovers and how they died.

Antony

Another problem is Antony. He dies at his own hands with limited tragic motive for his death – because he believes Cleopatra has betrayed him and killed herself. He attempts suicide on impulse, one of his many impulsive actions during the play. Unlike some of Shakespeare's great tragic heroes, he doesn't articulate the reasons for his dilemma. Indeed, he only speaks his inner thoughts directly to the audience on a couple of occasions and seems to have limited self-knowledge. Antony's attempts at death towards the end of Act 4 are almost comic in their clumsiness. Eros refuses to kill his master, but efficiently dispatches himself. Antony makes a mess of his own effort. On stage Antony's words, **How? Not**

dead? Not dead? (4.14.103) may have a comic or at least an embarrassing effect. Antony then calls out for his guards to despatch him. Like three stooges, each in turn refuses him:

> **Not I.**
> **Nor I.**
> **Nor anyone.** *(4.14.108–10)*

They make a quick exit, while Decretas takes up Antony's bloody sword and runs off to show it to Caesar, leaving Antony mortally wounded and unable to respond. Diomedes enters and, instead of stabbing him with his own sword, as Antony requests, he stabs Antony with news that Cleopatra is not dead. Truly this adds insult to his mortal injury! The scene ends with Antony being carried off, to be hauled ignominiously up into Cleopatra's monument where she is hiding from his wrath and Caesar's advance. Shortly afterwards he dies in her arms.

If this were a traditional tragedy, with Antony as the main tragic character, the end of the play would be marked by his death, followed quickly by Cleopatra's (as in *Romeo and Juliet*). Shakespeare, however, merely marks his death and then moves on. He followed Plutarch's account of Antony's death, aware of the theatrical effect such a dying would have. Yet the change of mood that Shakespeare achieves between the deaths of Antony and Cleopatra helps define the play. The death of the play's tragic hero is not the high point of the play. It is almost forgotten as the events of Act 5 unfold before us.

Cleopatra: alternative interpretations

Cleopatra's death provides a third problem in viewing the play as a tragedy. Shakespeare's dramatisation of the death of Cleopatra offers alternative interpretations: it could be seen as a celebration of the Queen's indomitable spirit or a tragic tale of futile suicide. Shakespeare achieved this by developing the play, moving on from the death of the supposed hero Antony at the end of Act 4 and, while dramatising the events of the long final scene ending in Cleopatra's death, altering the mood and tone of language. If the death of Cleopatra is interpreted as a celebration rather than a failure, then the play is difficult to classify as a tragedy.

Yes, Cleopatra dies, but because she chooses the moment and the manner of her death, and it does not come about directly from a flaw or weakness in her character, her death does not fit the tragic tradition. Instead, the deadly bite of the royal cobra metaphorically gives her eternal life. So by achieving this immortality at her own hand she celebrates her final victory over Caesar and over death itself. As Enobarbus says of her in Act 2:

> **Age cannot wither her nor custom stale**
> **Her infinite variety.** *(2.2.230–1)*

Antony's death is almost forgotten by the end of the play and is given only passing reference by Caesar:

> **She shall be buried by her Antony.**
> **No grave upon the earth shall clip in it**
> **A pair so famous.** *(5.2.350–2)*

The play moves on to being all about Cleopatra. In the final act Shakespeare gives the drama a form that distinguishes it from all other tragedies: Antony's impulsive act is compared with Cleopatra's measured actions. The audience cannot accept Antony's tragic image of himself at his death until Cleopatra gives it validity.

Cleopatra dominates the final scene of the play, and ultimately the play itself, through her control of language and events. Her opening words set the tone of her redemption, despite her loss, despair and death:

> **My desolation does begin to make**
> **A better life.** *(5.2.1–2)*

She celebrates the life of Antony in a dream-like sequence beginning, **I dreamt there was an Emperor Antony** (5.2.76). In her lament, like a funeral oration over a great hero, Cleopatra puts on one of her great performances. This is as much for herself as it is for Dolabella. Her words are more potent and more poetic than are those spoken over Antony's body at the end of Act 4. She celebrates her life through Antony's and puts both herself and Antony on an illusory and unreachable level. She uses images of the heavens, the stars, the sun, the moon and the earth. She sees him as the Colossus, one of the seven wonders of the ancient world. Like a dolphin that can move majestically through the air, transcending its own natural element of water, so Antony can escape his earthly bounds. She realises that such a dream is too fantastical ever to come close to physical reality, but it is such a transformation that she wishes for herself:

> **It's past the size of dreaming. Nature wants stuff**
> **To vie strange forms with fancy** *(5.2.97–8)*

During this long and varied scene Cleopatra transforms herself in front of our eyes from the living creature who has mesmerised friends, enemies and the audience, to the timeless work of art that transcends her physical death:

> **My resolution's placed, and I have nothing**
> **Of woman in me. Now from head to foot**
> **I am marble-constant; now the fleeting moon**
> **No planet is of mine.** *(5.2.238–41)*

She manipulates our emotions and allows us to see her vision. If the audience accepts her view of 'a better life', then her death is no tragedy. If we look at her death as delusive, then perhaps she is a tragic figure. It is Shakespeare's skill that allows us to have simultaneous alternative interpretations of the meaning of her death.

The Clown episode

The final scene has several changes of mood. A most significant one arrives with the Clown, the **rural fellow** disguised as a fig seller, who brings Cleopatra the deadly snakes. His bitter humour is in sharp contrast with the serious events unfolding. During his exchanges he comically warns Cleopatra that snakes are dangerous and states with all seriousness that those who die from snake bites **do seldom or never recover** (2.5.246–7). He plays upon the meaning of words: what appears to be contradictory in **honest women ... given to lie** (2.5.250) would have been interpreted by Shakespeare's audience comically, as 'honest' and 'lie' both have sexual connotations. All his talk of the snake, or 'worm', would likewise have been interpreted sexually, as 'worm' was contemporary slang for the penis. The tone of the bawdy comments is darker than in Act 1, when there was light sexual banter between Cleopatra's ladies. Like all Clowns he is talkative, and despite Cleopatra's attempts to get rid of him he tells in the style of a medieval comedy routine how women might be corrupted. His homespun philosophy and bawdy comments provide a contrast to the events that follow. After the Clown leaves, Cleopatra echoes his word play when she says, **I have immortal longings in me** (5.2.273–4).

Images of sleep

Dressing in her robes as Queen of Egypt, Cleopatra once more associates herself with the goddess Isis, part of her transformation to an immortal. Her death is not a tragic painful death like Antony's – it is full of images of gentle sleep. The snake becomes **my baby at my breast that sucks the nurse asleep** (5.2.302–3). She dies with words **As sweet as balm, as soft as air, as gentle** – (5.2.304). Charmian continues this image of peaceful sleep: **Speak softly, wake her not** (5.2.313) and Caesar admits that she looks like sleep (5.2.338).

Alternative interpretations

So Cleopatra is dead and the play ends. The world of politics and intrigue carries on in Rome as we are left to interpret Cleopatra's death: is it a tragic loss through self-indulgence or a marvellous achievement of her spirit and imagination? Has she taken Antony's gruesome death and, with the power of her imagination, elevated him to the same immortal plane on which she forever exists? Shakespeare has taken the traditional tragic form and changed it, making even the separate deaths of the play's two heroes essentially different: Antony's was painful and impulsive, Cleopatra's sweet and planned. If Antony's death could be seen as traditionally tragic, despite the mess he makes of it, Cleopatra's death could be interpreted as raising her above this.

So, has Shakespeare written a tragedy? His play leaves us with a sense of the conflict between imagination, dreams and desires and the unbending limitations of cold reality. Throughout the play we have been offered ambivalent views of its two heroes. At the end there is still ambivalence. Does Shakespeare leave you with the pessimistic and tragic sense that love and vitality are always destroyed by the coldness of a hostile world? Or do the play's events give you a message that there is a better world beyond the sordid, selfish one that Cleopatra left behind?

The characters

MARK ANTONY
OCTAVIUS CAESAR } triumvirs
LEPIDUS

SEXTUS POMPEIUS

DOMITIUS ENOBARBUS
VENTIDIUS
EROS
SCARUS } friends and followers of Mark Antony
DECRETAS
DEMETRIUS
PHILO
CANIDIUS, lieutenant general to Antony
SILIUS, an officer in Ventidius' army
A SCHOOLMASTER, ambassador from Antony to Caesar

MAECENAS
AGRIPPA
DOLABELLA } friends and followers of Caesar
PROCULEIUS
THIDIAS
GALLUS
TAURUS, lieutenant general to Caesar

MENAS
MENECRATES } friends and followers of Sextus Pompeius
VARRIUS

ALEXAS
MARDIAN, a eunuch } attendants on Cleopatra
SELEUCUS
DIOMEDES
A SOOTHSAYER
A CLOWN

OCTAVIA, sister to Caesar and wife to Antony
CLEOPATRA, Queen of Egypt
CHARMIAN } attendants on Cleopatra
IRAS

Officers
Soldiers
Messengers
Attendants

1:1

Alexandria: the conflict between duty and love is immediately introduced when two Roman soldiers enter in the middle of an argument about Antony's behaviour.

1   *dotage of our general's* Antony's foolish infatuation (for a younger woman)
2   *O'erflows the measure* exceeds an acceptable limit.
3   *files and musters* assembled troops
4   *plated Mars* the Roman god of war armoured
5   *office* service
6   *tawny front* dark face (of Cleopatra), with wordplay on a battlefront
8   *reneges all temper* loses self-control, with wordplay on the hardness of a tempered sword
9   *bellows and the fan* sexual metaphors for Antony's exciting then cooling of Cleopatra's desires
10   *gypsy's lust* In Shakespeare's time it was believed that the Gypsies originated from Egypt and that Gypsy women were promiscuous cheats and liars.
12   *triple pillar of the world* Antony, one of the triumvirs (the three rulers of the Roman Empire, along with Caesar and Lepidus)
13   *strumpet's fool* a court jester who provides entertainment for a whore

Antony and Cleopatra enter in the middle of an animated conversation about love in which Cleopatra significantly takes the lead.

15   *There's beggary ... be reckoned* Antony takes Cleopatra's 'tell' as meaning 'reckoned' and replies there is no worth in a love that can be so measured.
16   *bourn* limit, boundary
17   *find out ... new earth* search out new limits
18   *Grates me! The sum* It irritates me, so be brief.
19   *them* the news
20   *Fulvia* Antony's wife in Rome   *perchance* perhaps
21   *scarce-bearded* Cleopatra scathingly comments on Caesar's youth, implying that he has only just grown a beard; at the time the play opens Antony was forty-two, Caesar twenty-three.
22   *mandate* instruction
23   *take in* take over   *enfranchise* liberate
24   *we* the ironic use by Cleopatra of the royal 'we'
      How, my love What are you saying?
26   *dismission* order for Antony to leave Egypt
28   *process* summons (to appear in court)
      Both! Cleopatra confuses (perhaps intentionally) Fulvia with Caesar.

Cleopatra is so annoyed at Antony's lack of response she even confuses (perhaps intentionally) Fulvia with Caesar (line 30), and then accuses both of having control over Antony. How might the actor playing Cleopatra best convey her annoyance, using voice, gesture and movement? What is Antony doing during her outburst?

31   *homager* one who owes homage to a superior (here Caesar)
      else so thy cheek pays shame or else your blushes pay homage (to Fulvia)
34   *ranged* wide

1:1   *Enter* **DEMETRIUS** *and* **PHILO**

PHILO   Nay, but this dotage of our general's
                 O'erflows the measure. Those his goodly eyes,
                 That o'er the files and musters of the war
                 Have glowed like plated Mars, now bend, now turn
                 The office and devotion of their view   5
                 Upon a tawny front. His captain's heart,
                 Which in the scuffles of great fights hath burst
                 The buckles on his breast, reneges all temper,
                 And is become the bellows and the fan
                 To cool a gypsy's lust.

               Flourish. Enter **ANTONY**, **CLEOPATRA**, *her* **LADIES**, *the* **TRAIN**,
                        with **EUNUCHS** *fanning her*

                                  Look where they come –   10
                 Take but good note, and you shall see in him
                 The triple pillar of the world transformed
                 Into a strumpet's fool. Behold and see.

CLEOPATRA   If it be love indeed, tell me how much.

ANTONY   There's beggary in the love that can be reckoned.   15

CLEOPATRA   I'll set a bourn how far to be beloved.

ANTONY   Then must thou needs find out new heaven, new earth.

                        Enter an **ATTENDANT**

ATTENDANT   News, my good lord, from Rome.

ANTONY   Grates me! The sum.

CLEOPATRA   Nay, hear them, Antony:
                 Fulvia perchance is angry; or who knows   20
                 If the scarce-bearded Caesar have not sent
                 His powerful mandate to you – 'Do this, or this;
                 Take in that kingdom, and enfranchise that.
                 Perform't, or else we damn thee.'

ANTONY   How, my love?

CLEOPATRA   Perchance? Nay, and most like.   25
                 You must not stay here longer. Your dismission
                 Is come from Caesar, therefore hear it, Antony.
                 Where's Fulvia's process? – Caesar's I would say! – Both!
                 Call in the messengers. As I am Egypt's Queen,
                 Thou blushest, Antony, and that blood of thine   30
                 Is Casesar's homager; else so thy cheek pays shame
                 When shrill-tongued Fulvia scolds. The messengers!

ANTONY   Let Rome in Tiber melt, and the wide arch
                 Of the ranged empire fall! Here is my space.
                 Kingdoms are clay: our dungy earth alike   35

19

37 *such a mutual pair* well-matched lovers

38 *such a twain can d'ot* such a couple can do it *bind* compel

39 *weet* recognise

> What gestures and movements might the actor playing Cleopatra use to show her conflicting emotions as she either turns aside to her Ladies to speak about Antony, or deliberately speaks to Antony using the third person?

42 *I'll seem the fool I am not* If I believe Antony I'll be seen as foolish

42–3 *Antony … himself* Antony on the other hand is foolish to believe himself

43 *stirred* aroused, both sexually and in anger

44 *her soft hours* the time granted them by Venus, the goddess of love

45 *confound … harsh* waste time quarrelling

46 *stretch* both draw out the time and physically stretch (with the association of sexual contact)

47 *sport* sexual pleasure

> As their brief bantering ends with Antony's wish to embrace the pleasures of the moment, notice how Cleopatra attempts once again to turn Antony's attention to hear the news from Rome.

48 *Fie* a rebuke, with a variety of meanings *wrangling* quarrelsome

49 *chide* rebuke

52 *No messenger … thine* I will listen to nobody but you

54 *qualities of people* characters

> How could the director most effectively stage the exit of Antony and Cleopatra so as to create a memorable first impression of the 'mutual pair'?

56 *Is Caesar … slight?* Does Antony have such little respect for Caesar?

58 *property* qualities

60 *approves the common liar* gives truth to the malicious rumours in Rome about Antony

> Rome's disapproving view of Antony and Cleopatra is heard. Antony shows us something of his greatness; Cleopatra something of her paradoxical nature. Antony decides to ignore the messages from Rome and follow his own path of pleasure with Cleopatra.

Feeds beast as man. The nobleness of life
Is to do thus, when such a mutual pair
And such a twain can do't – in which I bind,
On pain of punishment, the world to weet
We stand up peerless.

CLEOPATRA   Excellent falsehood!   40
Why did he marry Fulvia, and not love her?
I'll seem the fool I am not; Antony
Will be himself.

ANTONY   But stirred by Cleopatra.
Now for the love of Love and her soft hours,
Let's not confound the time with conference harsh –   45
There's not a minute of our lives should stretch
Without some pleasure now. What sport tonight?

CLEOPATRA   Hear the ambassadors.

ANTONY   Fie, wrangling queen!
Whom every thing becomes – to chide, to laugh,
To weep; whose every passion fully strives   50
To make itself, in thee, fair and admired!
No messenger but thine. And all alone
Tonight we'll wander through the streets and note
The qualities of people. Come, my queen;
Last night you did desire it. [*To the* ATTENDANT] Speak not to us.   55

[*Exeunt* ANTONY *and* CLEOPATRA *with their train*

DEMETRIUS   Is Caesar with Antonius prized so slight?

PHILO   Sir, sometimes, when he is not Antony,
He comes too short of that great property
Which still should go with Antony.

DEMETRIUS   I am full sorry
That he approves the common liar, who   60
Thus speaks of him at Rome; but I will hope
Of better deeds tomorrow. Rest you happy!

[*Exeunt*

1:2

The Roman view of Cleopatra's court is that it is decadent and idle, seeking after pleasure. This scene gives the audience the mood of the Egyptian court as Cleopatra's ladies relax with bantering conversation while having their fortunes told.

Two groups enter: the Roman one is led by Enobarbus; the other made up of close attendants of Cleopatra. How might the director use the entrances, costume and stage positioning of these two groups in order to visualise for the audience the contrast between Rome and Egypt?

> **2** *soothsayer* fortune-teller
>
> **3–4** *knew this … garlands!* Alexas, it appears, has been teasing Charmian, saying that if she married she would be frequently unfaithful.

The Soothsayer speaks in verse, the others in prose. Would the Soothsayer also adopt a more formal style of speaking to underline the difference? What other significant contrasts between the Soothsayer and the others might the director bring out in this scene?

> **10** *banquet* selection of light refreshments

There are several implicit stage directions in this scene, where the dialogue indicates a particular movement on stage:
* *At line 12, Charmian offers her hand to the Soothsayer so her fortune can be told, as does Iras at line 41;*
* *At line 10, Enobarbus asks for a banquet to be brought in, which it presumably is.*

> **15** *fairer* several meanings: the Soothsayer means greater quality of character; Charmian takes it as having a rounder figure; Iras takes it as more beautiful
>
> **17** *paint* cosmetics
>
> **19** *prescience* vision of the future
>
> **22** *heat my liver* Love and drink could inflame the liver, the source of passion. Charmian jokingly chooses drink over love.
>
> **26** *Herod of Jewry* a tyrant ruler in Judea, who tried to kill the infant Jesus
>
> **27** *companion me with my mistress* make me Cleopatra's equal
>
> **29** *figs* bawdy connotations with female genitals; Charmian jokes that she would prefer a long life to an active sex life
>
> **30** *proved* experienced
>
> **32** *belike my children shall have no names* probably they will be illegitimate
>
> **36** *I forgive thee for a witch* I know you are a false prophet

1:2 *Enter* ENOBARBUS, LAMPRIUS, *a* SOOTHSAYER, RANNIUS,
LUCILLIUS, CHARMIAN, IRAS, MARDIAN *the* EUNUCH, *and* ALEXAS

CHARMIAN	Lord Alexas, sweet Alexas, most any thing Alexas, almost most absolute Alexas, where's the soothsayer that you praised so to the Queen? O that I knew this husband, which you say must charge his horns with garlands!
ALEXAS	Soothsayer! 5
SOOTHSAYER	Your will?
CHARMIAN	Is this the man? Is't you, sir, that know things?
SOOTHSAYER	In Nature's infinite book of secrecy A little I can read.
ALEXAS	Show him your hand.
ENOBARBUS	Bring in the banquet quickly; wine enough 10 Cleopatra's health to drink.
CHARMIAN	Good sir, give me good fortune.
SOOTHSAYER	I make not, but foresee.
CHARMIAN	Pray then, foresee me one.
SOOTHSAYER	You shall be yet far fairer than you are. 15
CHARMIAN	He means in flesh.
IRAS	No, you shall paint when you are old.
CHARMIAN	Wrinkles forbid!
ALEXAS	Vex not his prescience; be attentive.
CHARMIAN	Hush! 20
SOOTHSAYER	You shall be more beloving than beloved.
CHARMIAN	I had rather heat my liver with drinking.
ALEXAS	Nay, hear him.
CHARMIAN	Good now, some excellent fortune! Let me be married to three kings in a forenoon, and widow them all. Let me have a child at fifty, to 25 whom Herod of Jewry may do homage. Find me to marry me with Octavius Caesar, and companion me with my mistress.
SOOTHSAYER	You shall outlive the lady whom you serve.
CHARMIAN	O, excellent! I love long life better than figs.
SOOTHSAYER	You have seen and proved a fairer former fortune 30 Than that which is to approach.
CHARMIAN	Then belike my children shall have no names. Prithee, how many boys and wenches must I have?
SOOTHSAYER	If every of your wishes had a womb, And fertile every wish, a million. 35
CHARMIAN	Out, fool! I forgive thee for a witch.

37 *privy to your wishes* know your innermost desires

> *Enobarbus' command at line 10, and a second reference to drink at line 40, are his only contributions to this part of the scene. How might his drinking be used by the director during the early part of the scene?*

41 *presages* is a prediction or warning

42 *o'erflowing Nilus presageth famine* Charmian is being ironic about Iras' chastity, as the Nile flooding led to an abundant harvest.

43 *wild* promiscuous

44 *oily palm* A moist or oily palm indicated a sexy nature.

　　fruitful prognostication predicts many children

45 *workyday* ordinary

> *The Soothsayer concludes his fortune-telling with a clear finality – the future is told; there is nothing you can do; there is nothing more to say. In the frivolity and light-heartedness of these moments, how might the director indicate to the audience that there is a serious dimension to his predictions?*

52 *husband's nose* bawdy reference to the penis

> *From lines 53 to 62 Charmian and Iras mockingly imitate the style of formal prayers in ridiculing Alexas. They insultingly call him ugly and wish his fortune to be a serial cuckold! What actions and gestures might each of the three actors use here to enhance the mood of light-hearted bawdiness?*

54 *go* reach sexual climax
　　Isis Egyptian goddess of fertility who used powers of sorcery; ironically Cleopatra associated herself strongly with Isis

55–6 *worse follow worse* a series of unsuccessful wives

60 *loose-wived* having an unfaithful wife

61 *foul* ugly

61–2 *keep decorum* do what is appropriate

64–5 *if it … they'd do't* if they had it in their power to make me a cuckold, they'd even become whores to ensure it

> *What reason could you suggest for Enobarbus mistaking Antony for Cleopatra at line 66? Is it due to his drinking throughout the scene?*

70 *A Roman thought* a thought about Rome, with the clear contrast between Rome's serious sobriety in contrast to Antony's Egyptian mirth

> *Why does Cleopatra not wish to see Antony as he arrives? Yet she asked if Antony had been seen and sent Enobarbus to find him. Have they been arguing over his duty to Rome again? What is the effect of the rapid entrances and exits here?*

ALEXAS	You think none but your sheets are privy to your wishes.
CHARMIAN	Nay, come, tell Iras hers.
ALEXAS	We'll know all our fortunes.
ENOBARBUS	Mine, and most of our fortunes, tonight shall be – drunk to bed. 40
IRAS	There's a palm presages chastity, if nothing else.
CHARMIAN	E'en as the o'erflowing Nilus presageth famine.
IRAS	Go, you wild bedfellow, you cannot soothsay.
CHARMIAN	Nay, if an oily palm be not a fruitful prognostication, I cannot scratch mine ear. Prithee, tell her but a workyday fortune. 45
SOOTHSAYER	Your fortunes are alike.
IRAS	But how, but how? Give me particulars.
SOOTHSAYER	I have said.
IRAS	Am I not an inch of fortune better than she?
CHARMIAN	Well, if you were but an inch of fortune better than I, where would 50 you choose it?
IRAS	Not in my husband's nose.
CHARMIAN	Our worser thoughts heavens mend! Alexas – come, his fortune, his fortune! O, let him marry a woman that cannot go, sweet Isis, I beseech thee, and let her die too, and give him a worse, and let worse follow 55 worse till the worst of all follow him laughing to his grave, fiftyfold a cuckold! Good Isis, hear me this prayer, though thou deny me a matter of more weight; good Isis, I beseech thee!
IRAS	Amen, dear goddess, hear that prayer of the people! For, as it is a heart-breaking to see a handsome man loose-wived, so it is a deadly 60 sorrow to behold a foul knave uncuckolded. Therefore, dear Isis, keep decorum, and fortune him accordingly!
CHARMIAN	Amen.
ALEXAS	Lo now, if it lay in their hands to make me a cuckold, they would make themselves whores but they'd do't. 65
ENOBARBUS	Hush! Here comes Antony.
CHARMIAN	Not he – the Queen.

Enter CLEOPATRA

CLEOPATRA	Saw you my lord?
ENOBARBUS	No, lady.
CLEOPATRA	Was he not here?
CHARMIAN	No, madam.
CLEOPATRA	He was disposed to mirth, but on the sudden A Roman thought hath struck him. Enobarbus! 70
ENOBARBUS	Madam?
CLEOPATRA	Seek him, and bring him hither. Where's Alexas?

75   *field* battlefield

> *Notice how the mood of the scene changes with what Cleopatra calls Antony's 'Roman thought' (line 70). How might the director convey to the audience the more serious mood of Roman politics?*

78   *time's state* the political needs of the moment

80   *better issue* greater success

81   *drave* drove them out

82   *The nature … teller* A modern version is, 'Don't shoot the messenger.'

86   *Labienus* Roman general who defected to the Parthians

88   *Extended Asia* captured the Roman province of Asia (part of modern Turkey)

90   *Lydia and to Ionia* parts of modern Turkey

93   *home* frankly, to the point
     mince … tongue don't lessen what is being said

94   *Name … Rome* Speak of Cleopatra as she is spoken of in Rome

95   *Rail thou in Fulvia's phrase* speak as angrily as Fulvia would

96   *With such full licence* without restraint

97–9 *then we bring … our earing* metaphors of weeds growing through inactivity and then being ploughed up by criticism

101 *Sicyon* a Greek city

105 *dotage* an echo of Philo's criticism of Antony in the first line of the play

ALEXAS	Here at your service. My lord approaches.
CLEOPATRA	We will not look upon him. Go with us.

[Exeunt

Enter ANTONY with a MESSENGER and ATTENDANTS

FIRST MESSENGER Fulvia thy wife first came into the field. 75

ANTONY Against my brother Lucius?

FIRST MESSENGER Ay –
But soon that war had end, and the time's state
Made friends of them, jointing their force 'gainst Caesar,
Whose better issue in the war, from Italy, 80
Upon the first encounter, drave them.

ANTONY   Well, what worst?

FIRST MESSENGER The nature of bad news infects the teller.

ANTONY   When it concerns the fool or coward. On!
Things that are past are done, with me. 'Tis thus;
Who tells me true, though in his tale lie death, 85
I hear him as he flattered.

FIRST MESSENGER   Labienus –
This is stiff news – hath with his Parthian force
Extended Asia: from Euphrates
His conquering banner shook, from Syria
To Lydia and to Ionia, 90
Whilst –

ANTONY   'Antony' thou wouldst say –

FIRST MESSENGER   O, my lord!

ANTONY   Speak to me home, mince not the general tongue:
Name Cleopatra as she is called in Rome.
Rail thou in Fulvia's phrase, and taunt my faults 95
With such full licence as both truth and malice
Have power to utter. O, then we bring forth weeds
When our quick winds lie still, and our ills told us
Is as our earing. Fare thee well awhile.

FIRST MESSENGER At your noble pleasure.   [*Exit* 100

ANTONY   From Sicyon how the news? Speak there!

FIRST ATTENDANT The man from Sicyon – is there such an one?

SECOND ATTENDANT He stays upon your will.

ANTONY   Let him appear.
These strong Egyptian fetters I must break,
Or lose myself in dotage.

Enter another MESSENGER, with a letter

What are you? 105

109 *Importeth thee* concerns you   *Forbear me* leave me alone

> Compare what Antony tells us here, about his feelings for Cleopatra and his wife, with what he said about them in Scene 1. He speaks his mind to the audience in a soliloquy (a dramatic device where a character, when alone on the stage, speaks aloud his or her honest inner thoughts). Does this mean that he now speaks more truthfully about his love for Cleopatra and his feelings for his wife?

111–12 *our contempts ... again* we wish we still had those things we had thrown away in contempt

112–14 *The present ... itself* on life's wheel of Fortune pleasure revolves into pain

115 *could* would like to

116 *enchanting* as under the spell of a witch

117–18 *Ten thousand ... hatch* my time of idleness with Cleopatra will cause innumerable unknown problems

118 *idleness* perhaps with connotations of sexual pleasure

119 *'What's your pleasure, sir?'* Enobarbus enters with an innocuous greeting. Is this an ironic comment on Antony's lascivious idleness and pleasure, which he now regrets? During this scene Enobarbus makes many bawdy references, beginning with his comments on dying. In addition to the usual meaning for Shakespeare's audience, 'dying' would have had an alternative bawdy meaning of sexual orgasm.

126 *noise* awareness

127–8 *upon far poorer moment* for much slighter cause

128 *mettle* spirit, vigour

129 *celerity* speed

133 *almanacs* leaflets giving horoscopes and predictions for the weather

134 *Jove* Roman god of the weather, worshipped as a rain god

136 *wonderful piece of work* masterpiece

137 *discredited your travel* lost your reputation as a traveller

> Enobarbus continues his bawdy wordplay, discussing Fulvia's death: 'tailors' and 'robes' are metaphors for sexual relations, the words 'cut' and 'case' refer to the female sex organs, as 'member' does to the male. The modern audience would not pick up on the bawdy wordplay that Enobarbus indulges in without the actor using some graphic movement or gesture to make clear his sexual innuendo.

SECOND MESSENGER	Fulvia thy wife is dead.
ANTONY	Where died she?
SECOND MESSENGER	In Sicyon:

    Her length of sickness, with what else more serious
    Importeth thee to know, this bears. [*Gives the letter*]

ANTONY   Forbear me.

                         [*Exeunt* MESSENGER *and* ATTENDANTS

    There's a great spirit gone! Thus did I desire it.   110
    What our contempts doth often hurl from us,
    We wish it ours again. The present pleasure,
    By revolution lowering, does become
    The opposite of itself. She's good, being gone;
    The hand could pluck her back that shoved her on.   115
    I must from this enchanting queen break off.
    Ten thousand harms, more than the ills I know,
    My idleness doth hatch. Ho now, Enobarbus!

                  Enter ENOBARBUS

ENOBARBUS What's your pleasure, sir?

ANTONY   I must with haste from hence.   120

ENOBARBUS Why, then we kill all our women. We see how mortal an
    unkindness is to them. If they suffer our departure, death's the word.

ANTONY   I must be gone.

ENOBARBUS Under a compelling occasion let women die. It were pity to cast
    them away for nothing, though between them and a great cause they   125
    should be esteemed nothing. Cleopatra, catching but the least noise of
    this, dies instantly. I have seen her die twenty times upon far poorer
    moment. I do think there is mettle in death, which commits some
    loving act upon her, she hath such a celerity in dying.

ANTONY   She is cunning past man's thought.   130

ENOBARBUS Alack, sir, no – her passions are made of nothing but the finest part
    of pure love. We cannot call her winds and waters sighs and tears; they
    are greater storms and tempests than almanacs can report. This cannot
    be cunning in her; if it be, she makes a shower of rain as well as Jove.

ANTONY   Would I had never seen her!   135

ENOBARBUS O, sir, you had then left unseen a wonderful piece of work, which
    not to have been blessed withal would have discredited your travel.

ANTONY   Fulvia is dead.

ENOBARBUS Sir?

ANTONY   Fulvia is dead.   140

ENOBARBUS Fulvia?

ANTONY   Dead.

ENOBARBUS Why, sir, give the gods a thankful sacrifice. When it pleaseth their

144–5 *it shows … earth* it shows man that gods are the world's tailors, i.e. the gods control life and death

148–9 *your old smock … new petticoat* Antony's replacement of the old (Fulvia) with the new (Cleopatra) is represented by the female garments

149–50 *the tears … sorrow* any tears are false

151 *business she hath broachèd* political undertakings Cleopatra has started out on

153 *business … broached* Enobarbus plays on the bawdy meanings of 'broached' and 'business'.

154 *abode* remaining here

> The sexual bantering is quickly ended with Antony's switch from prose to verse at the command to stop the crude comments ('No more light answers'). He also uses the royal 'we' (speaking of himself in the first person plural). In what other ways might the actor indicate the shift to more serious matters? What has the audience learned of the relationship between the two during their conversation?

157 *expedience* rushed departure

158 *leave to part* permission to leave   *alone* only

159 *touches* reasons

161 *contriving* helpful

162 *Petition us at home* urge us to return Rome
Sextus Pompeius the son of Pompey the Great

163 *given the dare to* challenged

164 *The empire of the sea* sea power
slippery people fickle Roman mob

165–6 *Whose love … past* they never give their (political) support to the one who deserves it until his time has gone

166–7 *throw … dignities* shower Pompey the Great's titles and honour on the son, Sextus Pompeius

169 *blood and life* spirit and energy

169–70 *stands up … soldier* shows himself as the greatest warrior

170–1 *whose quality … danger* his inclinations (to fight) may endanger the world (i.e. the Roman Empire)

171–3 *Much is … poison* According to folklore, a horsehair left in standing water would turn into a creature. Antony uses it as a metaphor to say that his neglect of his political duties has become potentially dangerous for Rome, but he can salvage the situation.

173–5 *Say our … hence* He orders a quick departure of his army for Rome.

> The scene begins in a light-hearted mood, but this changes with Cleopatra's reference to Antony's 'Roman thought'. After a succession of messengers with bad news, Antony is left alone speaking of his wife's death and his entanglement with Cleopatra. The scene ends with Antony imposing his authority. We wonder if he has decided to reject love for duty as he leaves Egypt for Rome.

deities to take the wife of a man from him, it shows to man the tailors
of the earth; comforting therein, that when old robes are worn out,   **145**
there are members to make new. If there were no more women but
Fulvia, then had you indeed a cut, and the case to be lamented. This
grief is crowned with consolation: your old smock brings forth a new
petticoat – and indeed the tears live in an onion that should water this
sorrow.   **150**

ANTONY   The business she hath broachèd in the state
Cannot endure my absence.

ENOBARBUS   And the business you have broached here cannot be without you –
especially that of Cleopatra's, which wholly depends on your abode.

ANTONY   No more light answers. Let our officers   **155**
Have notice what we purpose. I shall break
The cause of our expedience to the Queen
And get her leave to part. For not alone
The death of Fulvia with more urgent touches
Do strongly speak to us, but the letters too   **160**
Of many our contriving friends in Rome
Petition us at home. Sextus Pompeius
Hath given the dare to Caesar and commands
The empire of the sea. Our slippery people –
Whose love is never linked to the deserver   **165**
Till his deserts are past – begin to throw
Pompey the Great and all his dignities
Upon his son; who, high in name and power,
Higher than both in blood and life, stands up
For the main soldier; whose quality, going on,   **170**
The sides o'the world may danger. Much is breeding
Which, like the courser's hair, hath yet but life
And not a serpent's poison. Say our pleasure,
To such whose place is under us, requires
Our quick remove from hence.   **175**

ENOBARBUS   I shall do't.

                                                                          [*Exeunt*

1:3

Cleopatra, anxious about Antony's planned departure, uses all her womanly wiles to stop him leaving for Rome.

Cleopatra shows anxiety with her opening question followed by quick-fire instructions to Alexas. What movements might highlight the opening mood of the scene? Notice what she tells Alexas to do in order to catch Antony's attention.

11 *Tempt* test *I wish, forbear* I beg you to refrain (from testing him)

How might the director choose to use Cleopatra's 'I am sick and sullen' (line 13)? Is it an aside to Charmian, a comment to Antony, a reminder to herself on her tactics with Antony or a true statement? Is her falling simply for effect in order to gain Antony's sympathy, or is she truly physically overwhelmed by Antony's intended departure?

14 *breathing to my purpose* speak my intentions

16–17 *It cannot … sustain it* I cannot put up with this, my body will not take it

19 *that same eye* the look in your eyes

20 *the married woman* a sarcastic reference to Fulvia, his wife

25–6 *Yet at … planted* I saw your treachery from the first moment

28 *in swearing … gods* oaths of fidelity sworn to the gods so loudly that it made them shake

30–1 *mouth-made … in swearing* empty vows broken as soon as they are made

1:3   *Enter* CLEOPATRA, CHARMIAN, CHARMIAN *and* IRAS

CLEOPATRA   Where is he?

CHARMIAN   I did not see him since.

CLEOPATRA   See where he is, who's with him, what he does –
            I did not send you. If you find him sad,
            Say I am dancing; if in mirth, report
            That I am sudden sick. Quick, and return.   [*Exit* ALEXAS   5

CHARMIAN   Madam, methinks, if you did love him dearly,
            You do not hold the method to enforce
            The like from him.

CLEOPATRA   What should I do, I do not?

CHARMIAN   In each thing give him way. Cross him in nothing.

CLEOPATRA   Thou teachest like a fool the way to lose him.   10

CHARMIAN   Tempt him not so too far. I wish, forbear.
            In time we hate that which we often fear.

                        Enter ANTONY

        But here comes Antony.

CLEOPATRA   I am sick and sullen.

ANTONY   I am sorry to give breathing to my purpose –

CLEOPATRA   Help me away, dear Charmian, I shall fall.   15
            It cannot be thus long, the sides of nature
            Will not sustain it.

ANTONY   Now, my dearest queen –

CLEOPATRA   Pray you, stand farther from me.

ANTONY   What's the matter?

CLEOPATRA   I know by that same eye there's some good news,
            What, says the married woman you may go?   20
            Would she had never given you leave to come!
            Let her not say 'tis I that keep you here.
            I have no power upon you – hers you are.

ANTONY   The gods best know –

CLEOPATRA   O, never was there queen
            So mightily betrayed! Yet at the first   25
            I saw the treasons planted.

ANTONY   Cleopatra –

CLEOPATRA   Why should I think you can be mine, and true –
            Though you in swearing shake the thronèd gods –
            Who have been false to Fulvia? Riotous madness,
            To be entangled with those mouth-made vows   30
            Which break themselves in swearing!

32   *colour* excuse
33   *sued* begged

> Compare Cleopatra's speech on eternal love with Antony's in Scene 1. Is she
> ironically referring back to his comments, as she calls Antony 'the greatest liar'?
> Notice how she uses the royal 'we' in order to demonstrate her queenly qualities.

36   *brows' bent* the shape of the eyebrow
36–7   *none … heaven* all of my features, no matter how insignificant,
         were thought heavenly
40   *had thy inches* either (1) was a man, or (2) was as tall as you are
41   *Egypt* Cleopatra refers to herself as her country.

*From line 19 Cleopatra has hardly given Antony chance to say a word in
explanation or defence. What movements and gestures might convey the
whirlwind of her words?
What directions would you give to the actor playing Antony on how to respond
to Cleopatra? Would he stand still, showing quiet restraint, or show detached
amusement or become increasingly exasperated?*

44   *in use with you* yours
45   *civil swords* swords drawn in civil war
47–8   *Equality … faction* two groups disputing power in one country lead
         to quarrels over little things
48–9   *the hated … love* those once hated become loved as they acquire
         political strength
49   *condemned* outlawed
50   *apace* rapidly
51–2   *thrived Upon* flourished under
53–4   *And quietness … change* The image is taken from a popular
         contemporary cure for ailments – bloodletting. Rome at peace has
         become ill through discontent and its health can only be restored
         by bloodletting (war).
54   *more particular* more concerns me
55   *safe* save you worrying about
57–8   *Though age … childishness* though my age did not stop me from
         the folly (of falling in love), but it does stop me childishly believing
         what you tell me (about Fulvia)

*There is an implicit stage direction in 'Look here' at line 60, when Antony asks
her to read the letter giving news of Fulvia's death. Cleopatra must scan the letter
while Antony speaks, before replying that she does not believe his love is true.
Do you think she believes what she says or is it part of her cunning deception?*

61   *garboils* disturbances   *at the last, best* best news of all
63   *sacred vials* small bottles of tears placed in the tombs of loved ones
65   *mine* my death
68–9   *By the fire … slime* Antony swears by the sun that gives life to the
         Nile valley.
71   *affects* feels, wishes

ANTONY   Most sweet queen –

CLEOPATRA   Nay, pray you seek no colour for your going,
         But bid farewell, and go. When you sued staying,
         Then was the time for words. No going then!
         Eternity was in our lips and eyes,   **35**
         Bliss in our brows' bent; none our parts so poor
         But was a race of heaven. They are so still,
         Or thou, the greatest soldier of the world,
         Art turned the greatest liar.

ANTONY   How now, lady?

CLEOPATRA   I would I had thy inches. Thou shouldst know   **40**
         There were a heart in Egypt.

ANTONY   Hear me, Queen:
         The strong necessity of time commands
         Our services awhile, but my full heart
         Remains in use with you. Our Italy
         Shines o'er with civil swords. Sextus Pompeius   **45**
         Makes his approaches to the port of Rome.
         Equality of two domestic powers
         Breed scrupulous faction; the hated, grown to strength,
         Are newly grown to love. The condemned Pompey,
         Rich in his father's honour, creeps apace   **50**
         Into the hearts of such as have not thrived
         Upon the present state, whose numbers threaten;
         And quietness, grown sick of rest, would purge
         By any desperate change. My more particular,
         And that which most with you should safe my going,   **55**
         Is Fulvia's death.

CLEOPATRA   Though age from folly could not give me freedom,
         It does from childishness. Can Fulvia die?

ANTONY   She's dead, my Queen.
         Look here, and at thy sovereign leisure read   **60**
         The garboils she awaked; at the last, best,
         See when and where she died.

CLEOPATRA   O most false love!
         Where be the sacred vials thou shouldst fill
         With sorrowful water? Now I see, I see,
         In Fulvia's death, how mine received shall be.   **65**

ANTONY   Quarrel no more, but be prepared to know
         The purposes I bear; which are, or cease,
         As you shall give the advice. By the fire
         That quickens Nilus' slime, I go from hence
         Thy soldier, servant, making peace or war   **70**
         As thou affects.

CLEOPATRA   Cut my lace, Charmian, come –

35

Antony and Cleopatra

Hercules.

73   *So Antony loves* either (1) If Antony loves me, I am well; or (2) His love is as changeable as my health
      forbear stop (behaving like this)

74   *stands* withstands

75   *trial* test   *told* taught

78   *Egypt* Cleopatra   *Good now* Please

79   *dissembling* pretence, disguise

80   *heat my blood* make me angry

81   *meetly* quite good

82   *target* shield

82   *mends* improves (his performance)

84   *Herculean* Antony thought himself a descendant of Hercules.

84–5   *does ... chafe* plays well the role of an angry man

> *Cleopatra angers Antony by sarcastically asking him to play a scene of pretended anger. She provokes him to fury with her taunting reference to 'honour' and then turns his angry 'by my sword' into a commonplace saying. What gestures and movements might best accompany Cleopatra's goading remarks?*
> *As Antony moves to leave (line 86), note the change in Cleopatra as she struggles with what to say. What change of tone of voice and accompanying gestures or movements might the actor use to show her turbulent emotions?*

91–2   *But that ... subject* If it were not clear that you are in control of yourself being the queen of foolishness

96   *becomings* change of mood

97   *Eye* look

100   *laurel* a wreath signifying victory

102–4   *Our separation ... remain with thee* Antony replies gallantly using paradox, a device popular with Elizabethan writers.

Cleopatra uses all her wiles to try to keep Antony with her, but as he is determined to leave for Rome she gives up her taunting mockery and graciously wishes him well. Where will the next scene take us? Will we follow Antony, or stay with Cleopatra in Alexandria?

But let it be. I am quickly ill and well,
So Antony loves.

ANTONY   My precious queen, forbear,
And give true evidence to his love, which stands
An honourable trial.

CLEOPATRA   So Fulvia told me.   75
I prithee turn aside and weep for her,
Then bid adieu to me and say the tears
Belong to Egypt. Good now, play one scene
Of excellent dissembling, and let it look
Like perfect honour.

ANTONY   You'll heat my blood – no more!   80

CLEOPATRA   You can do better yet; but this is meetly.

ANTONY   Now by my sword –

CLEOPATRA   And target. Still he mends.
But this is not the best. Look, prithee, Charmian,
How this Herculean Roman does become
The carriage of his chafe.   85

ANTONY   I'll leave you, lady!

CLEOPATRA   Courteous lord, one word:
Sir, you and I must part – but that's not it.
Sir, you and I have loved – but there's not it;
That you know well. Something it is I would –
O, my oblivion is a very Antony,   90
And I am all forgotten.

ANTONY   But that your royalty
Holds idleness your subject, I should take you
For idleness itself.

CLEOPATRA   'Tis sweating labour
To bear such idleness so near the heart
As Cleopatra this. But, sir, forgive me,   95
Since my becomings kill me when they do not
Eye well to you. Your honour calls you hence,
Therefore be deaf to my unpitied folly,
And all the gods go with you! Upon your sword
Sit laurel victory, and smooth success   100
Be strewed before your feet!

ANTONY   Let us go. Come.
Our separation so abides and flies
That thou, residing here, goes yet with me;
And I, hence fleeting, here remain with thee.
Away!   105

[*Exeunt*

1:4

The scene jumps ahead of Antony to Rome where we are introduced to Caesar and Lepidus, the two other members of the ruling group, the triumvirate. They enter with Caesar denouncing Antony as he reads of his behaviour in Alexandria with Cleopatra.

  3 *competitor* associate (in the triumvirate)
  6 *Ptolemy* Cleopatra had married her brother (see page 8)
  7 *gave audience* refers back to Antony's refusal in Scene 1 to listen to the messenger from Rome

The letter provides a focus for the discussion of Antony's faults and it appears there is a direction for Caesar to show or give the letter to Lepidus in line 8. Lepidus is less critical of Antony than Caesar. Notice how Caesar refers to himself with the royal 'we'. In what ways might Caesar's relationship with Lepidus as 'first among equals' be shown?

  9–10 *abstract ... follow* perfect example of all human faults
  11 *enow* enough
  12 *spots* stars
  14 *purchased* acquired
  18 *mirth* joke
  19 *turn of tippling* drinking (toasts) in rounds
  20 *reel* drunken stagger *stand the buffet* endure being pushed or punched
  22 *composure* character
  24 *foils* blemishes
  24–5 *bear ... lightness* carry a heavy burden because of his frivolous behaviour
  26 *vacancy* free time *voluptuousness* sexual pleasures
  27 *full surfeits* disorders caused by excess
       dryness of his bones a reference to old age, or to syphilis (a sexually transmitted disease)
  28 *Call on him for't* will make him pay (for his excesses) *confound* waste
  29 *drums* calls to *sport* affair with Cleopatra
  29–30 *speaks ... ours* is as important as his and our positions (as triumvirs)
  30–3 *chid ... judgement* told off, as we would tell off young men, who should know better, who ignore the dangers involved in enjoying instant pleasures

The action is propelled forward with the news from the Messenger about the threat to Rome from Pompey. Reports of how Pompey's reputation strikes fear remind Caesar of Antony's reputation for courage. This provides a contrast with Caesar's earlier criticisms of Antony's behaviour.

  39 *discontents repair* discontented citizens go to
  40 *Give him much wronged* say he has been badly treated (by the triumvirs)

1:4   *Enter* OCTAVIUS CAESAR, *reading a letter,* LEPIDUS, *and their train*

CAESAR	You may see, Lepidus, and henceforth know
	It is not Caesar's natural vice to hate
	Our great competitor. From Alexandria
	This is the news: he fishes, he drinks, and wastes
	The lamps of night in revel; is not more manlike 5
	Than Cleopatra, nor the queen of Ptolemy
	More womanly than he; hardy gave audience, or
	Vouchsafed to think he had partners. You shall find there
	A man who is the abstract of all faults
	That all men follow.

LEPIDUS   I must not think there are   10
Evils enow to darken all his goodness.
His faults, in him, seem as the spots of heaven –
More fiery by night's blackness – hereditary
Rather than purchased, what he cannot change
Than what he chooses.   15

CAESAR   You are too indulgent. Let's grant it is not
Amiss to tumble on the bed of Ptolemy,
To give a kingdom for a mirth, to sit
And keep the turn of tippling with a slave,
To reel the streets at noon, and stand the buffet   20
With knaves that smells of sweat. Say this becomes him –
As his composure must be rare indeed
Whom these cannot blemish – yet must Antony
No way excuse his foils, when we do bear
So great weight in his lightness. If he filled   25
His vacancy with his voluptuousness,
Full surfeits and the dryness of his bones
Call on him for't. But to confound such time
That drums him from his sport and speaks as loud
As his own state and ours – 'tis to be chid   30
As we rate boys who, being mature in knowledge,
Pawn their experience to their present pleasure,
And so rebel to judgement.

Enter a MESSENGER

LEPIDUS   Here's more news.

MESSENGER   Thy biddings have been done, and every hour,
Most noble Caesar, shalt thou have report   35
How 'tis abroad. Pompey is strong at sea,
And it appears he is beloved of those
That only have feared Caesar; to the ports
The discontents repair, and men's reports
Give him much wronged.

41 *primal state* from the first

42–4 *That he … being lacked* people's enthusiasm for a new ruler only lasts until he achieves power; while the unpopular ruler is not appreciated until he is removed from power, when he regains popularity

44 *common body* common people

45 *vagabond flag* drifting water plant

46 *lackeying* like the servant following the master
varying changing

47 *motion* changing position

48 *famous* infamous, notorious

49 *ear* plough

51 *borders maritime* coastal regions

52 *Lack blood* turn pale (with fear of invasion)
flush lusty, vigorous

54–5 *strikes … resisted* creates more fear than an actual attack

56 *wassails* drunken revels

> Caesar contrasts Antony's 'lascivious wassails' with his soldierly
> behaviour in surviving defeat in battle and the famine that followed.
> What directions might be given to the actor playing Caesar to add
> impact in his address to Antony? What might be added to the
> actor's descriptions of what Antony did to survive the famine in
> order to make them more expressive?

57–9 *Modena … famine follow* Although he killed two consuls, Antony was defeated by armies sent from Rome in 43 BC. A severe famine followed.

59 *whom* this refers to the famine

60 *daintily* with civilised and refined tastes *patience* tenacity

62 *stale* urine *gilded* shining surface froth

63 *cough at* refuse to drink
palate then did deign didn't refuse to eat

64 *roughest, rudest* wildest, least cultivated

66 *browsed* ate (like an animal)

71 *So … not* did not become thin

74 *field* i.e. of battle

78–9 *Both … time* what land and sea forces I can gather to confront the enemy

CAESAR   I should have known no less.   **40**
  It hath been taught us from the primal state
  That he which is was wished until he were;
  And the ebbed man, ne'er loved till ne'er worth love,
  Comes deared by being lacked. This common body –
  Like to a vagabond flag upon the stream –   **45**
  Goes to and back, lackeying the varying tide,
  To rot itself with motion.

MESSENGER   Caesar, I bring thee word
  Menecrates and Menas, famous pirates,
  Makes the sea serve them, which they ear and wound
  With keels of every kind. Many hot inroads   **50**
  They make in Italy – the borders maritime
  Lack blood to think on't, and flush youth revolt;
  No vessel can peep forth but 'tis as soon
  Taken as seen, for Pompey's name strikes more
  Than could his war resisted.

CAESAR   Antony,   **55**
  Leave thy lascivious wassails. When thou once
  Was beaten from Modena – where thou slew'st
  Hirtius and Pansa, consuls – at thy heel
  Did famine follow, whom thou fought'st against,
  Though daintily brought up, with patience more   **60**
  Than savages could suffer. Thou didst drink
  The stale of horses and the gilded puddle
  Which beasts would cough at. Thy palate then did deign
  The roughest berry on the rudest hedge –
  Yea, like the stag when snow the pasture sheets,   **65**
  The barks of trees thou browsed. On the Alps
  It is reported thou didst eat strange flesh,
  Which some did die to look on. And all this –
  It wounds thine honour that I speak it now –
  Was borne so like a soldier that thy cheek   **70**
  So much as lanked not.

LEPIDUS   'Tis pity of him.

CAESAR   Let his shames quickly
  Drive him to Rome. 'Tis time we twain
  Did show ourselves i'the field, and to that end
  Assemble we immediate council. Pompey   **75**
  Thrives in our idleness.

LEPIDUS   Tomorrow, Caesar,
  I shall be furnished to inform you rightly
  Both what by sea and land I can be able
  To front this present time.

CAESAR   Till which encounter,

82   *stirs* happenings

Caesar criticises Antony's behaviour to a more sympathetic Lepidus. We hear Caesar's analysis of the contrasts in Antony's character. The scene shows Caesar to be clear thinking and decisive; it ends with both Caesar and Lepidus preparing to go to war against Pompey.

1:5

After the politics and preparation for war in Rome, we return to Alexandria where the contrast in mood is clear from the opening lines. Cleopatra openly describes how she is missing Antony, who is still en route for Rome.

4   *mandragora* powerful drug

8   *eunuch* male with his testicles removed

9   *to hear thee sing* eunuchs known as castrati were admired for their clear voices

11   *unseminared* without virility, i.e. castrated

12   *affections* sexual thoughts

16   *honest* chaste

18   *What Venus did with Mars* a classical allusion to passionate lovers; here Antony and Cleopatra. (Antony was compared to Mars in the opening lines of the play.)

Here is another example of Cleopatra the actress. How might Cleopatra play this part of the scene for most effect? Is her small stage audience sitting around her? Is she sitting down for the earlier part of this scene before standing to deliver lines 18–34? She asks both her stage and theatre audience to look on her as a great lover with her past affairs. How might she illustrate the erotic suggestiveness in lines 21–2 which describe the horse bearing Antony's weight?

22   *wot'st thou* do you know

23   *demi-Atlas* another classical allusion – to Atlas, a Titan who supported the heavens; Antony as a triumvir supports Rome

Compare Cleopatra's allusion to Antony being a godlike creature supporting the Roman world with the words of Philo in the opening lines of Scene 1. There he describes Antony as a 'triple pillar of the world', but goes on to criticise him for allowing the 'strumpet', Cleopatra, to turn him into her plaything. The contrast between Antony's greatness and his weakness for Cleopatra is present throughout the play.

23–4   *arm and burgonet* the complete soldier in both attack and defence
24   *burgonet* helmet

It is my business too. Farewell. 80

LEPIDUS   Farewell, my lord. What you shall know meantime
Of stirs abroad, I shall beseech you, sir,
To let me be partaker.

CAESAR   Doubt not, sir;
I know it for my bond.

                                                        [*Exeunt*

1:5   *Enter* CLEOPATRA, CHARMIAN, IRAS *and* MARDIAN

CLEOPATRA   Charmian!

CHARMIAN   Madam?

CLEOPATRA [*Yawning*] Ha, ha.
Give me to drink mandragora.

CHARMIAN   Why, madam?

CLEOPATRA   That I might sleep out this great gap of time 5
My Antony is away.

CHARMIAN   You think of him too much.

CLEOPATRA   O, 'tis treason!

CHARMIAN   Madam, I trust not so.

CLEOPATRA   Thou, eunuch Mardian!

MARDIAN   What's your highness' pleasure?

CLEOPATRA   Not now to hear thee sing – I take no pleasure
In aught an eunuch has. 'Tis well for thee 10
That, being unseminared, thy freer thoughts
May not fly forth of Egypt. Has thou affections?

MARDIAN   Yes, gracious madam.

CLEOPATRA   Indeed?

MARDIAN   Not in deed, madam, for I can do nothing 15
But what indeed is honest to be done.
Yet have I fierce affections, and think
What Venus did with Mars.

CLEOPATRA   O, Charmian!
Where think'st thou he is now? Stands he, or sits he?
Or does he walk? Or is he on his horse? 20
O happy horse, to bear the weight of Antony!
Do bravely, horse, for wot'st thou whom thou mov'st? –
The demi-Atlas of this earth, the arm
And burgonet of men. He's speaking now,
Or murmuring 'Where's my serpent of old Nile?' 25

27 *delicious poison* an oxymoron describing the pleasure and pain of Antony's absence

28 *Pheobus' amorous pinches* Cleopatra sees her skin darkened by the rays of her lover (the sun god)

29 *Broad-fronted Caesar* Julius Caesar, Antony's friend, was Cleopatra's lover; reputedly he had a broad face

31 *morsel* a tasty dish *Pompey* her second lover Gnaeus, son of Pompey the Great and brother to the Pompey (Sextus) now threatening Rome

33 *anchor his aspect* fix his gaze

Throughout this scene there are examples of Cleopatra's sexual longing. In describing Pompey's love she uses words that could have sexual connotations. Cleopatra would perhaps have to add suggestive movements to make their bawdy meaning as clear to a modern audience as they would have been to Shakespeare's.

36 *great med'cine* a metaphor from alchemy – the search for the secret elixir that could turn base metal into gold
tinct colouring; another term for the elixir

41 *orient* brightly shining

43 *firm* constant *great Egypt* Cleopatra

45 *mend* make amends for *piece* add to

48 *arm-gaunt steed* lean war-horse

50 *beastly dumbed by him* wiped out by the horse's neighing

53 *well-divided disposition* balanced temperament

There is obvious emotion in Cleopatra's repetition of 'Note him'. What emotions do you think Cleopatra would be feeling when she receives Antony's gift and hears his message? How might the actor most effectively show them?

54 *'tis the man* that's him

Compare the parallels between the compliments Cleopatra pays Antony in lines 59–61 and those Antony pays her in Scene 1, lines 48–51.

56 *make their looks by his* follow his moods

60 *violence* extreme

61 *posts* messengers

62 *several* different

63 *thick* frequently

For so he calls me. Now I feed myself
With most delicious poison. Think on me,
That am with Phoebus' amorous pinches black
And wrinkled deep in time. Broad-fronted Caesar,
When thou wast here above the ground, I was   30
A morsel for a monarch; and great Pompey
Would stand and make his eyes grow in my brow –
There would he anchor his aspect, and die
With looking on his life.

Enter ALEXAS

ALEXAS   Sovereign of Egypt, hail!

CLEOPATRA   How much unlike art thou Mark Antony!   35
Yet, coming from him, that great med'cine hath
With his tinct gilded thee.
How goes it with my brave Mark Antony?

ALEXAS   Last thing he did, dear Queen,
He kissed – the last of many doubled kisses –   40
This orient pearl. His speech sticks in my heart.

CLEOPATRA   Mine ear must pluck it thence.

ALEXAS   'Good friend,' quoth he,
'Say the firm Roman to great Egypt sends
This treasure of an oyster; at whose foot,
To mend the petty present, I will piece   45
Her opulent throne with kingdoms. All the east,
Say thou, shall call her mistress.' So he nodded,
And soberly did mount an arm-gaunt steed,
Who neighed so high that what I would have spoke
Was beastly dumbed by him.

CLEOPATRA   What, was he sad, or merry?   50

ALEXAS   Like to the time o'the year between the extremes
Of hot and cold, he was nor sad nor merry.

CLEOPATRA   O well-divided disposition! Note him,
Note him, good Charmian, 'tis the man; but note him!
He was not sad, for he would shine on those   55
That make their looks by his; he was not merry,
Which seemed to tell them his remembrance lay
In Egypt with his joy; but between both.
O heavenly mingle! Be'st thou sad or merry,
The violence of either thee becomes,   60
So does it no man else. Met'st thou my posts?

ALEXAS   Ay, madam, twenty several messengers.
Why do you send so thick?

68 *Be choked … emphasis* may you choke if you again praise Caesar with such passion
70 *Isis* Egyptian goddess of fertility
71 *paragon* compare
73 *I sing but after you* I only copy you (as in singing a 'round', where the second voice repeats the words of the first)

Compare what Charmian seems to be doing to Cleopatra towards the end of this scene with what Cleopatra did to Antony in Scene 3. Is Charmian merely mocking Cleopatra over her love affair with Caesar? Cleopatra's threats about giving Charmian 'bloody teeth' and Charmian being 'choked' might have more than a playful edge about them. As Cleopatra defends her more mature love for Antony against Charmian's gibes, how do you think the relationship between the two might be best played here?

73 *salad days* youthful inexperience
74 *green* immature   *cold in blood* not yet sexually hot
77 *a several* many
78 *unpeople Egypt* send every Egyptian as a messenger

The goddess Isis, depicted as having a cow's head, which associates her with Hathor, the goddess of creation. The infant is her son Horus.

Compare the exits of this scene with the previous one in Rome. Here Cleopatra leaves to write love letters to Antony; in the previous scene Caesar and Lepidus exited preparing for war.

We are seeing Cleopatra absorbed in thinking of Antony. His message of love merely heightens her emotional state. She compares Antony with her previous lovers and states how superior he is to them.
In Act 1 we are introduced to the two main characters, Antony and Cleopatra, and shown something of the intensity of their relationship. We are given different perspectives on Antony. In contrast to his great qualities, we also hear the disapproving voices of Rome. Life in Alexandria is contrasted sharply with life in Rome. Eventually Antony leaves behind his leisured life with Cleopatra. Act 1 ends with him en route to save Rome from invading armies.

CLEOPATRA   Who's born that day
　　　　When I forget to send to Antony
　　　　Shall die a beggar. Ink and paper, Charmian.
　　　　Welcome, my good Alexas. Did I, Charmian,   65
　　　　Ever love Caesar so?

CHARMIAN   O that brave Caesar!

CLEOPATRA   Be choked with such another emphasis! –
　　　　Say 'the brave Antony'.

CHARMIAN   The valiant Caesar!

CLEOPATRA   By Isis, I will give thee bloody teeth
　　　　If thou with Caesar paragon again   70
　　　　My man of men.

CHARMIAN   By your most gracious pardon,
　　　　I sing but after you.

CLEOPATRA   My salad days,
　　　　When I was green in judgement, cold in blood,
　　　　To say as I said then. But come, away,
　　　　Get me ink and paper.   75
　　　　He shall have every day a several greeting,
　　　　Or I'll unpeople Egypt!

[*Exeunt*

2:1

The scene moves to the coast of Italy and the audience is introduced to Pompey. In his assessment of his enemies he provides us with another view of Antony.

Pompey, alongside notorious pirates Menecrates and Menas, strikes fear into his enemies, according to the messenger in Act 1 Scene 4. How might the director best use the stage direction 'in warlike manner' in order to show the audience their fearsome appearance?

1 *shall* will

3 *That ... deny* a delay from the gods is not a refusal (of our wishes)

4–5 *Whiles ... sue for* even while we are making our requests it is ceasing to exist

6 *Beg ... harms* ask for things harmful to us *wise powers* gods

7 *profit* gain

8 *losing of our prayers* having our prayers unanswered

> **Compare Pompey's assessment of how the people love him with Caesar's in Act 1 Scene 4, lines 40–7.**

10 *crescent* growing (as the moon waxes) *auguring* prophesying

11–13 *Mark Antony ... doors* While listening to Pompey's comments on Antony and Cleopatra it must be remembered that his father had an affair with Cleopatra in her 'salad days'. How might that colour his opinion of both Cleopatra and her new lover, Antony? His food imagery has sensual and probably sexual connotations.

13 *without doors* outside (a jibe at Antony, whose only wars are sexual ones)

13–14 *gets money ... loses hearts* raising taxes lose him popularity

15–16 *neither loves ... for him* loves neither Antony nor Caesar, nor they him

17 *in the field* assembled for battle

20 *Looking* waiting *charms* spells

21 *Salt* tasty

21 *wan'd* faded

23 *Tie up ... feasts* tether Antony like an animal in a rich pasture

24 *fuming* confused *Epicurean* self-indulgence in food and drink

25 *cloyless* cannot be satisfied

26 *prorogue his honour* postpone the time when he will act honourably

27 *Lethe'd* forgetful (an allusion to the classical underworld's river Lethe which caused those who drank from it to forget their past)

30 *Since he went from Egypt* Antony's long journey from Egypt to Rome has taken place off-stage during this and the last two scenes. The switching between Italy and Egypt gives the audience the sense of time passing, so making Antony's journey more theatrically acceptable.

31 *A space for farther travel* time to travel further than he has already done

33 *amorous surfeiter* an over-indulgent lover (Antony)
donned his helm put on his helmet

2:1   *Enter* POMPEY, MENECRATES, *and* MENAS, *in war-like manner*

POMPEY   If the great gods be just, they shall assist
The deeds of justest men.

MENECRATES   Know, worthy Pompey,
That what they do delay they not deny.

POMPEY   Whiles we are suitors to their throne, decays
The thing we sue for.

MENECRATES   We, ignorant of ourselves,   5
Beg often our own harms, which the wise powers
Deny us for our good; so find we profit
By losing of our prayers.

POMPEY   I shall do well.
The people love me, and the sea is mine;
My powers are crescent, and my auguring hope   10
Says it will come to the full. Mark Antony
In Egypt sits at dinner, and will make
No wars without doors. Caesar gets money where
He loses hearts. Lepidus flatters both,
Of both is flattered – but he neither loves,   15
Nor either cares for him.

MENAS   Caesar and Lepidus
Are in the field; a mighty strength they carry.

POMPEY   Where have you this? – 'tis false.

MENAS   From Silvius, sir.

POMPEY   He dreams. I know they are in Rome together
Looking for Antony. But all the charms of love,   20
Salt Cleopatra, soften thy wan'd lip!
Let witchcraft join with beauty, lust with both,
Tie up the libertine in a field of feasts,
Keep his brain fuming. Epicurean cooks
Sharpen with cloyless sauce his appetite,   25
That sleep and feeding may prorogue his honour
Even till a Lethe'd dullness –

Enter VARRIUS

How now, Varrius?

VARRIUS   This is most certain that I shall deliver:
Mark Antony is every hour in Rome
Expected. Since he went from Egypt, 'tis   30
A space for farther travel.

POMPEY   I could have given less matter
A better ear. Menas, I did not think
This amorous surfeiter would have donned his helm

49

35   *rear* raise
36   *opinion* opinion of ourselves
38   *hope* believe
39   *well greet* meet as friends
40   *did trespasses to* committed offences against
41   *warred upon* fought against
42   *moved* encouraged
43   *lesser ... greater* smaller quarrels are forgotten in the face of a greater threat
45   *pregnant* obvious   *square* fight
46   *entertainèd* received
48   *cement their divisions* join them together
50–1   *It only ... hands* our lives depend upon our bravery

Pompey's confidence is a little deflated with the news of Antony, whom he recognises as the main threat to his success. Despite some uncertainty, Pompey thinks that the divisions within the triumvirate will help his cause. This prepares us for the meeting of the triumvirs that follows.

2:2

The scene moves to Rome where Pompey's opponents are patching up their political differences. It opens with Lepidus advising Enobarbus about Antony's behaviour in the meeting. We see that the power struggle is between Antony and Caesar; Lepidus is the least of the triumvirs.

4   *like himself* as suits a man of his greatness   *move* angers
5   *look over Caesar's head* treat Caesar as man of less stature (than him)
6   *Mars* god of war with a reputation for a loud voice
      By Jupiter an oath on the principal Roman god
7–8   *Were I ... today* If I were Antony I would be defiant with Caesar
7   *Antonio* familiar form of Antony
9   *private stomaching* personal resentment
9–10 *Every time ... in't* there's a time for everything (proverbial)

For such a petty war – his soldiership
Is twice the other twain. But let us rear   35
The higher our opinion, that our stirring
Can from the lap of Egypt's widow pluck
The ne'er-lust-wearied Antony.

MENAS   I cannot hope
Caesar and Antony shall well greet together:
His wife that's dead did trespasses to Caesar,   40
His brother warred upon him – although I think
Not moved by Antony.

POMPEY   I know not, Menas,
How lesser enmities may give way to greater.
Were't not that we stand up against them all,
'Twere pregnant they should square between themselves,   45
For they have entertainèd cause enough
To draw their swords. But how the fear of us
May cement their divisions and bind up
The petty difference, we yet not know.
Be't as our gods will have't! It only stands   50
Our lives upon to use our strongest hands.
Come, Menas.

                                                            [*Exeunt*

2:2   *Enter* ENOBARBUS *and* LEPIDUS

LEPIDUS   Good Enobarbus, 'tis a worthy deed,
And shall become you well, to entreat your captain
To soft and gentle speech.

ENOBARBUS   I shall entreat him
To answer like himself. If Caesar move him,
Let Antony look over Caesar's head   5
And speak as loud as Mars. By Jupiter,
Were I the wearer of Antonio's beard,
I would not shave't today.

LEPIDUS   'Tis not a time
For private stomaching.

ENOBARBUS   Every time
Serves for the matter that is then born in't.   10

Compare what Lepidus says about putting personal rivalries aside for the greater good with the fears Pompey expresses in the previous scene: that 'lesser enmities would give way to greater' and lead Caesar and Antony to 'bind up the petty differences' between them.

12 *passion* too emotional

13 *stir no embers up* don't encourage trouble

How Antony and Caesar enter is important. Entering from different sides, their rivalry is signalled to the audience. Are they deliberately ignoring each other as they continue their conversations? Lepidus in lines 17–25 is again the peacemaker, asking for compromise between the rivals.

15 *compose* reach agreement

19 *leaner* slighter   *rend* split

20–2 *When we ... wounds* when we argue over small matters we make things worse

25 *Nor ... matter* do not let disrespectful behaviour worsen the situation

Does Antony offer a handshake or embrace of friendship to Caesar with the words 'I should do thus'? If so, there is still tension in the rivalry of the exchange that follows over who should sit first! The request to sit also implies that chairs and possibly a table for negotiations to take place around were brought on, either at the start of the scene or during the arrivals of Antony and Caesar.

29 *learn* understand

30 *being* if they are

31 *or ... or* either ... or

32 *myself* I was

34 *derogately* disparagingly or critically

LEPIDUS	But small to greater matters must give way.
ENOBARBUS	Not if the small come first.
LEPIDUS	Your speech is passion –

But, pray you, stir no embers up. Here comes
The noble Antony.

Enter ANTONY *and* VENTIDIUS

ENOBARBUS   And yonder Caesar.

Enter CAESAR, MAECENAS *and* AGRIPPA

ANTONY   If we compose well here, to Parthia.   **15**
Hark, Ventidius.

CAESAR   I do not know,
Maecenas – ask Agrippa.

LEPIDUS   Noble friends,
That which combined us was most great, and let not
A leaner action rend us. What's amiss,
May it be gently heard. When we debate   **20**
Our trivial difference loud, we do commit
Murder in healing wounds. Then, noble partners,
The rather for I earnestly beseech,
Touch you the sourest points with sweetest terms,
Nor curstness grow to the matter.

ANTONY   'Tis spoken well.   **25**
Were we before our enemies, and to fight,
I should do thus.

                                                      [*Flourish*

CAESAR   Welcome to Rome.

ANTONY   Thank you.

CAESAR   Sit.

ANTONY   Sit, sir.

CAESAR   Nay then.

ANTONY   I learn you take things ill which are not so;
Or, being, concern you not.

CAESAR   I must be laughed at   **30**
If, or for nothing or a little, I
Should say myself offended, and with you
Chiefly i'the world; more laughed at that I should
Once name you derogately, when to sound your name
It not concerned me.

ANTONY   My being in Egypt, Caesar,   **35**
What was't to you?

CAESAR   No more than my residing here at Rome
Might be to you in Egypt. Yet if you there

39 *practise … state* scheme to undermine my authority

40 *How intend you?* What do you mean?

41 *catch at* figure out

43–4 *their contestation … you* their uprising was on your behalf

46 *inquire* investigate

49 *with yours* against your authority

50 *stomach* wishes

51 *Having … cause?* having the same cause as you have against me

52–4 *If you'll … with this* if you insist on picking a quarrel, there are better causes that this

52–6 *patch … patched* Caesar picks up Antony's meaning of 'putting together hastily'

57–8 *I know … thought* I am sure you must have been aware

60 *graceful* favourable   *attend* look upon

61 *fronted* confronted, opposed

> *Antony criticises his wife's uncontrollable behaviour as a means of explanation. How might Antony's tone change as he moves from accusing his brother to the age-old technique of blaming the wife?*

62 *I would you* If you
      such another a wife of your own (then you'd understand)

63 *snaffle* a means of light control (of a horse)

64 *pace easily* train to walk at a steady pace (of a horse)

> *Is Enobarbus' ironic observation meant for the audience or the characters on stage? It's not an aside, yet Antony seems to ignore it completely as he continues describing his wife's behaviour by using images from breaking in a horse.*

67 *uncurbable* not controllable (of a horse)
      garboils disturbances

68 *not wanted* did not lack

69 *Shrewdness of policy* political cunning, with some deviousness
      grant agree

71 *But* nevertheless

> *Caesar interrupts Antony with another criticism. How might the actor playing Caesar react during Antony's explanation of his actions leading up to his 'I wrote to you'?*

72 *rioting* revelling

74 *gibe … audience* mock my messenger out of your presence

75 *fell … then* burst in on me without permission

76–7 *newly feasted … morning* been feasting with the night before and had a hangover

78–9 *of myself … pardon* explained why I was not myself, by way of apology

	Did practise on my state, your being in Egypt	
	Might be my question.	
ANTONY	How intend you – practised?	40
CAESAR	You may be pleased to catch at mine intent	
	By what did here befall me. Your wife and brother	
	Made wars upon me, and their contestation	
	Was theme for you. You were the word of war.	
ANTONY	You do mistake your business. My brother never	45
	Did urge me in his act. I did inquire it,	
	And have my learning from some true reports	
	That drew their swords with you. Did he not rather	
	Discredit my authority with yours,	
	And make the wars alike against my stomach,	50
	Having alike your cause? Of this, my letters	
	Before did satisfy you. If you'll patch a quarrel,	
	As a matter whole you have to make it with,	
	It must not be with this.	
CAESAR	You praise yourself	
	By laying defects of judgement to me, but	55
	You patched up your excuses.	
ANTONY	Not so, not so.	
	I know you could not lack, I am certain on't,	
	Very necessity of this thought, that I,	
	Your partner in the cause 'gainst which he fought,	
	Could not with graceful eyes attend those wars	60
	Which fronted mine own peace. As for my wife,	
	I would you had her spirit in such another;	
	The third o'the world is yours, which with a snaffle	
	You may pace easy, but not such a wife.	
ENOBARBUS	Would we had all such wives, that the men might go to wars with the women!	65
ANTONY	So much uncurbable, her garboils, Caesar,	
	Made out of her impatience – which not wanted	
	Shrewdness of policy too – I grieving grant	
	Did you too much disquiet. For that you must	70
	But say I could not help it.	
CAESAR	I wrote to you.	
	When rioting in Alexandria you	
	Did pocket up my letters, and with taunts	
	Did gibe my missive out of audience.	
ANTONY	Sir,	
	He fell upon me, ere admitted, then.	75
	Three kings I had newly feasted, and did want	
	Of what I was i'the morning; but next day	
	I told him of myself, which was as much	

55

80–1 *nothing … wipe him* no reason for a quarrel; let's keep this incident (of the messenger) out of our dispute

82 *article* terms *oath* taken as a member of the triumvirate

83 *Have tongue to charge* be able to accuse

> With Enobarbus' 'Soft', a warning to Caesar to 'Take it easy', we see a worsening situation. How might the stage furniture be used here to demonstrate increasing tension? Perhaps Caesar leaves his seat and moves across to Antony, until restrained by Enobarbus?

Compare the formal and legalistic tone of the language used by Antony and Caesar with the style of Cleopatra's words as she imagines Antony speaking in Act 1 Scene 5, lines 19–34. The legalistic tone is exemplified in Antony's substitution of 'neglected' for Caesar's word 'denied'. This very precise use of words is the style of politicians or lawyers.

90 *poisoned* either drunken, or the time spent with Cleopatra which 'poisoned' me

90–1 *bound me up … knowledge* kept me from knowing what I was doing

92–4 *but mine … without it* even though I'm going to be honest, I'm not going to impoverish my nobility, nor the power that comes from it

96 *ignorant motive* unwitting cause

100 *griefs* grievances

100–2 *quite … you* completely, as the situation requires you to be as one

> Enobarbus speaks without tact, prophetically saying there will be a time for renewed conflict between Antony and Caesar. Antony tells him twice to 'speak no more'. What gestures might Antony use to show his reaction to Enobarbus' words?
> Does this exchange heighten or reduce the tension?

108 *wrong this presence* offend this dignified company

109 *Go … stone* a dismissal of himself as thinking, but unspeaking (impertinent)

111 *his* Antony's, not Enobarbus'

112–13 *our conditions … acts* our natures result in different behaviour

114 *hoop* metal band around a cask *staunch* fast together

As to have asked him pardon. Let this fellow
Be nothing of our strife; if we contend,   **80**
Out of our question wipe him.

CAESAR   You have broken
The article of your oath, which you shall never
Have tongue to charge me with.

LEPIDUS   Soft, Caesar!

ANTONY   No, Lepidus, let him speak.
The honour is sacred which he talks on now,   **85**
Supposing that I lacked it. But on, Caesar –
The article of my oath.

CAESAR   To lend me arms and aid when I required them,
The which you both denied.

ANTONY   Neglected, rather –
And then when poisoned hours had bound me up   **90**
From mine own knowledge. As nearly as I may,
I'll play the penitent to you; but mine honesty
Shall not make poor my greatness, nor my power
Work without it. Truth is that Fulvia,
To have me out of Egypt, made wars here,   **95**
For which myself – the ignorant motive – do
So far ask pardon as befits mine honour
To stoop in such a case.

LEPIDUS   'Tis noble spoken.

MAECENAS   If it might please you to enforce no further
The griefs between ye: to forget them quite   **100**
Were to remember that the present need
Speaks to atone you.

LEPIDUS   Worthily spoken, Maecenas.

ENOBARBUS   Or, if you borrow one another's love for the instant, you may, when
you hear no more words of Pompey, return it again. You shall have time
to wrangle in when you have nothing else to do.   **105**

ANTONY   Thou art a soldier only – speak no more.

ENOBARBUS   That truth should be silent, I had almost forgot.

ANTONY   You wrong this presence, therefore speak no more.

ENOBARBUS   Go to, then; your considerate stone.

CAESAR   I do not much dislike the matter, but   **110**
The manner of his speech; for't cannot be
We shall remain in friendship, our conditions
So differing in their acts. Yet if I knew
What hoop should hold us staunch from edge to edge
O'the world, I would pursue it.

AGRIPPA   Give me leave, Caesar.   **115**

> Compare Antony's easy dismissal of his relationship with Cleopatra (line 122) after Caesar's discreet, if ironic, comment, with his opening words of the play (Act 1 Scene 1, lines 33–5). Is he untrue to Cleopatra or merely putting on a show to deceive the others?

123	*perpetual amity*	eternal friendship
125	*take Antony*	let Antony take
130	*jealousies*	suspicions
132–3	*Truths … be truths*	reports (of internal conflicts) will be dismissed; whereas now, all malicious rumours are believed
136	*present*	sudden
137	*ruminated*	thought on

A solution has been 'put on the table'. Antony waits for Caesar's reaction, Caesar waits for Antony's. How might this part of the scene be played? Are there long pauses after Agrippa's speech and before each of the protagonists speaks?

138	*touched*	influenced
144	*impediment*	obstacle (impediment is the word used in the marriage service)
145	*Further*	to confirm
151	*Fly … again!*	Let our friendship again desert us!

CAESAR	Speak, Agrippa.
AGRIPPA	Thou hast a sister by the mother's side,
	Admired Octavia. Great Mark Antony
	Is now a widower.
CAESAR	Say not so, Agrippa –
	If Cleopatra heard you, your reproof
	Where well deserved of rashness.

ANTONY   I am not married, Caesar. Let me hear Agrippa further speak.

AGRIPPA   To hold you in perpetual amity,
To make you brothers, and to knit your hearts
With an unslipping knot, take Antony   125
Octavia to his wife; whose beauty claims
No worse a husband than the best of men;
Whose virtue and whose general graces speak
That which none else can utter. By this marriage
All little jealousies, which now seem great,   130
And all great fears, which now import their dangers,
Would then be nothing. Truths would be tales,
Where now half-tales be truths. Her love to both
Would each to other, and all loves to both,
Draw after her. Pardon what I have spoke,   135
For 'tis a studied, not a present thought,
By duty ruminated.

ANTONY   Will Caesar speak?

CAESAR   Not till he hears how Antony is touched
With what is spoke already.

ANTONY   What power is in Agrippa,
If I would say 'Agrippa, be it so',   140
To make this good?

CAESAR   The power of Caesar, and
His power unto Octavia.

ANTONY   May I never
To this good purpose, that so fairly shows,
Dream of impediment! Let me have thy hand
Further this act of grace; and from this hour   145
The heart of brothers govern in our loves
And sway our great designs!

CAESAR   There's my hand.
A sister I bequeath you whom no brother
Did ever love so dearly. Let her live
To join our kingdoms and our hearts; and never   150
Fly off our loves again!

LEPIDUS   Happily, amen!

ANTONY   I did not think to draw my sword 'gainst Pompey,

153 *strange* exceptional

155 *my remembrance … report* my forgetfulness appears as ungratefulness

156 *At the heel of that* once that's done
defy him attack him

157 *presently* immediately

159 *Mount Misena* a southern Italian port

161 *fame* report

162 *spoke together* joined battle

165 *my sister's view* see my sister

With the exits of Antony and Caesar there is a change of tone in the scene. The removal of part or all of the furniture used during the previous negotiations might indicate this change.

170 *Half … Caesar* being one of Caesar's closest friends, Agrippa the other

173 *digested* arranged

174 *stayed well by't* a military phrase meaning 'stood up well to it'; here ironically refers to surviving the easy life in Egypt

175 *did … countenance* darkened the day by sleeping through it

176 *light* meaning includes both 'bright' and 'light-headed from drinking'

179 *This … eagle* this was nothing, like comparing a fly to an eagle (proverbial)

181 *square* fair, true

182 *pursed up* pocketed, i.e. captured

183 *Cydnus* now in modern Turkey

184 *devised* invented

Antony and Cleopatra meet for the first time.

The famous speech of Enobarbus (lines 185–200) describes in extravagant and imaginative language Cleopatra's appearance on the barge, an appearance that captures Antony's heart. What lighting techniques might a modern director use to enhance the speech's evocative and sensual beauty?

For he hath laid strange courtesies and great
Of late upon me. I must thank him only,
Lest my remembrance suffer ill report –   155
At heel of that, defy him.

LEPIDUS   Time calls upon's.
Of us must Pompey presently be sought,
Or else he seeks out us.

ANTONY   Where lies he?

CAESAR   About the Mount Misena.

ANTONY   What is his strength
By land?

CAESAR   Great, and increasing; but by sea   160
He is an absolute master.

ANTONY   So is the fame.
Would we had spoke together! Haste we for it.
Yet, ere we put ourselves in arms, dispatch we
The business we have talked of.

CAESAR   With most gladness;   165
And do invite you to my sister's view,
Whither straight I'll lead you.

ANTONY   Let us, Lepidus,
Not lack your company.

LEPIDUS   Noble Antony,
Not sickness should detain me.

                    [*Flourish. Exeunt all but* ENOBARBUS, AGRIPPA *and* MAECENAS

MAECENAS   Welcome from Egypt, sir.

ENOBARBUS   Half the heart of Caesar, worthy Maecenas! My honourable friend   170
Agrippa!

AGRIPPA   Good Enobarbus!

MAECENAS   We have cause to be glad, that matters are so well digested. You
stayed well by't in Egypt.

ENOBARBUS   Ay, sir, we did sleep day out of countenance and made the night   175
light with drinking.

MAECENAS   Eight wild boars roasted whole at breakfast, and but twelve persons
there – is this true?

ENOBARBUS   This was but as a fly by an eagle. We had much more monstrous
matter of feast, which worthily deserved noting.   180

MAECENAS   She's a most triumphant lady, if report be square to her.

ENOBARBUS   When she first met Mark Antony, she pursed up his heart upon the
river of Cydnus.

AGRIPPA   There she appeared indeed! – or my reporter devised well for her.

186 *barge* ceremonial river boat *burnished* polished brilliantly

192 *As amorous of their strokes* as if in love with their caresses

194 *cloth-of-gold, of tissue* rich, yet delicate, fabric with gold thread woven into it

195–6 *O'erpicturing … nature* surpassing even portraits where artists used their imaginations to picture Venus (the goddess of love)

198 *divers-coloured* many-coloured

199 *To glow* flushed

200 *undid did* paradox: the fans, in cooling, induced warm colours in the face

---

Compare how the image of the fan that can both cool and inflame is used here and by Philo, in his opening speech of the play (1.1.9–10).

---

200 *rare* what a rare vision

201 *Nereides* sea-nymphs

202 *So* like, as if *tended … eyes* attended her closely

203 *made … adornings* their graceful movements were pleasurable to watch

204 *seeming mermaid steers* one of the gentlewomen appears to steer the barge *tackle* sails, ropes and rigging

206 *yarely … office* nimbly perform their tasks

208 *wharfs* riverbanks

208–9 *cast … upon her* emptied to watch her

211 *but for vacancy* except that it would have created a vacuum

213 *a gap in nature* a vacuum that nature detests

Compare the use of 'Egyptian' in line 213 with Philo's 'gypsy' in line 10 of the play's opening scene. In Shakespeare's time both words were synonymous, often used in association with fickle and devious women. Here the use of 'rare', meaning priceless, in 'rare Egyptian' creates an oxymoron – a figure of speech involving two normally contradictory terms

---

220 *ordinary* supper

221 *Royal wench* another oxymoron, as a wench was a woman of low status

222–3 *She made … cropped* Two images are at work here: in the first, war becomes peace, as swords turn into ploughshares; the second is sexual, as their child (Caesarion) is the fruit of Caesar's sexual intercourse with Cleopatra.

223 *cropped* bore fruit

ENOBARBUS   I will tell you.   **185**
        The barge she sat in, like a burnished throne,
        Burned on the water. The poop was beaten gold;
        Purple the sails, and so perfumed that
        The winds were lovesick with them. The oars were silver,
        Which to the tune of flutes kept stroke, and made   **190**
        The water which they beat to follow faster,
        As amorous of their strokes. For her own person,
        It beggared all description. She did lie
        In her pavilion – cloth-of-gold, of tissue –
        O'erpicturing that Venus where we see   **195**
        The fancy outwork nature. On each side her
        Stood pretty dimpled boys, like smiling Cupids,
        With divers-coloured fans, whose wind did seem
        To glow the delicate cheeks which they did cool,
        And what they undid did.

AGRIPPA   O, rare for Antony!   **200**

ENOBARBUS   Her gentlewomen, like the Nereides,
        So many mermaids, tended her i'the eyes,
        And made their bends adornings. At the helm
        A seeming mermaid steers. The silken tackle
        Swell with the touches of those flower-soft hands,   **205**
        That yarely frame the office. From the barge
        A strange invisible perfume hits the sense
        Of the adjacent wharfs. The city cast
        Her people out upon her; and Antony,
        Enthroned i' the market-place, did sit alone,   **210**
        Whistling to the air; which, but for vacancy,
        Had gone to gaze on Cleopatra too
        And made a gap in nature.

AGRIPPA   Rare Egyptian!

ENOBARBUS   Upon her landing, Antony sent to her,
        Invited her to supper. She replied   **215**
        It should be better be became her guest;
        Which she entreated. Our courteous Antony,
        Whom ne'er the word of 'No' woman heard speak,
        Being barbered ten times o'er, goes to the feast,
        And, for his ordinary, pays his heart   **220**
        For what his eyes eat only.

AGRIPPA   Royal wench! –
        She made great Caesar lay his sword to bed.
        He ploughed her and she cropped.

ENOBARBUS   I saw her once
        Hop forty paces through the public street,
        And – having lost her breath – she spoke, and panted,   **225**

226 *defect perfection* paradoxically made an attraction out of her weakness (breathlessness)
227 *breathless … forth* even breathing so, she creates an image of power
230 *custom stale* familiarity will never make her dull and dry

> Compare Enobarbus' image of satisfying sexual appetites in lines 230–3 with Pompey's description in Act 2 Scene 1, lines 20–7.

234 *Become themselves in her* she makes beautiful
235 *riggish* lustful
238 *lottery* prize

Antony and Caesar settle their differences, using Antony's marriage to Caesar's sister Octavia. Enobarbus immediately undermines this alliance for the audience with his emphatic belief in Antony's bond with Cleopatra, and her power over him. Will Enobarbus' prediction prove true?

2:3

The audience now sees how sincere Antony is about his acceptance of Octavia and his seeming rejection of Cleopatra. Or will Enobarbus' predictions be realised?

The stage direction that Octavia enters between Antony and Caesar indicates the emotional divide between brother and husband that Octavia will finds herself in. It is interesting that the first words Antony speaks are an apology for future absence. Is 'the world' perhaps an unconscious reference to Egypt?

1 *world* Roman Empire, i.e. official business
5 *Read not … report* don't believe popular reports of my faults
6 *kept my square* behaved correctly
7 *the rule* correctly; both 'square' and 'rule' are metaphors of measurement

What does the audience read into Octavia leaving with her brother rather than staying with Antony? Perhaps a pause before the entrance of the Soothsayer would give time for Antony to show his emotional state, as his first words are about being in Egypt?

10 *sirrah* term of address to inferiors

That she did make defect perfection,
And, breathless, power breathe forth.

MAECENAS   Now Antony must leave her utterly.

ENOBARBUS   Never; he will not.
Age cannot wither her nor custom stale   230
Her infinite variety. Other women cloy
The appetites they feed, but she makes hungry
Where most she satisfies. For vilest things
Become themselves in her, that the holy priests
Bless her when she is riggish.   235

MAECENAS   If beauty, wisdom, modesty, can settle
The heart of Antony, Octavia is
A blessèd lottery to him.

AGRIPPA   Let us go.
Good Enobarbus, make yourself my guest
Whilst you abide here.

ENOBARBUS   Humbly, sir, I thank you.   240

[*Exeunt*

2:3   *Enter* **ANTONY** *and* **CAESAR**, *with* **OCTAVIA** *between them*

ANTONY   The world, and my great office, will sometimes
Divide me from your bosom.

OCTAVIA   All which time,
Before the gods my knee shall bow my prayers
To them for you.

ANTONY   Good night, sir. My Octavia,
Read not my blemishes in the world's report.   5
I have not kept my square, but that to come
Shall all be done by the rule. Good night, dear lady.

OCTAVIA   Good night, sir.

CAESAR   Good night.

[*Exeunt* **CAESAR** *and* **OCTAVIA**

Enter the **SOOTHSAYER**

ANTONY   Now, sirrah: you do wish yourself in Egypt?   10

SOOTHSAYER Would I had never come from thence, nor you thither.

ANTONY   If you can, your reason?

13   *see it in my motion* know it intuitively *hie* hurry

18   *daemon* guarding spirit

> What lighting might a director use in order to enhance the Soothsayer's warning? His dangerous advice seems to disturb Antony. Is that because it voices Antony's deeper feelings?

23   *no more but when* only

25   *of* because of

26   *lustre thickens* glory dims

28   *govern* protect

29   *But ... noble* when Caesar is not near, your guarding sprit again is noble

31   *Parthia* a kingdom south-east of the Caspian Sea

> With the exit of the Soothsayer we see one of the few occasions when Antony is alone declaring his real intentions. Does he speak directly to the audience or consider his words, as though thinking aloud?

31   *Be it ... hap* whether it is skill or chance

32   *him* Caesar

33–4   *my better ... chance* my superior skill cannot beat his luck

34   *speeds* wins

35–7   *His cocks ... at odds* his fighting cocks and fighting quails beat mine against heavy odds in my favour

37   *inhooped* a ring or hoop for fighting birds

38   *peace* for political purposes

> Enobarbus is shown to be right in predicting that Antony would never reject Cleopatra. We are made aware of the forthcoming military action, but how will Antony deal with Octavia, Caesar and the threat of Pompey? And how will Cleopatra react to the news about Antony and Octavia?

SOOTHSAYER I see it in my motion, have it not in my tongue; but yet hie you to
Egypt again.

ANTONY   Say to me, whose fortunes shall rise higher – Caesar's or mine?   **15**

SOOTHSAYER Caesar's.
Therefore, O Antony, stay not by his side.
Thy daemon – that thy spirit which keeps thee – is
Noble, courageous, high, unmatchable,
Where Caesar's is not. But near him thy angel   **20**
Becomes afeard, as being o'erpowered. Therefore
Make space enough between you.

ANTONY   Speak this no more.

SOOTHSAYER To none but thee; no more but when to thee.
If thou dost play with him at any game,
Thou art sure to lose; and of that natural luck,   **25**
He beats thee 'gainst the odds. Thy lustre thickens
When he shines by. I say again, they spirit
Is all afraid to govern thee near him;
But he away, 'tis noble.

ANTONY   Get thee gone –
Say to Ventidius I would speak with him.   **30**
He shall to Parthia.

                                    [*Exit* **SOOTHSAYER**

                    Be it art or hap,
He hath spoken true. The very dice obey him,
And in our sports my better cunning faints
Under his chance. If we draw lots, he speeds;
His cocks do win the battle still of mine   **35**
When it is all to nought; and his quails ever
Beat mine, inhooped, at odds. I will to Egypt;
And though I make this marriage for my peace,
I'the East my pleasure lies.

                Enter **VENTIDIUS**

                    O come, Ventidius,
You must to Parthia. Your commission's ready –   **40**
Follow me and receive't.

                                    [*Exeunt*

Antony and Cleopatra

2:4

In this short scene the audience are reminded of the political activity going on and the long distances involved in the military action.

2 *Your ... after* after your generals
3 *e'en but* just
6 *conceive* understand
   the Mount Mount Misena, as mentioned by Caesar in Act 2 Scene 2
8 *My ... about* my plans involve the longer route

The Roman generals are on their way to confront Pompey, but what of Cleopatra?

2:5

The setting reverts to the luxurious, languid atmosphere of Alexandria, a sharp contrast with the political intrigues and military activity of Rome.

Stage furniture, such as couches to lounge on, might be brought on at the start of this scene. It is difficult to be languid standing up!

1 *moody* melancholy, a mood often associated with love

Cleopatra first asks for music, then dismisses it and instead requests a game. She uses sexual innuendo with Mardian, the eunuch. To stress her moods what movements might the actor playing Cleopatra use in the opening lines of this scene?

5–6 *as well ... woman* There is sexual innuendo in her meaning: there is no difference between a eunuch and a woman in 'playing with a woman'.
8 *will* continues the bawdy references of the previous 'playing'; here it refers to the penis and/or sexual desire   *come too short* continues the bawdy sexual imagery
9 *actor* another bawdy reference – the 'act' is the sexual act
10 *angle* fishing tackle
11 *betray* deceive

68

2:4

Enter **Lepidus, Maecenas** *and* **Agrippa**

Lepidus   Trouble yourselves no further. Pray you, hasten
Your generals after.

Agrippa   Sir, Mark Antony
Will e'en but kiss Octavia, and we'll follow.

Lepidus   Till I shall see you in your soldier's dress,
Which will become you both, farewell.

Maecenas   We shall,   5
As I conceive the journey, be at the Mount
Before you, Lepidus.

Lepidus   Your way is shorter;
My purposes do draw me much about –
You'll win two days upon me.

Maecenas *and* **Agrippa**   Sir, good success!

Lepidus   Farewell.   10

                                              [*Exeunt*

2:5

Enter **Cleopatra, Charmian, Iras** *and* **Alexas**

Cleopatra   Give me some music – music, moody food
Of us that trade in love.

All   The music, ho!

Enter **Mardian,** *the eunuch*

Cleopatra   Let it alone! Let's to billiards – come, Charmian.

Charmian   My arm is sore; best play with Mardian.

Cleopatra   As well a woman with an eunuch played   5
As with a woman. Come you'll play with me, sir?

Mardian   As well as I can, madam.

Cleopatra   And when good will is showed, though't come too short,
The actor may plead pardon. I'll none now.
Give me mine angle, we'll to the river – there,   10
My music playing far off, I will betray
Tawny-finned fishes; my bended hook shall pierce

Antony and Cleopatra

> Charmian and Cleopatra recall happier times when Cleopatra
> tricked Antony in a fishing contest and then, after a night of revelry,
> dressed him in her clothes while she wore his sword. The physical
> depiction of these events by the two actors would heighten the
> happy mood of this part of the scene.

17 *salt-fish* dried fish

18 *fervency* excitement

21 *Ere ... hour* before 9 a.m.

22 *tires* head-dresses   *mantles* clothes

23 *sword Philippan* Antony's sword commemorating the victory at
Philippi

> The arrival of the messenger immediately changes Cleopatra's
> mood. There is dramatic irony in that the audience already knows
> the bad news that the messenger fears to give Cleopatra. The
> tension builds as the messenger is hardly given a chance to respond
> to Cleopatra's anxious interrogation.

28 *yield him* deliver news of him

30 *lipped* put their lips to

33 *well* in that they are dead   *Bring ... that* if that's what you mean

36 *go to* go on

38 *so tart a favour* so sour an expression

39 *trumpet* declare

40 *Fury* an allusion to the Furies – goddesses of vengeance, associated
with madness, who were depicted with snakes twined in their hair

41 *formal* normal

> There is much potential for action between the two as Cleopatra
> offers the luckless messenger a mixture of threats of dire
> punishments and promises of rich rewards, depending on his news
> about Antony. What advice might the director give to the two actors
> about playing this part of the scene?

Their slimy jaws, and as I draw them up
I'll think them every one an Antony,
And say, 'Ah, ha! Y'are caught!'

CHARMIAN   'Twas merry when   **15**
You wagered on your angling, when your diver
Did hang a salt-fish on his hook; which he
With fervency drew up.

CLEOPATRA   That time – O times! –
I laughed him out of patience; and that night
I laughed him into patience, and next morn,   **20**
Ere the ninth hour, I drunk him to his bed;
Then put my tires and mantles on him, whilst
I wore his sword Philippan.

Enter a MESSENGER

              O, from Italy!
Ram thou thy fruitful tidings in mine ears,
That long time have been barren.

MESSENGER   Madam, madam –   **25**

CLEOPATRA   Antonio's dead! – If thou say so, villain,
Thou kill'st thy mistress; but well and free,
If thou so yield him, there is gold and here
My bluest veins to kiss, a hand that kings
Have lipped, and trembled kissing.   **30**

MESSENGER   First, madam, he is well.

CLEOPATRA   Why, there's more gold.
But, sirrah, mark, we use
To say the dead are well. Bring it to that,
The gold I give thee will I melt and pour
Down thy ill-uttering throat.   **35**

MESSENGER   Good madam, hear me.

CLEOPATRA   Well, go to, I will.
But there's no goodness in thy face if Antony
Be free and healthful – so tart a favour
To trumpet such good tidings! If not well,
Thou shouldst come like a Fury crowned with snakes,   **40**
Not like a formal man.

MESSENGER   Will't please you hear me?

CLEOPATRA   I have a mind to strike thee ere thou speak'st.
Yet, if thou say Antony lives, is well,
Or friends with Caesar, or not captive to him,
I'll set thee in a shower of gold, and hail   **45**
Rich pearls upon thee.

MESSENGER   Madam, he's well.

50–51 *does allay … precedence* spoils what seemed promising

53 *malefactor* wrong-doer

54 *pack of matter* everything

58 *bound* married; Cleopatra takes 'bound' to mean Antony owes her a favour

59 *turn* With black humour the messenger makes a sexual pun on 'turn'.

> The messenger finally delivers the news of Antony's marriage with an ill-advised joke. Cleopatra goes into a violent rage, beating him and threatening him with a knife. The scene with the messenger can be played for either knockabout comedy or sadistic violence, or both.

63 *spurn* kick

64 *hales (stage direction)* drags

71 *boot* reward

71–2 *what gift … beg* whatever gifts a man of your humble expectations could ask

CLEOPATRA	Well said.
MESSENGER	And friends with Caesar.
CLEOPATRA	Th'art an honest man.
MESSENGER	Caesar and he are greater friends than ever.
CLEOPATRA	Make thee a fortune from me.
MESSENGER	But yet, madam –

CLEOPATRA   I do not like 'But yet' – it does allay   50
    The good precedence. Fie upon 'But yet'!
    'But yet' is as a gaoler to bring forth
    Some monstrous malefactor. Prithee, friend,
    Pour out the pack of matter to mine ear,
    The good and bad together: he's friends with Caesar,   55
    In state of health, thou sayst, and, thou sayst, free.

MESSENGER   Free, madam? – no, I made no such report;
    He's bound unto Octavia.

CLEOPATRA   For what good turn?

MESSENGER   For the best turn i'the bed.

CLEOPATRA   I am pale, Charmian.

MESSENGER   Madam, he's married to Octavia.   60

CLEOPATRA   The most infectious pestilence upon thee!

                                                  [Strike him down

MESSENGER   Good madam, patience.

CLEOPATRA   What say you? Hence,

                                              [Strikes him
    Horrible villain, or I'll spurn thine eyes
    Like balls before me! I'll unhair thy head!

                              [She hales him up and down
    Thou shalt be whipped with wire and stewed in brine,   65
    Smarting in lingering pickle!

MESSENGER   Gracious madam,
    I that do bring the news made not the match.

CLEOPATRA   Say 'tis not so, a province I will give thee,
    And make thy fortunes proud. The blow thou hadst
    Shall make thy peace for moving me to rage,   70
    And I will boot thee with what gift beside
    Thy modesty can beg.

MESSENGER   He's married, madam.

CLEOPATRA   Rogue, thou hast lived too long.

                                              [Draws a knife

MESSENGER   Nay, then I'll run.
    What mean you, madam? I have made no fault.

                                              [Exit

75   *keep … yourself* control yourself

77   *'scape* escape

78   *kindly* natural

Compare Cleopatra's cry 'Melt Egypt into Nile' with Antony's pledge that he would rather 'Let Rome in Tiber melt' (1.1.33) than give up Cleopatra. In her agony at being deserted she wishes for the end of the world, when every creature turns into a serpent.

Cleopatra regrets her treatment of the messenger as being unworthy of a woman of her nobility. But how does Charmian know the messenger is scared to come back in? Is he cowering at the edge of the stage, or does Charmian go to the side and, without exiting, look for him?

83   *meaner* servant

85–6   *it is … news* it is dangerous to bring bad news (often messengers of bad news were killed on the spot)

86–8   *Give … be felt* give good news, but bad news becomes known by its effects

92   *confound* destroy   *Dost … still?* Are you sticking to that story?

94   *So* even if

95   *cistern* lake

96   *Narcissus* in Greek mythology, a beautiful youth who loved his own reflection

99–101   *Take … unequal* don't be offended that I'm unwilling to offend you, but it seems unfair to punish me for answering you

102   *his fault* Antony's crime (of marriage)   *knave* rogue

103   *That … sure of!* you're not as bad as the news you bring

105   *dear* emotionally costly

106   *Lie … 'em!* may you be unable to sell your goods and so be ruined by them

---

The actor playing Cleopatra has shown a sweeping range of emotions during this scene. After her aggressive violence, we now see her suffering rejection, desperate to know about her rival, wanting to forget Antony, and yet being unable to do so. How might the audience's sympathy be affected during the final moments of this scene?

CHARMIAN   Good madam, keep yourself within yourself –   75
   The man is innocent.

CLEOPATRA   Some innocents 'scape not the thunderbolt.
   Melt Egypt into Nile, and kindly creatures
   Turn all to serpents! Call the slave again.
   Though I am mad, I will not bite him. Call!   80

CHARMIAN   He is afeard to come.

CLEOPATRA   I will not hurt him.
   These hands do lack nobility, that they strike
   A meaner than myself; since I myself
   Have given myself the cause.

      Enter the MESSENGER *again*

       Come hither, sir.
   Thought it be honest, it is never good   85
   To bring bad news. Give to a gracious message
   An host of tongues, but let ill tidings tell
   Themselves, when they be felt.

MESSENGER   I have done my duty.

CLEOPATRA   Is he married?
   I cannot hate thee worser than I do   90
   If thou again say 'Yes'.

MESSENGER   He's married, madam.

CLEOPATRA   The gods confound thee! Dost thou hold there still?

MESSENGER   Should I lie, madam?

CLEOPATRA   O, I would thou didst,
   So half my Egypt were submerged and made
   A cistern for scaled snakes! Go get thee hence –   95
   Hadst thou Narcissus in thy face, to me
   Thou wouldst appear most ugly. He is married?

MESSENGER   I crave your highness' pardon.

CLEOPATRA   He is married?

MESSENGER   Take no offence that I would not offend you;
   To punish me for what you make me do   100
   Seems much unequal. He's married to Octavia.

CLEOPATRA   O that his fault should make a knave of thee,
   That art not what th'art sure of! Get thee hence.
   The merchandise which thou hast brought from Rome
   Are all too dear for me: 105
   Lie they upon thy hand, and be undone by 'em!

         [*Exit* MESSENGER

CHARMIAN   Good your highness, patience.

CLEOPATRA   In praising Antony, I have dispraised Caesar.

113 *feature* physical features
114 *inclination* kind of person she is
116 *him* Antony
117 *painted one way … Gorgon* one side of Antony is like a monster. The Gorgon was a hideous mythical monster, with snakes for hair, whose look could turn victims to stone.
118 *The … Mars* on his other side Antony is a magnificent figure of a man

We see several aspects of Cleopatra's tempestuous character in this short scene. She remembers fondly some good times with Antony, yet the news of his marriage drives her to violence. Her dilemma is that she wants to forget Antony, but she cannot. Does the audience hope that Antony will return soon, knowing that he has already rejected Octavia? But what about the war against Pompey?

2:6

Back in Italy, Pompey meets the triumvirs. Will it be war or peace?

To highlight the conflict between the two groups, each enters at opposite doors. To create the military mood, Pompey's entrance is heralded with drum and trumpet, while marching soldiers accompany the triumvirs.

2 *meet* suitable
3 *come to words* a play on 'come to blows'
4 *purposes* proposals
6 *tie up* keep (swords in the scabbard)
7 *tall* brave
9 *world* Roman Empire
10 *factors* representatives
11 *Wherefore* why *want* lack

From lines 10 to 23 Pompey argues that he is entitled to avenge his father's death, in the same way that Julius Caesar was avenged. How might Pompey emphasise his account of recent Roman history? How might the triumvirs react to his angry argument?

13 *Brutus* along with Cassius, he assassinated Julius Caesar
    ghosted haunted (by Julius Caesar's ghost)
14 *labouring* fighting

CHARMIAN Many times, madam.

CLEOPATRA I am paid for't now. Lead me from hence – I faint,   **110**
    O Iras! Charmian! – 'Tis no matter.
    Go to the fellow, good Alexas, bid him
    Report the feature of Octavia, her years,
    Her inclination, let him not leave out
    The colour of her hair. Bring me word quickly.   **115**

                                        [*Exit* ALEXAS

    Let him for ever go! – Let him not, Charmian:
    Though he be painted one way like a Gorgon,
    The other way's a Mars. [*To* MARDIAN] Bid you Alexas
    Bring me word how tall she is. Pity me, Charmian,
    But do not speak to me. Lead me to my chamber.   **120**

                                        [*Exeunt*

2:6 *Flourish. Enter* POMPEY *and* MENAS *at one door, with drum and trumpet;*
  at another, CAESAR, LEPIDUS, ANTONY, ENOBARBUS, MAECENAS, AGRIPPA,
    with soldiers marching

POMPEY Your hostages I have, so have you mine;
    And we shall talk before we fight.

CAESAR   Most meet
    That first we come to words; and therefore have we
    Our written purposes before us sent,
    Which if thou hast considered, let us know   **5**
    If 'twill tie up thy discontented sword
    And carry back to Sicily much tall youth
    That else must perish here.

POMPEY   To you all three,
    The senators alone of this great world,
    Chief factors for the gods: I do not know   **10**
    Wherefore my father should revengers want,
    Having a son and friends, since Julius Caesar,
    Who at Philippi the good Brutus ghosted,
    There saw you labouring for him. What was't
    That moved pale Cassius to conspire? And what   **15**
    Made the all-honoured, honest Roman, Brutus,

17   *rest* others   *courtiers* wooers

18   *drench* with the blood of Julius Caesar

18–19   *but ... man* they only wanted men to be equal (i.e. no monarch or dictator)

20   *rig* equip

22   *despiteful* cruel

> Is Caesar's 'Take your time' spoken sarcastically, or is he genuinely concerned, advising Pompey to calm himself? How might the actor emphasise this by his looks to Antony and Lepidus?

24   *fear* frighten

25   *speak with* encounter you (in battle)

26   *o'ercount* outnumber

26–7   *At land ... house* Pompey puns on 'o'ercount', reminding Antony that he bought but did not pay for Pompey's father's house.

28   *But since ... himself* Pompey alludes to the cuckoo laying eggs in another's nest.

29   *as thou mayst* while you can

> Pompey turns to personal insults with Antony, especially with his 'cuckoo' reference. Does Lepidus intervene physically as well as verbally?

30   *from the present* beside the point

32–3   *Which do ... embraced* don't be persuaded to accept our offer, but think carefully about what you will gain

33–4   *And ... fortune* what the consequences will be if you try something more ambitious

> Does Pompey read the offer of the triumvirs from a scroll? Might a reading have a more dramatic impact as Pompey recites the proposals?

37   *'greed* agreed

38   *part* depart   *unhacked edges* unused swords

39   *targes undinted* undamaged shields

43   *praise of* credit for

47   *studied* prepared

With the armed rest, courtiers of beauteous freedom,
To drench the Capitol, but that they would
Have one man but a man? And that is it
Hath made me rig my navy, at whose burden   20
The angered ocean foams; with which I meant
To scourge th'ingratitude that despiteful Rome
Cast on my noble father.

CAESAR   Take your time.

ANTONY   Thou canst not fear us, Pompey, with thy sails.
We'll speak with thee at sea. At land thou know'st   25
How much we do o'ercount thee.

POMPEY   At land indeed
Thou dost o'ercount me of my father's house;
But since the cuckoo builds not for himself,
Remain in't as thou mayst.

LEPIDUS   Be pleased to tell us –
For this is from the present – how you take   30
The offers we have sent you.

CAESAR   There's the point.

ANTONY   Which do not be entreated to, but weigh
What it is worth embraced.

CAESAR   And what may follow,
To try a larger fortune.

POMPEY   You have made me offer
Of Sicily, Sardinia; and I must   35
Rid all the sea of pirates; then, to send
Measures of wheat to Rome; this 'greed upon,
To part with unhacked edges and bear back
Our targes undinted.

ALL THE TRIUMVIRS   That's our offer.

POMPEY   Know, then,
I came before you here a man prepared   40
To take this offer. But Mark Antony
Put me to some impatience. Though I lose
The praise of it by telling, you must know,
When Caesar and your brother were at blows,
Your mother came to Sicily and did find   45
Her welcome friendly.

ANTONY   I have heard it, Pompey,
And am well studied for a liberal thanks,
Which I do owe you.

POMPEY   Let me have your hand –
I did not think, sir, to have met you here.

51	*timelier ... purpose* sooner than I intended
52	*gained by't* profited by it
53–4	*I know ... face* whatever experiences may have marked my face
55	*she* Fortune (experiences)
56	*vassal* slave
58	*composition* agreement, treaty
61	*That will I* I'll go first
62	*take the lot* accept the results of the drawing of lots

Is Pompey's tactlessness intentional? Why does he use an implied sexual indulgence in 'Grew fat with feasting there' when he mentions Julius Caesar, Cleopatra's previous lover? Enobarbus relieves the tension by taking Pompey away from Antony's hearing.

68	*Apollodorus* a reference to the famous incident when Cleopatra as a young girl seduced Caesar after having Apollodorus smuggle her into his presence hidden in a carpet
71	*How far'st thou* How are you faring?
73	*toward* impending
78	*Enjoy thy plainness* indulge in your blunt speaking
79	*It ... thee* it suits you

| ANTONY | The beds i'the East are soft; and thanks to you, | **50** |

ANTONY   The beds i'the East are soft; and thanks to you,   **50**
            That called me timelier than my purpose hither,
            For I have gained by't.

CAESAR   Since I saw you last
            There is a change upon you.

POMPEY   Well, I know not
            What counts harsh Fortune casts upon my face,
            But in my bosom shall she never come   **55**
            To make my heart her vassal.

LEPIDUS   Well met here.

POMPEY   I hope so, Lepidus. Thus we are agreed.
            I crave our composition may be written
            And sealed between us.

CAESAR   That's the next to do.

POMPEY   We'll feast each other ere we part, and let's   **60**
            Draw lots who shall begin.

ANTONY   That will I, Pompey.

POMPEY   No, Antony, take the lot. But first or last,
            Your fine Egyptian cookery shall have
            The fame. I have heard that Julius Caesar
            Grew fat with feasting there.

ANTONY   You have heard much.   **65**

POMPEY   I have fair meanings, sir.

ANTONY   And fair words to them.

POMPEY   Then so much have I heard.
            And I have heard Apollodorus carried –

ENOBARBUS   No more of that: he did so.

POMPEY   What, I pray you?

ENOBARBUS   A certain queen to Caesar in a mattress.   **70**

POMPEY   I know thee now. How far'st thou, soldier?

ENOBARBUS   Well –
            And well am like to do, for I perceive
            Four feasts are toward.

POMPEY   Let me shake thy hand,
            I never hated thee. I have seen thee fight
            When I have envied thy behaviour.

ENOBARBUS   Sir,   **75**
            I never loved you much; but I ha' praised ye
            When you have well deserved ten times as much
            As I have said you did.

POMPEY   Enjoy thy plainness,
            It nothing ill becomes thee.

> *Are Menas and Enobarbus standing apart as the four main
> characters exit? Menas' first comment on the treaty is an aside
> before he speaks to Enobarbus.*

83 *have known* met before

95 *take* arrest *kissing* clasping hands in embrace

96 *true* both honest and an accurate indication of character

97 *true* plain, without make-up

> *There is an implicit stage direction about handshakes and an
> indication of a friendlier, closer manner in the conversation that
> follows.*

98 *No slander* it's true

103 *Y'have said* you're right

107 *Marcus Antonius* Antony

108 *Pray ye* I beg your pardon

> *Menas cannot believe what he has just heard. He thought Antony
> was married to Cleopatra, not Caesar's sister. How might he show
> his incredulity at this news?*

111 *If I … prophesy so* if I were forced to predict the outcome, I
wouldn't (i.e. it won't last)

112 *policy* political convenience

Compare the play on the word 'band' (line 114), a marriage ring and a
'strangler' (line 115), with Act 2 Scene 2, line 114, where the play is on a
marriage ring and a confining hoop.

Aboard my galley I invite you all.   **80**
Will you lead, lords?

ALL THE TRIUMVIRS   Show's the way, sir.

POMPEY   Come.

[*Exeunt all but* ENOBARBUS *and* MENAS

MENAS [*Aside*] Thy father, Pompey, would ne'er have made this treaty. – You and
I have known, sir.

ENOBARBUS   At sea, I think.

MENAS   We have, sir.   **85**

ENOBARBUS   You have done well by water.

MENAS   And you by land.

ENOBARBUS   I will praise any man that will praise me – though it cannot be
denied what I have done by land.

MENAS   Nor what I have done by water.   **90**

ENOBARBUS   Yes, something you can deny for your own safety: you have been a
great thief by sea.

MENAS   And you by land.

ENOBARBUS   There I deny my land service. But give me your hand, Menas. If our
eyes had authority, here they might take two thieves kissing.   **95**

MENAS   All men's faces are true, whatsome'er their hands are.

ENOBARBUS   But there is never a fair woman has a true face.

MENAS   No slander, they steal hearts.

ENOBARBUS   We came hither to fight with you.

MENAS   For my part, I am sorry it is turned to a drinking. Pompey doth this **100**
day laugh away his fortune.

ENOBARBUS   If he do, sure he cannot weep't back again.

MENAS   Y'have said, sir. We looked not for Mark Antony here. Pray you, is
he married to Cleopatra?

ENOBARBUS   Caesar's sister is called Octavia.   **105**

MENAS   True, sir; she was the wife of Caius Marcellus.

ENOBARBUS   But she is now the wife of Marcus Antonius.

MENAS   Pray ye, sir?

ENOBARBUS   'Tis true.

MENAS   Then is Caesar and he for ever knit together.   **110**

ENOBARBUS   If I were bound to divine of this unity, I would not prophesy so.

MENAS   I think the policy of that purpose made more in the marriage than
the love of the parties.

ENOBARBUS   I think so too. But you shall find the band that seems to tie their
friendship together will be the very strangler of their amity. Octavia is **115**

116	*still conversation* quiet manner
119	*sighs* complaints *blow the fire up* enrage
120	*amity* friendship
121	*author of their variance* cause of their conflict
121–2	*use his affection* satisfy his sexual appetite
122	*where it is* i.e. with Cleopatra *married … his occasion* took a political opportunity, not married for love
123–4	*have a health for you* drink your health
125	*used* trained (with drinking)

Pompey accepts the peace terms and Enobarbus has predicted the breakdown of both Antony's marriage and his alliance with Caesar. Will his predictions come true?

2:7

The banquet to celebrate the peace treaty is in full swing on board Pompey's galley.

The richness of the banquet is indicated with the music and the entrance of the servants carrying trays of wine and food. Tables and seats need to be brought on at the same time. Before the banquet is shown, we are given a chance to see the great men of Rome through the eyes of humble servants.

1	*plants* word play on Latin for feet (the joke is about drunkenness)
3	*high-coloured* red-faced (from drinking)
4	*alms-drink* regular drinking from toasts
5	*pinch … disposition* annoy each other with their personalities
5–6	*No more* stop arguing
6	*reconciles … drink* persuades them to stop arguing and in return he drinks more
7	*discretion* common sense
8	*it is … fellowship* is what it is to be just a name among great men
8–10	*I had … heave* I would rather use a reed than a spear I couldn't throw
11–13	*into a huge … cheeks* to a high position and be seen to have no function there, is like having an eye socket with no eyes, which would ruin the face

The servants, after mocking Lepidus for his drunkenness and his weak position in the triumvirate, stand aside as the trumpet fanfare heralds the ceremonial entrance of the principals. Antony in mid-sentence is talking to a drunken Lepidus.

14	*take* measure
15	*scales* measuring marks *pyramid* obelisk (not what we recognise as a pyramid)
16	*dearth* famine
17	*foison* plent

of a holy, cold, and still conversation.

MENAS   Who would not have his wife so?

ENOBARBUS   Not he that himself is not so; which is Mark Antony. He will to his
             Egyptian dish again. Then shall the sighs of Octavia blow the fire up in
             Caesar, and – as I said before – that which is the strength of their amity   120
             shall prove the immediate author of their variance. Antony will use his
             affection where it is. He married but his occasion here.

MENAS   And thus it may be. Come, sir, will you aboard? I have a health for
             you.

ENOBARBUS   I shall take it, sir. We have used our throats in Egypt.   125

MENAS   Come, let's away.

                                                                          [*Exeunt*

2:7   *Music plays. Enter two or three* SERVANTS *with a banquet*

FIRST SERVANT   Here they'll be, man. Some o'their plants are ill-rooted already,
                 the least wind i'the world will blow them down.

SECOND SERVANT   Lepidus is high-coloured.

FIRST SERVANT   They have made him drink alms-drink.

SECOND SERVANT   As they pinch one another by the disposition, he cries out 'No   5
                 more'; reconciles them to his entreaty, and himself to the drink.

FIRST SERVANT   But it raises the greater war between him and his discretion.

SECOND SERVANT   Why, this it is to have a name in great men's fellowship. I had
                 as lief have a reed that will do me no service as a partisan I could not
                 heave.   10

FIRST SERVANT   To be called into a huge sphere, and not to be seen to move
                 in't, are the holes where eyes should be, which pitifully disaster the
                 cheeks.

             A sennet sounded. Enter CAESAR, ANTONY, POMPEY, LEPIDUS, AGRIPPA,
                 MAECENAS, ENOBARBUS, MENAS, *with other captains*

ANTONY   Thus do they, sir: they take the flow o'the Nile
             By certain scales i'the pyramid. They know   15
             By the height, the lowness, or the mean if dearth
             Or foison follow. The higher Nilus swells,
             The more it promises; as it ebbs, the seedsman
             Upon the slime and ooze scatters his grain,

20 *shortly* soon

With the repetition of 'your' we see Lepidus showing off. In what ways might the actor convey this drunken manner?

27 *out* stop drinking
28 *in* both 'drunk' and 'in the drinking session'
29 *Ptolemies* Egyptian royal family
    pyramises (drunken slurring of) pyramids

The exchanges between Menas and Pompey during the next twenty-five lines are spoken against a background of drinking and other conversations breaking into theirs. How might this be achieved?

33 *Forsake* leave
34 *Forbear me till anon* leave it until later

While Antony has some fun at Lepidus' drunken expense, Caesar hardly takes part in the conversations. Is he isolated, observing the scene, or joining in, smiling but watchful?

38 *it own* its
39 *the elements ... transmigrates* when it dies, its soul passes into another
45 *epicure* (1) a heavy drinker, (2) non-believer in transmigration
48 *merit* my past service
51 *ever ... fortunes* always been faithful to you

When Antony speaks of 'quicksands' he is referring to Lepidus' drunken state, but it may be a metaphor for the political conspiracy being plotted at that very moment. How might the audience be made aware of this secondary meaning?

An obelisk at Alexandria.

		20

And shortly comes to harvest.

LEPIDUS   Y'have strange serpents there?

ANTONY   Ay, Lepidus.

LEPIDUS   Your serpent of Egypt is bred now of your mud by the operation of your sun; so is your crocodile.

ANTONY   They are so.   25

POMPEY   Sit – and some wine! A health to Lepidus!

LEPIDUS   I am not so well as I should be, but I'll ne'er out.

ENOBARBUS   Not till you have slept; I fear me you'll be in till then.

LEPIDUS   Nay, certainly, I have heard the Ptolemies' pyramises are very goodly things; without contradiction I have heard that.   30

MENAS [*Aside to* **POMPEY**] Pompey, a word.

POMPEY [*Aside to* **MENAS**] Say in mine ear, what is't?

MENAS [*Aside to* **POMPEY**] Forsake thy seat, I do beseech thee, captain, And hear me speak a word.

POMPEY [*Aside to* **MENAS**]   Forbear me till anon.
[*Aloud*] This wine for Lepidus!   35
                              [**MENAS** *whispers in his ear*

LEPIDUS   What manner o'thing is your crocodile?

ANTONY   It is shaped, sir, like itself, and it is as broad as it has breadth. It is just so high as it is, and moves with it own organs. It lives by that which nourisheth it, and the elements once out of it, it transmigrates.

LEPIDUS   What colour is it of?   40

ANTONY   Of it own colour too.

LEPIDUS   'Tis a strange serpent.

ANTONY   'Tis so, and the tears of it are wet.

CAESAR   Will this description satisfy him?

ANTONY   With the health that Pompey gives him, else he is a very epicure.   45

POMPEY [*Aside to* **MENAS**] Go hang, sir, hang! Tell me of that? Away! Do as I bid you. [*Aloud*] Where's this cup I called for?

MENAS [*Aside to* **POMPEY**] If for the sake of merit thou wilt hear me, Rise from thy stool.

POMPEY [*Aside to* **MENAS**] I think th'art mad. The matter?   50
                              [*Rises and walks aside*

MENAS   I have ever held my cap off to thy fortunes.

POMPEY   Thou hast served me with much faith. What's else to say? Be jolly, lords.

ANTONY   These quicksands, Lepidus, Keep off them, for you sink.

MENAS   Wilt thou be lord of all the world?

57 *entertain* consider

59 *Will* who will *Hast … well?* Are you drunk?

61 *earthly Jove* king of the world, an allusion to Jove, the supreme ruler of the heavens

62 *pales* encloses *inclips* embraces

66 *fall to* cut

68 *In me* for me to do it

71 *Mine honour, it* it is my honour, not profit, directing me

72 *betrayed thine act* revealed your intentions
Being done unknown if it had been done without me knowing

75 *palled* decayed, weakened

76 *Who* whoever

After dismissing Menas' plot to assassinate the triumvirs, Pompey ironically toasts the unconscious Lepidus. What is Menas' reaction to this false good humour?

78 *pledge it* reply (to the salute or toast, with a drink)

86 *go on wheels* run so fast

87 *reels* drunken dancing

POMPEY	What sayst thou?	55

MENAS   Wilt thou be lord of the whole world? That's twice.

POMPEY   How should that be?

MENAS   But entertain it,
And though thou think me poor, I am the man
Will give thee all the world.

POMPEY   Hast thou drunk well?

MENAS   No, Pompey, I have kept me from the cup.   60
Thou art, if thou dar'st be, the earthly Jove;
Whate'er the ocean pales, or sky inclips,
Is thine, if thou wilt ha't.

POMPEY   Show me which way.

MENAS   These three world-sharers, these competitors,
Are in thy vessel. Let me cut the cable,   65
And when we are put off, fall to their throats.
All there is thine.

POMPEY   Ah, this thou shouldst have done,
And not have spoke on't! In me 'tis villainy;
In thee't had been good service. Thou must know
'Tis not my profit that does lead mine honour;   70
Mine honour, it. Repent that e'er thy tongue
Hath so betrayed thine act. Being done unknown,
I should have found it afterwards well done,
But must condemn it now. Desist, and drink.

MENAS [*Aside*] For this, I'll never follow thy palled fortunes more.   75
Who seeks and will not take, when one 'tis offered,
Shall never find it more.

POMPEY   This health to Lepidus!

ANTONY   Bear him ashore. I'll pledge it for him, Pompey.

ENOBARBUS   Here's to thee, Menas!

MENAS   Enobarbus, welcome!

POMPEY   Fill till the cup be hid.   80

ENOBARBUS   [*Pointing to the servant who carries off* LEPIDUS] There's a strong fellow,
Menas.

MENAS   Why?

ENOBARBUS   'A bears the third part of the world, man; seest not?

MENAS   The third part, then, is drunk. Would it were all,   85
That it might go on wheels!

ENOBARBUS   Drink thou; increase the reels.

MENAS   Come.

POMPEY   This is not yet an Alexandrian feast.

A Roman banquet.

90 *Strike the vessels* a toast or salute with a drink
91 *well forbear't* do without it (drinking the toast)
92 *wash my brain* getting drunk
93 *fouler* clogs it up
    Be a child o'the time give in and join us (in drinking)
94 *Possess … answer* my answer is, overcome the urge
97 *bacchanals* dances to celebrate Bachhus, the god of wine
98 *celebrate* sanctify
101 *Lethe* allusion to the river of forgetfulness
103 *place you* position you (for the dance)
104 *holding* singing refrain
105 *volley* produce noise

There is a lot of potential entertainment in Enobarbus arranging and choreographing a drunken ring-dance. While the rest stamp out the rhythm of the boy's drinking song, Caesar continues to stand apart both literally and metaphorically.

107 *pink eyne* half-closed eyes
108 *fats* vats
110 *Cup us* fill our drinks
113 *request you off* ask you to come ashore (with me)
115 *burnt our cheeks* red with drinking
117 *Splits what it speaks* trips over his words
117–18 *The wild … us all* this drinking has almost made us all fools
119 *try you* test your drinking ability

As the main party leaves to be rowed ashore by boat, Pompey and Antony show a drunken friendship. How might their intoxicated leave-taking be most effectively played? After their exit Menas orders the fanfare of trumpets and drums.

ANTONY	It ripens towards it. Strike the vessels, ho!	90
	Here's to Caesar!	

CAESAR   I could well forbear't.
It's monstrous labour when I wash my brain
And it grows fouler.

ANTONY   Be a child o'the time.

CAESAR   Possess it, I'll make answer –
But I had rather fast from all, four days,   95
Than drink so much in one.

ENOBARBUS   [*To* ANTONY]   Ha, my brave emperor,
Shall we dance now the Egyptian bacchanals
And celebrate our drink?

POMPEY   Let's ha't, good soldier.

ANTONY   Come, let's all take hands
Till that the conquering wine hath steeped our sense   100
In soft and delicate Lethe.

ENOBARBUS   All take hands.
Make battery to our ears with the loud music;
The while I'll place you; then the boy shall sing.
The holding every man shall beat as loud
As his strong sides can volley.   105

                    [*Music plays.* ENOBARBUS *places them hand in hand*

BOY [*Sings*] Come, thou monarch of the vine,
        Plumpy Bacchus with pink eyne!
        In thy fats our cares be drowned,
        With thy grapes our hairs be crowned.
            Cup us till the world go round,   110
            Cup us till the world go round!

CAESAR   What would you more? Pompey, good night. [*To* ANTONY] Good
brother,
Let me request you off – our graver business
Frowns at this levity. Gentle lords, let's part.
You see we have burnt our cheeks. Strong Enobarb   115
Is weaker than the wine, and mine own tongue
Splits what it speaks. The wild disguise hath almost
Anticked us all. What needs more words? Good night.
Good Antony, your hand.

POMPEY   I'll try you on the shore.

ANTONY   And shall, sir. Give's your hand.

POMPEY   O, Antony,   120
You have my father's house. But what, we are friends!
Come down into the boat.

123   *I'll not* I won't be going

125   *Neptune* Roman god of the sea

126   *sound out* an order to the musicians to play the fanfare

▌▌ *Enobarbus and Menas exit, perhaps mimicking both the noise and the playing of trumpets.*

During this mainly comic scene we see the Roman leaders revelling in drink, behaving in a manner they criticised the Egyptians for. The peace accord has been celebrated, but the villainy that lies beneath the surface of the various drunken friendships has been revealed.

Act 2 is concerned with the political and military threat of Pompey and its resolution. With Antony's marriage to Octavia there is some reconciliation between Antony and Caesar. But Cleopatra awaits Antony. We go into Act 3 wondering about the peace between Caesar and Antony and his choice between Cleopatra and Octavia.

ENOBARBUS   Take heed you fall not.

[*Exeunt all but* ENOBARBUS *and* MENAS

        Menas, I'll not on shore.

MENAS   No, to my cabin.
        These drums! These trumpets, flutes! What!
        Let Neptune hear we bid a loud farewell   125
        To these great fellows. Sound and be hanged, sound out!

[*Sound a flourish, with drums*

ENOBARBUS   Hoo, says 'a. There's my cap.

MENAS   Hoo! Noble captain, come.

[*Exeunt*

3:1

This scene, set on the frontiers of the Roman Empire in Syria, provides a comment on the activities of Rome's political leaders. We are given another perspective on Antony's character, this time from the viewpoint of his subordinates.

The stage direction tells the actors to enter exultantly. Yet the dead body borne in front is a sober reminder for the audience of the realities of war. What stage lighting would best set the mood for this scene?

1	*darting* a reference to the use of darts and arrows by the Parthians
2	*Marcus Crassus* Roman leader killed by the Parthian king Orodes
4	*Pacorus* son of Orodes
7	*fugitive ... follow* pursue the fleeing Parthians *Spur* race swiftly
12	*a lower place* a subordinate
13	*make ... act* become too successful
15	*him ... away* in Antony's absence
16	*ever* always
17	*in their ... person* by their military officers than themselves *Sossius* a soldier of the same rank as Ventidius
18 and 20	*his* Antony's (lieutenant)
19	*For ... renown* Because he acquired fame quickly
20	*by the minute* continually
23–4	*rather ... him* prefers loss of fame to loss of his leader's favour
27–9	*that ... distinction* that quality of discretion that separates the thinking soldier from the unthinking sword
31	*magical word* Antony's reputation
34	*jaded* driven like worn-out horses (jades)
35	*purposeth* proposes
35–6	*whither ... permit* there, with as much speed as our spoils of war will allow us

Compare this scene with other scenes where the reality of political survival is hidden beneath fine words and deceitful behaviour, such as Act 2 Scene 7.

Some directors cut this short scene, but without it the audience cannot see how jealously Antony defends his fame against any challenges from victorious subordinates.

3:1   *Enter* VENTIDIUS, *as it were in triumph, the dead body of*
PACORUS *borne before him; with* SILIUS *and other Romans, officers and soldiers*

VENTIDIUS   Now, darting Parthia, art thou struck; and now
              Pleased Fortune does of Marcus Crassus' death
              Make me revenger. Bear the king's son's body
              Before our army. Thy Pacorus, Orodes,
              Pays this for Marcus Crassus.

SILIUS   Noble Ventidius,   5
              Whilst yet with Parthian blood thy sword is warm,
              The fugitive Parthians follow. Spur through Media,
              Mesopotamia, and the shelters whither
              The routed fly. So thy grand captain Antony
              Shall set thee on triumphant chariots, and   10
              Put garlands on thy head.

VENTIDIUS   O Silius, Silius,
              I have done enough. A lower place, note well,
              May make too great an act. For learn this, Silius:
              Better to leave undone than by our deed
              Acquire too high a fame, when him we serve's away.   15
              Caesar and Antony have ever won
              More in their officer than person. Sossius,
              One of my place in Syria, his lieutenant,
              For quick accumulation of renown,
              Which he achieved by the minute, lost his favour.   20
              Who does i'the wars more than his captain can,
              Becomes his captain's captain; and ambition,
              The soldier's virtue, rather makes choice of loss
              Than gain which darkens him.
              I could do more to do Antonius good,   25
              But 'twould offend him, and in his offence
              Should my performance perish.

SILIUS   Thou hast, Ventidius, that
              Without the which a soldier and his sword
              Grants scarce distinction. Thou wilt write to Antony?

VENTIDIUS   I'll humbly signify what in his name,   30
              That magical word of war, we have effected –
              How, with his banners and his well-paid ranks,
              The ne'er-yet-beaten horse of Parthia
              We have jaded out o'the field.

SILIUS   Where is he now?

VENTIDIUS   He purposeth to Athens, whither, with what haste   35
              The weight we must convey with's will permit,
              We shall appear before him. On, there! Pass along!

                                              [*Exeunt*

3:2

Back in Rome the audience sees a sharp contrast with the previous scene. The leaders prepare their farewells, but first we hear mocking comments from Enobarbus and Agrippa.

  1 *brothers* Antony and Caesar *parted* departed
  2 *dispatched* finished their business
  3 *other three* the triumvirs
      sealing literally putting their seals on the peace agreement
  6 *green-sickness* love-sickness in young women (Enobarbus mocks Lepidus' hangover as being a result of his love for Caesar and Antony)

From ''Tis a noble Lepidus' at line 6 to line 20 the actors playing Enobarbus and Agrippa are given scope to display their ability to mock the weaknesses of Lepidus by imitating the way he flatters Antony and Caesar in his speech and mannerisms.

  9 *Jupiter* the principal Roman god
 11 *How!* What! *nonpareil* incomparable
 12 *Arabian bird* allusion to the legendary phoenix; an immortal bird, of which only one existed, which was reborn from its own ashes
16–17 *hearts ... number* Enobarbus employs the effective rhetorical device of listing. The two lists are paired; each of the nouns in the first list has its corresponding verb in the second.
 16 *figures* to do with mathematics or horoscopes
 17 *cast* calculate *number* put into lines of verse
 20 *shards* patches of dung between which the dung beetle (Lepidus) crawls

The trumpet sounding off stage is a signal for Antony's soldiers to mount their horses. It also heralds movement on stage with the entrance of the triumvirate and Octavia.

 23 *No further, sir* we must separate here
 25 *Use ... in't* use my sister well (as you would me)
 26 *As ... thee* as I think you will
26–7 *my farthest ... thy approof* I stake anything you will prove (to be a good wife)

How might the two actors during lines 24–36 try to hide the underlying distrust that still exists between Caesar and Antony? Notice how Caesar uses legal and military terms when talking about Octavia's marriage to Antony.

 28 *piece* masterpiece
 29 *cement* union
 30 *builded* intact
 32 *mean* intermediary *both parts* both of us
 33 *This* Octavia
 34 *In* by

3:2   *Enter* AGRIPPA *at one door,* ENOBARBUS *at another*

AGRIPPA   What, are the brothers parted?

ENOBARBUS   They have dispatched with Pompey; he is gone;
                      The other three are sealing. Octavia weeps
                      To part from Rome; Caesar is sad, and Lepidus
                      Since Pompey's feast, as Menas says, is troubled   5
                      With the green-sickness.

AGRIPPA   'Tis a noble Lepidus.

ENOBARBUS   A very fine one. O, how he loves Caesar!

AGRIPPA   Nay, but how dearly he adores Mark Antony!

ENOBARBUS   Caesar? Why he's the Jupiter of men.

AGRIPPA   What's Antony? The god of Jupiter.   10

ENOBARBUS   Spake you of Caesar? How! The nonpareil!

AGRIPPA   O Antony! O thou Arabian bird!

ENOBARBUS   Would you praise Caesar, say 'Caesar' – go no further.

AGRIPPA   Indeed, he plied them both with excellent praises.

ENOBARBUS   But he loves Caesar best, yet he loves Antony –   15
                      Hoo! hearts, tongues, figures, scribes, bards, poets cannot
                      Think, speak, cast, write, sing, number – hoo!
                      His love to Antony. But as for Caesar,
                      Kneel down, kneel down, and wonder.

AGRIPPA   Both he loves.

ENOBARBUS   They are his shards, and he their beetle. [*Trumpet within*] So –   20
                      This is to horse. Adieu, noble Agrippa.

AGRIPPA   Good fortune, worthy soldier, and farewell.

                    Enter CAESAR, ANTONY, LEPIDUS *and* OCTAVIA

ANTONY   No further, sir.

CAESAR   You take from me a great part of myself;
                      Use me well in't. Sister, prove such a wife   25
                      As my thoughts make thee, and as my farthest band
                      Shall pass on thy approof. Most noble Antony,
                      Let not the piece of virtue which is set
                      Betwixt us, and the cement of our love
                      To keep it builded, be the ram to batter   30
                      The fortress of it; for better might we
                      Have loved without this mean, if on both parts
                      This be not cherished.

ANTONY   Make me not offended
                      In your distrust.

CAESAR   I have said.

35   *curious* too inquisitive and sensitive (over Octavia)

> The sad parting of Octavia and Caesar is touching, and made
> especially so with the dramatic irony of the audience's knowledge
> of Antony's intentions concerning Cleopatra. As Octavia and Caesar
> embrace and weep, what is Antony doing, particularly as Octavia
> whispers in Caesar's ear?

43   *The April's* tears   *love's spring* start of love for Antony

48–50   *the swan's … inclines* an image of Octavia: a swan caught
between two strong forces

51   *cloud* sad look

52   *a horse* A horse with a 'cloud' (without a white blaze) was
considered inferior.

> As Octavia and Caesar weep, Enobarbus and Agrippa stand aside. In
> mocking the tears of Caesar and Antony they remind the audience
> to question the honesty of the emotions on display.

56   *Philippi* the battle at which Brutus died
Brutus enemy of Antony, murderer of Julius Caesar

57   *rheum* complaint in which eyes water

58   *confound* destroy

> Antony jokingly turns his farewell embrace with Caesar into a
> wrestling match over who loves Octavia more. Does the audience
> see any irony in this grappling?
> Caesar says little in response to Antony's over-enthusiastic embrace;
> what point is Antony trying to make?

64   *give … gods* put you in the care of the gods

*The mocking comments by Agrippa and Enobarbus in this scene cast some
doubts about the honesty of the emotions witnessed. Cleopatra still awaits
Antony, so where does he go from here?*

ANTONY   You shall not find,
     Though you be therein curious, the least cause   35
     For what you seem to fear. So, the gods keep you,
     And make the hearts of Romans serve your ends!
     We will here part.

CAESAR   Farewell, my dearest sister, fare thee well –
     The elements be kind to thee, and make   40
     Thy spirits all of comfort. Fare thee well.

OCTAVIA   My noble brother!

ANTONY   The April's in her eyes – it is love's spring,
     And these the showers to bring it on. Be cheerful.

OCTAVIA   Sir, look well to my husband's house; and –

CAESAR   What, Octavia?   45

OCTAVIA   I'll tell you in your ear.

ANTONY   Her tongue will not obey her heart, nor can
     Her heart inform her tongue – the swan's-down feather,
     That stands upon the swell at the full of tide,
     And neither way inclines.   50

ENOBARBUS [*Aside to* AGRIPPA] Will Caesar weep?

AGRIPPA [*Aside to* ENOBARBUS]   He has a cloud in's face.

ENOBARBUS [*Aside to* AGRIPPA] He were the worse for that, were he a horse;
     So is he, being a man.

AGRIPPA [*Aside to* ENOBARBUS]   Why, Enobarbus?
     When Antony found Julius Caesar dead,
     He cried almost to roaring; and he wept   55
     When at Philippi he found Brutus slain.

ENOBARBUS [*Aside to* AGRIPPA] That year, indeed, he was troubled with a rheum.
     What willingly he did confound, he wailed –
     Believe't – till I wept too.

CAESAR   No, sweet Octavia,
     You shall hear from me still; the time shall not   60
     Outgo my thinking on you.

ANTONY   Come, sir, come,
     I'll wrestle with you in my strength of love.
     Look, here I have you; thus I let you go,
     And give you to the gods.

CAESAR   Adieu; be happy!

LEPIDUS   Let all the number of the stars give light   65
     To thy fair way!

CAESAR   Farewell, farewell!   [*Kisses* OCTAVIA

ANTONY   Farewell!

                                   [*Trumpets sound. Exeunt*

3:3

The questions asked about the future of Octavia in the previous scene are still in the audience's mind as the setting moves immediately back to Alexandria, where Cleopatra still awaits news of Antony.

The audience is quickly reminded of the comedy and violence of Act 2 Scene 5, as Cleopatra, perhaps pacing up and down, awaits the return of the same unfortunate messenger. There is an opportunity for visual humour as the messenger enters in the same apprehensive manner. How might he use furniture and the space for comic effect?

4   *Herod's head* probably alluding to St John the Baptist, whose head was given to Salome by Herod

5   *but* except

The audience will be amused at how Cleopatra quickly switches from initial dismay into the pleasure of mocking Octavia's height, voice and posture. How might visual humour be added here?

17   *gait* walk, movement

19   *motion* walking   *station* standing

20   *shows a body* seems lifeless   *life* something alive

21   *breather* living thing

22   *observance* powers of observation
       Three in Egypt i.e. Charmian, Iras and Alexas

23   *knowing* aware

24   *nothing in her* no quality in her

The messenger shows he has learned how to indulge Cleopatra, appealing to her vanity when describing Octavia. There are opportunities for humour in their exchanges. When he thinks he's on safe ground by saying 'And I do think she's thirty' (unaware that Cleopatra is thirty-eight), Cleopatra ignores this and asks instead for a description of Octavia's face!

3:3	*Enter* **Cleopatra**, **Charmian**, **Iras** *and* **Alexas**

Cleopatra Where is the fellow?

Alexas   Half afeard to come.

Cleopatra Go to, go to. Come hither, sir.

Enter the **Messenger** *as before*

Alexas   Good majesty,
    Herod of Jewry dare not look upon you
    But when you are well pleased.

Cleopatra   That Herod's head
    I'll have; but how, when Antony is gone,   5
    Through whom I might command it? – Come thou near.

Messenger Most gracious majesty!

Cleopatra   Didst thou behold Octavia?

Messenger Ay, dread queen.

Cleopatra   Where?

Messenger   Madam, in Rome.
    I looked her in the face, and saw her led
    Between her brother and Mark Antony.   10

Cleopatra Is she as tall as me?

Messenger   She is not, madam.

Cleopatra Did hear her speak? – is she shrill-tongued or low?

Messenger Madam, I heard her speak; she is low-voiced.

Cleopatra That's not so good. He cannot like her long.

Charmian Like her? O Isis! 'tis impossible.   15

Cleopatra I think so, Charmian. Dull of tongue, and dwarfish!
    What majesty is in her gait? Remember,
    If e'er thou look'st on majesty.

Messenger   She creeps –
    Her motion and her station are as one.
    She shows a body rather than a life,   20
    A statue than a breather.

Cleopatra   Is this certain?

Messenger Or I have no observance.

Charmian   Three in Egypt
    Cannot make better note.

Cleopatra   He's very knowing,
    I do perceive't; there's nothing in her yet.
    The fellow has good judgement.

Charmian   Excellent.   25

33 *As low* Low foreheads were unattractive, considered a sign of poor breeding.

34 *former sharpness* her violence to him in Act 2 Scene 5

35 *back* as my messenger to Rome

The messenger has learned to give the 'correct' information to Cleopatra! As he leaves with Cleopatra's letters for Antony, compare the treatment he received at her hands in Act 2 Scene 5. What does the comparison between the two scenes tell you about Cleopatra's strong emotions?

---

39 *by* according to

40 *This … thing* Octavia's nothing to worry about (as a rival)

42 *Isis else defend* an oath – god (Isis) defend us

47 *I warrant you* I'll be bound

In this comic scene we see that the messenger, who had been terrified in Act 2 Scene 5 by Cleopatra's rage at hearing the 'wrong' news, has now learned how to deliver the 'right' news! What was the last thing that Cleopatra wanted to ask the messenger? She asks Charmian to bring him to her, where she will give him another letter to Antony. As the scene ends, Cleopatra seems a little unsure of herself.

CLEOPATRA   Guess at her years, I prithee.

MESSENGER   Madam,
     She was a widow –

CLEOPATRA   Widow? Charmian, hark.

MESSENGER   And I do think she's thirty.

CLEOPATRA   Bear'st thou her face in mind? – is't long or round?

MESSENGER   Round, even to faultiness.   30

CLEOPATRA   For the most part, too, they are foolish that are so.
     Her hair what colour?

MESSENGER   Brown, madam; and her forehead
     As low as she would wish it.

CLEOPATRA   There's gold for thee.
     Thou must not take my former sharpness ill,
     I will employ thee back again; I find thee   35
     Most fit for business. Go, make thee ready –
     Our letters are prepared.

                                  [*Exit* MESSENGER

CHARMIAN   A proper man.

CLEOPATRA   Indeed he is so: I repent me much
     That so I harried him. Why, methinks by him,
     This creature's no such thing.

CHARMIAN   Nothing, madam.   40

CLEOPATRA   The man hath seen some majesty, and should know.

CHARMIAN   Hath he seen majesty? Isis else defend,
     And serving you so long!

CLEOPATRA   I have one thing more to ask him yet, good Charmian –
     But 'tis no matter. Thou shalt bring him to me   45
     Where I will write. All may be well enough.

CHARMIAN   I warrant you, madam.

                                  [*Exeunt*

3:4

After hearing critical remarks about Octavia in the previous scene, we immediately see her and make up our own minds. Set in Athens, this scene opens with negative words. Antony's argument with Octavia shows the strains in the alliance between himself and Caesar.

3	*semblable import* similar importance
4	*New wars* the peace treaty with Pompey was fruitless
4–5	*made his will … ear* in order to gain public favour made public his will
6	*scantly* grudgingly
6–8	*when perforce … lent me* when he was obliged to speak honourably of me, he was unenthusiastic, giving me little regard
9	*hint* opportunity
10	*from his teeth* without feeling
12	*Stomach not all* don't be insulted
13	*division* i.e. between Antony and Caesar *chance* happens
15	*presently* immediately

Octavia tells how the growing conflict between her husband and her brother is tearing her apart. How might her sorrows be most effectively expressed? What feelings does Antony show as she describes her dilemma?

21	*draw* be drawn (like a magnet) *point* compass (point)
24	*branchless* bare (of honour)
25	*go between's* be our go-between (mediator)
27	*raise the preparation of* prepare for *stain* darken (as during a solar eclipse)
29	*Jove* Roman god
30	*reconciler* mediator *you twain* you two (Antony and Caesar)
31	*cleave* fall apart
32	*solder* repair
33	*it appears … begins* you know who started this
34	*our* i.e. Antony and Caesar's
36	*Provide* prepare
37	*command what cost* spend what

Antony complains to his wife about Caesar and threatens a war against him, unless she can mediate between them. Octavia is caught between love for her husband and her brother. Enobarbus' prediction seems to be coming true.

3:4   *Enter* **ANTONY** *and* **OCTAVIA**

ANTONY   Nay, nay, Octavia, not only that –
             There were excusable, that and thousands more
             Of semblable import – but he hath waged
             New wars 'gainst Pompey; made his will, and read it
             To public ear;   5
             Spoke scantly of me; when perforce he could not
             But pay me terms of honour, cold and sickly
             He vented them, most narrow measure lent me;
             When the best hint was given him, he not took't,
             Or did it from his teeth.

OCTAVIA   O my good lord,   10
             Believe not all, or if you must believe,
             Stomach not all. A more unhappy lady,
             If this division chance, ne'er stood between,
             Praying for both parts.
             The good gods will mock me presently,   15
             When I shall pray 'O, bless my lord and husband!',
             Undo that prayer by crying out as loud
             'O, bless my brother!' Husband win, win brother,
             Prays, and destroys the prayer – no midway
             'Twixt these extremes at all.

ANTONY   Gentle Octavia,   20
             Let your best love draw to that point which seeks
             Best to preserve it. If I lose mine honour,
             I lose myself; better I were not yours
             Than yours so branchless. But, as you requested,
             Yourself shall go between's. The meantime, lady,   25
             I'll raise the preparation of a war
             Shall stain your brother. Make your soonest haste;
             So your desires are yours.

OCTAVIA   Thanks to my lord.
             The Jove of power make me most weak, most weak,
             Your reconciler! Wars 'twixt you twain would be   30
             As if the world should cleave, and that slain men
             Should solder up the rift.

ANTONY   When it appears to you where this begins,
             Turn your displeasure that way, for our faults
             Can never be so equal that your love   35
             Can equally move with them. Provide your going,
             Choose your own company, and command what cost
             Your heart has mind to.

                                                    [*Exeunt*

3:5

Back in Alexandria Enobarbus learns of Caesar's removal of one of the triumvirate, Lepidus.

5	*success* outcome
7	*presently* immediately *rivality* his place in the triumvirate
8	*resting here* stopping there
9	*his own appeal* on Caesar's own accusations
9–10	*poor third is up* the weakest (of the triumvirs) is shut up (imprisoned)
10	*enlarge his confine* sets him free
11	*chaps* chops, jaws
13	*grind the one the other* neither will be satisfied
14	*spurns* kicks
15	*rush* (1) something of no value, (2) straw strewn on the floor

Eros mimics Antony's style of walking in the garden, then suddenly kicking at things close by and shouting out.

16	*throat* life *that* that of
17	*rigged* prepared
18	*For* ready for *Domitius* Enobarbus
20	*naught* nothing of importance
21	*let it be* never mind

Although Antony is back in Alexandria after leaving Octavia, this is not the main reason for the breakdown in relations between Caesar and Antony. Caesar for his part has been gathering power. War between Antony and Caesar seems unavoidable.

3:6

In Rome, Caesar condemns Antony. Enobarbus' predictions are realised. The alliance is finished.

1	*Contemning* despising
3	*tribunal silvered* raised platform, silver-plated
7	*unlawful issue* illegitimate children

3:5   *Enter* ENOBARBUS *and* EROS

ENOBARBUS   How now, friend Eros?

EROS   There's strange news come, sir.

ENOBARBUS   What, man?

EROS   Caesar and Lepidus have made wars upon Pompey.

ENOBARBUS   This is old – what is the success?   5

EROS   Caesar, having made use of him in the wars 'gainst Pompey,
            presently denied him rivality, would not let him partake in the glory of
            the action; and not resting here, accuses him of letters he had formerly
            wrote to Pompey; upon his own appeal, seizes him; so the poor third is
            up, till death enlarge his confine.   10

ENOBARBUS   Then, world, thou hast a pair of chaps, no more;
            And throw between them all the food thou hast,
            They'll grind the one the other. Where's Antony?

EROS   He's walking in the garden – thus, and spurns
            The rush that lies before him; cries 'Fool Lepidus!'   15
            And threats the throat of that his officer
            That murdered Pompey.

ENOBARBUS   Our great navy's rigged.

EROS   For Italy and Caesar. More, Domitius.
            My lord desires you presently. My news
            I might have told hereafter.

ENOBARBUS   'Twill be naught,   20
            But let it be. Bring me to Antony.

EROS   Come, sir.

                                                                      [*Exeunt*

3:6   *Enter* AGRIPPA, MAECENAS *and* CAESAR

CAESAR   Contemning Rome, he has done all this and more
            In Alexandria. Here's the manner of't:
            I'the market-place, on a tribunal silvered,
            Cleopatra and himself in chairs of gold
            Were publicly enthroned; at the feet sat   5
            Caesarion, whom they call my father's son,
            And all the unlawful issue that their lust

9   *stablishment* possession
12 *showplace* public place
17 *habiliments* robes
19 *so* so dressed
20 *Who, queasy with* those, disgusted by
21 *call from him* be cancelled
22 *The people* i.e. of Rome   *received* heard
25 *spoiled* plundered   *rated* allotted
27 *unrestored* not returned
29 *being* because of that
34 *change* i.e. of fortune and status
37 *the like* the same

How does Octavia's entrance add to the mood of the scene? It is important for the audience to see how Caesar greets her. No stage directions are given, but it seems that some physical contact would be needed to show their emotions.

40 *castaway* rejected
42 *stol'n* arrived furtively

Since then hath made between them. Unto her
He gave the stablishment of Egypt; made her
Of Lower Syria, Cyprus, Lydia,   10
Absolute queen.

MAECENAS   This in the public eye?

CAESAR   I'the common showplace, where they exercise.
His sons he there proclaimed the kings of kings;
Great Media, Parthia, and Armenia
He gave to Alexander; to Ptolemy he assigned   15
Syria, Cilicia, and Phoenicia. She
In the habiliments of the goddess Isis
That day appeared, and oft before gave audience,
As 'tis reported, so.

MAECENAS   Let Rome be thus informed.

AGRIPPA   Who, queasy with his insolence already,   20
Will their good thoughts call from him.

CAESAR   The people knows it, and have now received
His accusations.

AGRIPPA   Who does he accuse?

CAESAR   Caesar – and that, having in Sicily
Sextus Pompeius spoiled, we had not rated him   25
His part o'the isle. Then does he say he lent me
Some shipping, unrestored. Lastly, he frets
That Lepidus of the triumvirate
Should be deposed; and, being, that we detain
All his revenue.

AGRIPPA   Sir, this should be answered.   30

CAESAR   'Tis done already, and the messenger gone.
I have told him Lepidus was grown too cruel,
That he his high authority abused,
And did deserve his change. For what I have conquered,
I grant him part; but then in his Armenia,   35
And other of his conquered kingdoms, I
Demand the like.

MAECENAS   He'll never yield to that.

CAESAR   Nor must not then be yielded to in this.

Enter **OCTAVIA** *with her train*

OCTAVIA   Hail, Caesar, and my lord! Hail, most dear Caesar!

CAESAR   That ever I should call thee castaway!   40

OCTAVIA   You have not called me so, nor have you cause.

CAESAR   Why have you stol'n upon us thus? You come not
Like Caesar's sister. The wife of Antony
Should have an army for an usher, and

46 *way* wayside

47 *borne* been full of   *expectation* those waiting

50 *populous* many

52 *ostentation* public display

53 *left unloved* considered not to be felt

54 *stage* resting places (on a journey)

55 *augmented* increased

56 *constrained* compelled, forced

60 *pardon* permission

61 *abstract* obstruction   *his lust* i.e. Cleopatra

62 *eyes* i.e. spies

63 *on the wind* swiftly

66 *nodded* summoned him with a nod of her head (as she would a servant)

67 *who* they

Caesar shows increasing anger as he describes how his sister should have been welcomed on her return and her mistreatment by Antony. Is he angry for his sister or for the slight on his honour? Notice how he slips into the more forceful 'I have eyes on him' instead of his normal use of the royal 'we'. What might Caesar be doing as he shows what angers him most by listing the allies Antony has assembled? Perhaps he reads the list from one of his spies' reports.

76 *more larger* The use of a double comparative was common in Shakespeare's time.   *sceptres* kings

77 *parted* split

78 *does* do   *afflict* harm

79 *withhold … forth* delayed my action (i.e. declaration of war)

81 *negligent danger* danger from doing nothing

With his 'Cheer your heart' and repetition of 'Welcome' Caesar reminds himself that he needs to offer some physical comfort to his distressed sister, rather than just storm on about Antony.

82 *the time* the state of affairs

82–3 *which drives … necessities* for these concerns outweigh your own happiness

The neighs of horse to tell of her approach   45
Long ere she did appear. The trees by the way
Should have borne men, and expectation fainted,
Longing for what it had not. Nay, the dust
Should have ascended to the roof of heaven,
Raised by your populous troops. But you are come   50
A market-maid to Rome, and have prevented
The ostentation of our love; which, left unshown,
Is often left unloved. We should have met you
By sea and land, supplying every stage
With an augmented greeting.

OCTAVIA   Good my lord,   55
To come thus was I not constrained, but did it
On my free will. My lord, Mark Antony,
Hearing that you prepared for war, acquainted
My grievèd ear withal; whereon I begged
His pardon for return.

CAESAR   Which soon he granted,   60
Being an abstract 'tween his lust and him.

OCTAVIA   Do not say so, my lord.

CAESAR   I have eyes upon him,
And his affairs come to me on the wind.
Where is he now?

OCTAVIA   My lord, in Athens.

CAESAR   No, my most wrongèd sister – Cleopatra   65
Hath nodded him to her. He hath given his empire
Up to a whore, who now are levying
The kings o'the earth for war. He hath assembled
Bocchus, the King of Libya; Archelaus,
Of Cappodocia; Philadelphos, King   70
Of Paphlagonia; the Thracian king, Adallas;
King Manchus of Arabia; King of Pont;
Herod of Jewry; Mithridates, King
Of Comagene; Polemon and Amyntas,
The kings of Mede and Lycaonia;   75
With a more larger list of sceptres.

OCTAVIA   Ay me most wretched,
That have my heart parted betwixt two friends
That does afflict each other!

CAESAR   Welcome hither.
Your letters did withhold our breaking forth
Till we perceived both how you were wrong led,   80
And we in negligent danger. Cheer your heart;
Be you not troubled with the time, which drives
O'er your content these strong necessities,

84–5 *let … way* allow the inevitable to happen without weeping
86 *abused* deceived
87 *the mark of thought* what can be imagined
88 *do* give *ministers* representatives

‖ *Both Agrippa and Maecenas stand to one side before offering to Octavia their*
‖ *simple 'Welcome', perhaps accompanied by a formal gesture, such as a bow.*

93–4 *large … abominations* open in his offensive behaviour
94 *turns* casts
95 *potent regiment* powerful authority *trull* whore
96 *noises it* cries out

Caesar denounces Antony's political and personal behaviour in Alexandria.
Then he is given additional cause to declare war on Antony with the
mistreatment of his sister, which Caesar takes as an insult to his own dignity.
His concerns for his sister's feelings come second to his need to take strong
action against Antony. With Lepidus out of the picture, the battle for who will
be the ultimate leader of Rome is imminent.

3:7

Events move quickly as we move to Antony's war camp where tactics are being
discussed.

Compare the way Cleopatra gets involved with important matters of war with
how Caesar advises his sister not to be 'troubled with the time'.

‖ *As they enter, Enobarbus' 'But why, why, why?' shows his irritation*
‖ *with Cleopatra in the argument they are engaged in.*

3 *forspoke* opposed
4 *fit* fitting
5 *denounced* declared (war) *us … we* Cleopatra uses the royal 'we'. The declaration of
war was made against her alone and not Antony.

‖ *Although Enobarbus' comments are marked as an aside, considering his characteristic*
‖ *frankness they could be spoken directly to Cleopatra, implying that her presence*
‖ *would be a distraction to Antony. Her answer might then be an indignant comment*
‖ *asking for clarification, rather than questioning why he is muttering to himself.*
‖ *If played as an aside, what does Cleopatra do while waiting for Enobarbus to*
‖ *answer her question?*

8–9 *would … horse* carry the soldiers and mate with the stallions
8 *merely* utterly (perhaps with a pun on mare)

112

But let determined things to destiny
Hold unbewailed their way. Welcome to Rome,   **85**
Nothing more dear to me. You are abused
Beyond the mark of thought; and the high gods,
To do you justice, makes his ministers
Of us and those that love you. Best of comfort,
And ever welcome to us.

AGRIPPA   Welcome, lady.   **90**

MAECENAS   Welcome, dear madam.
Each heart in Rome does love and pity you.
Only the adulterous Antony – most large
In his abominations – turns you off
And gives his potent regiment to a trull,   **95**
That noises it against us.

OCTAVIA   Is it so, sir?

CAESAR   Most certain. Sister, welcome; pray you,
Be ever known to patience. My dear'st sister!

                                                            [*Exeunt*

3:7   *Enter* CLEOPATRA *and* ENOBARBUS

CLEOPATRA   I will be even with thee, doubt it not.

ENOBARBUS   But why, why, why?

CLEOPATRA   Thou hast forspoke my being in these wars,
And sayst it is not fit.

ENOBARBUS   Well, is it, is it?

CLEOPATRA   If not denounced against us, why should not we   **5**
Be there in person?

ENOBARBUS [*Aside*]   Well, I could reply:
If we should serve with horse and mares together,
The horse were merely lost; the mares would bear
A soldier and his horse.

CLEOPATRA   What is't you say?

10 *puzzle* confuse

13 *Traduced* censured

14 *a eunuch* i.e. Mardian

16 *a charge* the expenses

18 *Appear there for* behave like

> As Cleopatra will not budge on this issue and ends the discussion, Antony enters with concerns about Caesar's speed of advance. In the light of Enobarbus' comments, might there be a change in the way that Cleopatra greets Antony?

21 *Tarentum and Brundusium* ports south-east of Rome

23 *take in* occupy   *Toryne* a port in western Greece

24–5 *Celerity … negligent* the best admirers of speed are the inefficient

26 *becomed* suited

27 *taunt at* criticise

29 *For that* because   *dares us to't* challenged us to it

> For honour's sake Antony will not refuse Caesar's formal challenge and decides to fight at sea. His advisers remind him that Caesar had already refused his challenge to fight in single combat. Are these signs of his weakness or strength? Perhaps a map would help visualise the arguments they put forward to persuade him.

33 *vantage* advantage   *shakes off* declines

35 *muleters* mule-drivers

36 *Ingrossed* gathered   *impress* being forced to enlist

38 *yare* quick and manoeuvrable

42 *absolute soldiership* military dominance

43 *Distract* divide   *most* mainly

ENOBARBUS   Your presence needs must puzzle Antony,   10
          Take from his heart, take from his brain, from's time,
          What should not then be spared. He is already
          Traduced for levity, and 'tis said in Rome
          That Photinus, an eunuch, and your maids
          Manage this war.

CLEOPATRA   Sink Rome, and their tongues rot   15
          That speak against us! A charge we bear i'the war,
          And as the president of my kingdom will
          Appear there for a man. Speak not against it,
          I will not stay behind.

                    Enter ANTONY *and* CANIDIUS

ENOBARBUS   Nay, I have done.
          Here comes the Emperor.

ANTONY   Is it not strange, Canidius,   20
          That from Tarentum and Brundusium
          He could so quickly cut the Ionian sea
          And take in Toryne? You have heard on't, sweet?

CLEOPATRA   Celerity is never more admired
          Than by the negligent.

ANTONY   A good rebuke,   25
          Which might have well becomed the best of men
          To taunt at slackness. Canidius, we
          Will fight with him by sea.

CLEOPATRA   By sea, what else?

CANIDIUS   Why will my lord do so?

ANTONY   For that he dares us to't.

ENOBARBUS   So hath my lord dared him to single fight.   30

CANIDIUS   Ay, and to wage this battle at Pharsalia,
          Where Caesar fought with Pompey. But these offers,
          Which serve not for his vantage, he shakes off –
          And so should you.

ENOBARBUS   Your ships are not well manned.
          Your mariners are muleters, reapers, people   35
          Ingrossed by swift impress. In Caesar's fleet
          Are those that often have 'gainst Pompey fought;
          Their ships are yare, yours heavy. No disgrace
          Shall fall you for refusing him at sea,
          Being prepared for land.

ANTONY   By sea, by sea.   40

ENOBARBUS   Most worthy sir, you therein throw away
          The absolute soldiership you have by land,
          Distract your army, which doth most consist

115

44   *war-marked footmen* experienced foot soldiers
      unexecuted unused

48   *firm security* a safe position

> How would you stage Antony's reaction to the intensity of their two
> sets of arguments, firstly that Caesar has the advantage fighting at
> sea, and secondly that Antony is throwing away his advantage by
> not fighting on land? Antony obstinately refuses to budge and offers
> no reasons for his decision. Why is this? How is Cleopatra reacting
> to all this as she supports Antony with her offer of sixty ships?

50   *overplus … burn* surplus unmanned ships were burned to prevent
      them falling into enemy hands

51   *head* headland

54   *descried* sighted

57   *power* forces

58   *hold* command

60   *Thetis* sea goddess, mother of the great warrior Achilles

62   *misdoubt* disbelieve

64   *go a-ducking* getting wet

65   *Have* are

> Antony is shocked by the speed of Caesar's advance, but takes heart
> in Cleopatra's support. After the advice he has ignored, the warning
> of the anonymous common soldier provides a powerful dramatic
> moment. Perhaps distracted by the attentions of Cleopatra, Antony
> chooses to ignore this warning of impending failure.

68–9 *his whole … on't* his plans ignore his military strengths

71   *whole* together

75   *Carries beyond belief* advances him unbelievably

76   *power* forces   *such distractions* small numbers

77   *Beguiled all spies* deceived Antony's spies

Of war-marked footmen, leave unexecuted
Your own renownèd knowledge, quite forgo   45
The way which promises assurance, and
Give up yourself merely to chance and hazard
From firm security.

ANTONY   I'll fight at sea.

CLEOPATRA   I have sixty sails, Caesar none better.

ANTONY   Our overplus of shipping will we burn,   50
And with the rest full-manned, from the head of Actium
Beat the approaching Caesar. But if we fail,
We then can do't at land.

                    Enter a MESSENGER

                    Thy business?

MESSENGER   The news is true, my lord, he is descried –
Caesar has taken Toryne.   55

ANTONY   Can he be there in person? 'Tis impossible;
Strange that his power should be. Canidius,
Our nineteen legions thou shalt hold by land
And our twelve thousand horse. We'll to our ship.
Away, my Thetis!

                    Enter a SOLDIER

                    How now, worthy soldier?   60

SOLDIER   O noble emperor, do not fight by sea.
Trust not to rotten planks. Do you misdoubt
This sword and these my wounds? Let the Egyptians
And the Phoenicians go a-ducking – we
Have used to conquer standing on the earth   65
And fighting foot to foot.

ANTONY   Well, well, away!

              [*Exeunt* ANTONY, CLEOPATRA *and* ENOBARBUS

SOLDIER   By Hercules, I think I am i'the right.

CANIDIUS   Soldier, thou art; but his whole action grows
Not in the power on't. So our leader's led,
And we are women's men.

SOLDIER   You keep by land   70
The legions and the horse whole, do you not?

CANIDIUS   Marcus Octavius, Marcus Justeius,
Publicola, and Caelius are for sea;
But we keep whole by land. This speed of Caesar's
Carries beyond belief.

SOLDIER   While he was yet in Rome,   75
His power went out in such distractions as
Beguiled all spies.

80–1   *With news ... some* it is so busy, every minute fresh news is born

After seeing Antony ignore his advisors and the warnings of the ordinary soldier, and seeing that Cleopatra supports him in his ill-advised decision, we are fearful of the coming sea battle with Caesar.

3:8

Scenes 8 and 9, the briefest of scenes, show the opposing forces lined up for battle near Actium.

3   *Strike not* don't attack   *whole* together
4   *done* won
5   *prescript* instructions
6   *jump* hazard

We leave Caesar knowing his plan of action.

A Roman galley.

3:9

We quickly move from Caesar's position to Antony's.

2   eye ... *battle* in sight of Caesar's line of battle

In these two short scenes we can compare Caesar's clear planning with Antony's more improvised approach.

CANIDIUS	Who's his lieutenant, hear you?
SOLDIER	They say one Taurus.
CANIDIUS	Well I know the man.

Enter a **MESSENGER**

MESSENGER	The Emperor calls Canidius.	
CANIDIUS	With news the time's in labour and throws forth,	80
	Each minute, some.	

[*Exeunt*

3:8   *Enter* **CAESAR** *with his army, marching*

CAESAR	Taurus!
TAURUS	My lord?
CAESAR	Strike not by land; keep whole; provoke not battle
	Till we have done at sea. Do not exceed
	The prescript of this scroll. Our fortune lies
	Upon this jump.

[*Exeunt*

5

3:9   *Enter* **ANTONY** *and* **ENOBARBUS**

ANTONY	Set we our squadrons on yond side o'the hill
	In eye of Caesar's battle; from which place
	We may the number of the ships behold,
	And so proceed accordingly.

[*Exeunt*

3:10

The sea battle is a disaster for Antony, as his advisers predicted.

Marching groups crossing over the stage, the sounds of fighting off-stage and alarm horns sounding all help create the sense of battle. In a modern theatre, sound effects along with smoke and lighting effects would all support this impression. Shakespeare's Globe might have relied on cannon fire to create 'the noise of a sea fight'. After this noisy opening, a troubled Enobarbus and then Scarus give the audience a graphic account of the battle.

1	*naught* ruined, lost
2	*admiral* flagship
3	*sixty* Cleopatra's ships
4	*blasted* damaged
5	*synod* assembly *thy passion* the cause of your distress
6	*cantle* segment of a sphere
7	*With very ignorance* through sheer stupidity

In the midst of the breathless graphic account by Scarus we see his frustration and anger in 'We have kissed away kingdoms and provinces.' He is certain that the battle has been lost because of Antony's poor military judgement and his obsession with Cleopatra. Here are opportunities for the actor to magnify with gesture and voice his scathing criticism of Cleopatra.

9	*tokened pestilence* marks of the plague
10	*ribaudred* lewd and foul *nag* whore
11	*leprosy* venereal disease
12–13	*vantage … same* equally balanced
13	*or … elder* with our slight advantage
14	*The breese … June* as if stung by a gadfly (an insect that stings cattle)
18	*loofed* some distance away
20	*Claps on his sea wings* immediately hoists sail *mallard* wild bird
21	*in heighth* at its height

Compare Scarus' speech with that of Philo in Act 1 Scene 1.

25	*out of breath* exhausted
27	*what he knew himself* his true self
28	*our flight* desertion
30	*are you thereabouts?* are you thinking of desertion?
30–1	*Why then, good night indeed* i.e. if so, it's all over
31	*Peloponnesus* southern Greece

3:10   CANIDIUS *marcheth with his land army one way over the stage, and*
TAURUS, *the lieutenant of Caesar, the other way. After their going*
in is heard the noise of a sea fight. Alarum. Enter ENOBARBUS

ENOBARBUS   Naught, naught, all naught! I can behold no longer.
The Antoniad, the Egyptian admiral,
With all their sixty, fly and turn the rudder.
To see't mine eyes are blasted.

Enter SCARUS

SCARUS   Gods and goddesses,
All the whole synod of them!

ENOBARBUS   What's thy passion?   5

SCARUS   The greater cantle of the world is lost
With very ignorance. We have kissed away
Kingdoms and provinces.

ENOBARBUS   How appears the fight?

SCARUS   On our side like the tokened pestilence,
Where death is sure. Yon ribaudred nag of Egypt –   10
Whom leprosy o'ertake! – i'the midst o'the fight,
When vantage like a pair of twins appeared
Both as the same, or rather ours the elder –
The breese upon her, like a cow in June –
Hoists sails and flies.   15

ENOBARBUS   That I beheld.
Mine eyes did sicken at the sight, and could not
Endure a further view.

SCARUS   She once being loofed,
The noble ruin of her magic, Antony,
Claps on his sea wing and – like a doting mallard –   20
Leaving the fight in heighth, flies after her.
I never saw an action of such shame.
Experience, manhood, honour, ne'er before
Did violate so itself.

ENOBARBUS   Alack, alack!

Enter CANIDIUS

CANIDIUS   Our fortune on the sea is out of breath,   25
And sinks most lamentably. Had our general
Been what he knew himself, it had gone well.
O, he has given example for our flight
Most grossly by his own.

ENOBARBUS   Ay, are you thereabouts? Why then, good night   30
Indeed.

CANIDIUS   Toward Peloponnesus are they fled.

32	*'Tis easy to't* it's easy to get to *attend* await
33	*render* surrender
35	*the way of yielding* how to surrender *yet* continue to
36	*chance* fortunes
36–7	*though … me* against my better judgement

Losing a battle is not a disreputable action, but to leave at the height of the conflict to chase after Cleopatra, leaving his men to fight on leaderless, offends the sense of honour of both Scarus and Canidius. Following Antony's example, Canidius deserts, preparing to surrender to Caesar. Enobarbus, however, chooses to remain loyal, but for how long?

3:11

We meet Antony after hearing about the disastrous defeat. How will he react after his shameful flight from the sea battle?

3	*lated* belated (an image of a lost traveller)

Antony offers his attendants gold and the chance to surrender to Caesar. Sad and despondent, they refuse. To appear authentic, their words of refusal should be less of a chorus and more individually spoken. Their body language should mirror Antony's feelings of despair and shame about his cowardly action.

7	*instructed* given an example to
8	*show their shoulders* show their backs (as they run away)
9	*resolved upon a course* i.e. suicide
12	*that* what
13	*mutiny* argue among themselves
13–15	*for the white … doting* i.e. experience blames immaturity for being impulsive, while immaturity blames experience for fear and foolishness
14	*they them* they (the brown hairs) blame them (the white hairs)
17	*Sweep* clear
18	*loathness* unwillingness *hint* opportunity
19	*proclaims* gives you
19–20	*Let that … leaves itself* leave the man (Antony) who is no longer what he was
21	*possess you of* give you

SCARUS   'Tis easy to't; and there I will attend
      What further comes.

CANIDIUS   To Caesar will I render
      My legions and my horse. Six kings already
      Show me the way of yielding.

ENOBARBUS   I'll yet follow   35
      The wounded chance of Antony, though my reason
      Sits in the wind against me.

                                         [*Exeunt*

3:11   Enter ANTONY *with attendants*

ANTONY   Hark, the land bids me tread no more upon't –
      It is ashamed to bear me. Friends, come hither.
      I am so lated in the world that I
      Have lost my way for ever. I have a ship
      Laden with gold – take that, divide it. Fly,   5
      And make your peace with Caesar.

ALL THE ATTENDANTS   Fly? Not we.

ANTONY   I have fled myself, and have instructed cowards
      To run and show their shoulders. Friends, be gone;
      I have myself resolved upon a course
      Which has no need of you. Be gone;   10
      My treasure's in the harbour – take it. O,
      I followed that I blush to look upon.
      My very hairs do mutiny, for the white
      Reprove the brown for rashness, and they them
      For fear and doting. Freinds, be gone; you shall   15
      Have letters from me to some friends, that will
      Sweep your way for you. Pray you, look not sad,
      Nor make replies of loathness; take the hint
      Which my despair proclaims. Let that be left
      Which leaves itself. To the seaside straightway –   20
      I will possess you of that ship and treasure.
      Leave me, I pray, a little. Pray you now,
      Nay, do so; for indeed I have lost command,
      Therefore I pray you. I'll see you by and by.

                                   [ANTONY *sits down*

Antony and Cleopatra

> The way Antony sits on the ground should demonstrate to the
> audience the overwhelming despair he feels. He is dismissing his
> faithful attendants and preparing for suicide. He is no longer in
> command, neither of his men nor himself. It is a powerful visual
> image when a great man breaks and slumps to the ground and
> there needs to be a pause to allow this image to affect the audience
> before the entrance of Cleopatra.

31	_fie_	term of contempt (for himself)

> There are rich possibilities of how this part of the scene might be
> played. Antony is wrapped up in his own despair and seems
> unaware that Cleopatra is near. Are his words directed to anyone on
> stage, or to an imaginary person?

35	_He_	Caesar
35–6	_kept … a dancer_	kept his sword in the scabbard, as a dancer would wear an ornament
37–8	_Cassius … Brutus_	Antony's memory is faulty: he didn't slay them, as both committed suicide
39	_dealt on lieutenantry_	made his subordinates fight for him
40	_brave squares_	splendid combat
44	_unqualitied_	without manliness

> These two vibrant characters sitting disconsolately on the ground is
> a sorry sight. Cleopatra's requests for help indicate either that she is
> trying to stand before moving towards Antony or that she is already
> standing and almost fainting.

45	_sustain_	support
47	_but_	unless
49	_offended_	ruined my
50	_unnoble_	an ironic echo of Eros' 'Most noble sir' of line 46
	swerving	deviation from the straight path
51	_Egypt_	Cleopatra

> Does Antony stand up before speaking of his dishonour? Does he
> turn his back on her or cover his face as he speaks lines 51–4?

51–4	_See … dishonour_	i.e. I try to hide my shame from your eyes, by thinking about what my dishonourable actions destroyed
55	_fearful sails_	the fear that made her galley flee
57	_strings_	heartstrings
60	_beck_	gesture of command (as in 'at your beck and call')

Enter CLEOPATRA, *led by* CHARMIAN *and* EROS; IRAS *following*

EROS	Nay, gentle madam, to him, comfort him.	25
IRAS	Do, most dear queen.	
CHARMIAN	Do; why, what else?	
CLEOPATRA	Let me sit down. O, Juno!	
ANTONY	No, no, no, no, no.	
EROS	See you here, sir?	30
ANTONY	O, fie, fie, fie!	
CHARMIAN	Madam!	
IRAS	Madam, O good Empress!	
EROS	Sir, sir!	

ANTONY Yes, my lord, yes. He at Philippi kept 35
His sword e'en like a dancer, while I struck
The lean and wrinkled Cassius; and 'twas I
That the mad Brutus ended. He alone
Dealt on lieutenantry, and no practice had
In the brave squares of war. Yet now – no matter. 40

CLEOPATRA Ah, stand by.

EROS The Queen, my lord, the Queen.

IRAS Go to him, madam, speak to him –
He's unqualitied with very shame.

CLEOPATRA Well then, sustain me. O! 45

EROS Most noble sir, arise. The Queen approaches.
Her head's declined, and death will seize her but
Your comfort makes the rescue.

ANTONY I have offended reputation,
A most unnoble swerving.

EROS   Sir, the Queen. 50

ANTONY O, whither hast thou led me, Egypt? See
How I convey my shame out of thine eyes,
By looking back what I have left behind
'Stroyed in dishonour.

CLEOPATRA   O my lord, my lord,
Forgive my fearful sails! I little thought 55
You would have followed.

ANTONY   Egypt, thou knew'st too well
My heart was to thy rudder tied by the strings,
And thou shouldst tow me after. O'er my spirit
Thy full supremacy thou knew'st, and that
Thy beck might from the bidding of the gods 60
Command me.

61	*my pardon* I beg pardon, forgive me
62	*young man* Caesar *treaties* terms of negotiation *dodge* shuffle about
63	*palter* haggle *shifts of lowness* the humiliation of those brought low
64	*bulk* ship's cargo *played* gamed, gambled
65	*marring* losing
67	*My sword, made weak* a play on sexual and military weakness *by my affection* passion
68	*on all cause* whatever the reason

║ *Cleopatra can only ask for his pardon and weep, and even one tear and one kiss are enough for Antony to forgive her for everything.*

69	*Fall not a tear* don't cry *rates* is worth
71	*Even this* this alone *schoolmaster* Euphronius, their children's tutor, has been negotiating with Caesar
72	*lead* heavy heart
73	*viands* food

We see this powerful high-flying pair literally brought to the ground. This is the lowest point in the play for Antony as he suffers the self-betrayal of his honour. Cleopatra tearfully begs his forgiveness, but can offer no reasons for her flight. Because of his undying love Antony forgives her, despite all that has happened.

3:12

║ *Antony realised that he would have to negotiate with Caesar over his and Cleopatra's future from a position of weakness. We now see these negotiations take place in Caesar's camp outside Alexandria.*

3	*An argument* this suggests *plucked* stripped (of all his authority)
4	*pinion* feather
5	*Which* who (i.e. Antony)
6	*Not ... gone by* not long ago
8	*petty to his ends* insignificant in his plans

║ *The ambassador, bowing low, must humbly acknowledge Caesar's power over the defeated Antony. In order to emphasise his control of the situation, Caesar might be seated on an ornate raised throne. For extra emphasis he may be flanked by several attendants.*

CLEOPATRA	O, my pardon!
ANTONY	Now I must

To the young man send humble treaties, dodge
And palter in the shifts of lowness, who
With half the bulk o'the world played as I pleased,
Making and marring fortunes. You did know   65
How much you were my conqueror, and that
My sword, made weak by my affection, would
Obey it on all cause.

CLEOPATRA	Pardon, pardon!
ANTONY	Fall not a tear, I say; one of them rates

All that is won and lost. Give me a kiss –   70
Even this repays me. We sent our schoolmaster;
Is 'a come back? Love, I am full of lead.
Some wine within there, and our viands! Fortune knows,
We scorn her most, when most she offers blows.

[*Exeunt*

3:12   *Enter* CAESAR, AGRIPPA, DOLABELLA, *and* THIDIAS, *with others*

CAESAR	Let him appear that's come from Antony.

Know you him?

DOLABELLA	Caesar, 'tis his schoolmaster:

An argument that he is plucked, when hither
He sends so poor a pinion of his wing,
Which had superfluous kings for messengers   5
Not many moons gone by.

Enter AMBASSADOR *from Antony*

CAESAR	Approach and speak.
AMBASSADOR	Such as I am, I come from Antony.

I was of late as petty to his ends
As is the morn-dew on the myrtle leaf
To his grand sea.

CAESAR	Be't so. Declare thine office. 10

12	*Requires* asks *which not* i.e. which if not
13	*sues* petitions
18	*circle of the Ptolemies* crown of Egypt
19	*hazarded to thy grace* dependent upon your wishes
20	*have no ears* will not listen
20–1	*The Queen … fail* I will give Cleopatra an audience and grant her wishes
21	*so* if
22	*drive her all-disgracèd friend* deport Antony
23	*take his life there* execute him
24	*unheard* in vain *So to them both* this is my reply to them
25	*Bring … bands* conduct him safely past the guards
26	*try thy eloquence* test your powers of persuasion *Despatch* leave quickly
28	*in our name* on my authority
28–9	*add more … offers* make other offers at your own discretion
29–31	*Women … vestal* women, even at their best, are not strong enough, when needs must, to resist breaking a vow, even one taken by the purest virgin
31	*cunning* skill
32–3	*Make thine … law* decide how much your efforts should be rewarded and it will be binding
34	*becomes his flaw* adapts to misfortune
35	*speaks* reveals
36	*every power that moves* every move he makes

Caesar refuses Antony's request, but agrees to Cleopatra's if she removes herself from Antony's influence. Caesar sends Thidias to the Queen instructing him to use whatever means necessary to win Cleopatra over to his side. Will Cleopatra be as weak as Caesar thinks all women are, when in need? Will she agree to his demands and discard Antony?

AMBASSADOR Lord of his fortunes he salutes thee, and
       Requires to live in Egypt; which not granted,
       He lessens his requests, and to thee sues
       To let him breathe between the heavens and earth,
       A private man in Athens. This for him.   **15**
       Next, Cleopatra does confess thy greatness,
       Submits her to thy might, and of thee craves
       The circle of the Ptolemies for her heirs,
       Now hazarded to thy grace.

CAESAR   For Antony,
       I have no ears to his request. The Queen   **20**
       Of audience nor desire shall fail, so she
       From Egypt drive her all-disgracèd friend
       Or take his life there. This if she perform,
       She shall not sue unheard. So to them both.

AMBASSADOR Fortune pursue thee!

CAESAR   Bring him through the bands.   **25**

                              [Exit **AMBASSADOR**

       (*To* **THIDIAS**) To try thy eloquence now 'tis time. Despatch.
       From Antony win Cleopatra. Promise,
       And in our name, what she requires; add more,
       From thine invention, offers. Women are not
       In their best fortunes strong, but want will perjure   **30**
       The ne'er-touched vestal. Try thy cunning, Thidias.
       Make thine own edict for thy pains, which we
       Will answer as a law.

THIDIAS   Caesar, I go.

CAESAR   Observe how Antony becomes his flaw,
       And what thou think'st his very action speaks   **35**
       In every power that moves.

THIDIAS   Caesar, I shall.

                                  [Exeunt

3:13

In the final scene of Act 3, set in Alexandria, Cleopatra and Antony have not yet heard Caesar's decision on their requests. Cleopatra asks advice from Enobarbus while awaiting Antony's arrival.

1	*Think, and die* i.e. die of shame thinking of what we have done
3–4	*that would … reason* because he let his desires rule his reason
5	*face of war* battle *ranges* lines of warships
7	*affection* sexual desire
8	*nicked his captainship* made him lose his military abilities
9	*half to … opposed* i.e. the battle for the Roman world between Antony and Caesar
10	*meréd question* sole cause of the dispute
11	*course* pursue
12	*gazing* looking in amazement at his action

Cleopatra listens as Enobarbus puts the blame for her troubles at the feet of Antony. She silences him as Antony enters in a state of growing anger at Caesar's response. Does Cleopatra move away from Enobarbus and embrace Antony or remain apart from him? Her actions tell the audience something about her thoughts in the light of Enobarbus' criticisms.

15	*courtesy* considerate treatment *so* so long as
16	*yield us up* Antony refers to himself with the royal 'we'
17	*send this grizzled head* i.e. Antony beheaded
19	*principalities* reward of lands
20	*To him* go to him
21	*from which* because he is young
21–2	*note Something particular* expect proof of some special quality
22–5	*His coin … Caesar* i.e. his great empire proves nothing about his personal qualities as it functions with or without him
26	*lay his gay comparisons apart* put his showy advantages to one side
27	*answer me declined* meet me in my state of misfortune

After Antony leaves, Enobarbus speaks an aside to the audience that is heavy in irony. His first words mean 'As if!' He laughs at how naïve Antony is to think Caesar would give up every advantage and risk fighting Antony in single combat. What is Cleopatra doing on stage as he laughs about Antony's growing failure of judgement?

29	*High-battled* commanding great armies
30	*Unstate his happiness* give up his fortunate position *staged to the show* put on public display
31	*sworder* gladiator
32	*parcel of* part of, i.e. affected by *things outward* external circumstances
33	*inward quality* inner character, personality
34	*suffer all alike* decay together

3:13   *Enter* CLEOPATRA, ENOBARBUS, CHARMIAN *and* IRAS

CLEOPATRA   What shall we do, Enobarbus?

ENOBARBUS   Think, and die.

CLEOPATRA   Is Antony or we in fault for this?

ENOBARBUS   Antony only, that would make his will
    Lord of his reason. What though you fled
    From that great face of war, whose several ranges   5
    Frighted each other? Why should he follow?
    The itch of his affection should not then
    Have nicked his captainship, at such a point,
    When half to half the world opposed, he being
    The merèd question. 'Twas a shame no less   10
    Than was his loss, to course your flying flags
    And leave his navy gazing.

CLEOPATRA   Prithee, peace.

Enter the AMBASSADOR, *with* ANTONY

ANTONY   Is that his answer?

AMBASSADOR   Ay, my lord.

ANTONY   The Queen shall then have courtesy, so she   15
    Will yield us up.

AMBASSADOR   He says so.

ANTONY   Let her know't.
    To the boy Caesar send this grizzled head,
    And he will fill thy wishes to the brim
    With principalities.

CLEOPATRA   That head, my lord?

ANTONY   To him again! Tell him he wears the rose   20
    Of youth upon him; from which the world should note
    Something particular. His coin, ships, legions,
    May be a coward's, whose ministers would prevail
    Under the service of a child as soon
    As i'the command of Caesar. I dare him therefore   25
    To lay his gay comparisons apart
    And answer me declined, sword against sword,
    Ourselves alone. I'll write it – follow me.

[Exeunt ANTONY *and* AMBASSADOR

ENOBARBUS *[Aside]* Yes, like enough! High-battled Caesar will
    Unstate his happiness and be staged to the show   30
    Against a sworder! I see men's judgements are
    A parcel of their fortunes, and things outward
    Do draw the inward quality after them
    To suffer all alike. That he should dream –

35 *Knowing all measures* having experienced every degree of fortune

35–6 *full Caesar … emptiness* an image echoing the saying 'Empty vessels make the most noise' – empty Antony is full of blustering sound and fury

37 *judgement too* as well as his troops, Antony's judgement has also been defeated

Cleopatra's angry response to the servant's abrupt entrance and lack of proper deference shows how she feels that she is a 'blown rose', losing power and therefore respectful treatment. Compare her rebuke of the servant with the violent way she treated the unfortunate messenger in Act 2 Scene 5.

38 *What, no more ceremony?* Am I now treated without respect?

39–40 *Against the blown rose … buds* The image shows the difference between the bud, full of promise, and the rose when withered. Cleopatra identifies herself with the 'blown rose'.

This part of the scene has a curious mood. Cleopatra is wrapped up in her own concerns, while Enobarbus speaks in asides to the audience. He becomes a chorus, commenting on the action and judging the characters.

41 *Mine honesty … square* my integrity and self-interest are in conflict

42–3 *The loyalty … folly* strong loyalty given to fools (like Antony) makes us foolish

43–5 *Yet he … master conquer* i.e. constant loyalty to a defeated lord overcomes even the one who conquered him

46 *story* history

47 *None … boldly* only friends are here – speak openly

48 *haply* perhaps

50 *Or needs not us* or Antony needs no friends at all (being powerless)

52 *Whose he is we are* whoever Antony befriends, so do we

54 *case* predicament, unfortunate situation

55 *Further than* except to remember   *he is Caesar* i.e. he is all-powerful, but generous

57 *as* because

59 *constrainèd blemishes* faults forced upon you (by Antony)

62 *merely* utterly

Enobarbus' final aside criticises Cleopatra's seeming abandonment of Antony. He could mimic sailors in a sinking ship before leaving the stage without either Cleopatra or Thidias seeming to notice his exit.

65 *dearest* i.e. Cleopatra

| | Knowing all measures – the full Caesar will | 35 |

Knowing all measures – the full Caesar will 35
Answer his emptiness! Caesar, thou hast subdued
His judgement too!

Enter a SERVANT

SERVANT A messenger from Caesar.

CLEOPATRA What, no more ceremony? See, my women,
Against the blown rose may they stop their nose
That kneeled unto the buds. Admit him, sir. [*Exit* SERVANT 40

ENOBARBUS [*Aside*] Mine honesty and I begin to square.
The loyalty well held to fools does make
Our faith mere folly. Yet he that can endure
To follow with allegiance a fallen lord,
Does conquer him that did his master conquer, 45
And earns a place i'the story.

Enter THIDIAS

CLEOPATRA Caesar's will?

THIDIAS Hear it apart.

CLEOPATRA None but friends – say boldly.

THIDIAS So haply are they friends to Antony.

ENOBARBUS He needs as many, sir, as Caesar has,
Or needs not us. If Caesar please, our master 50
Will leap to be his friend; for us, you know,
Whose he is we are, and that is Caesar's.

THIDIAS So.
Thus then, thou most renowned: Caesar entreats
Not to consider in what case thou stand'st
Further than he is Caesar.

CLEOPATRA Go on; right royal. 55

THIDIAS He knows that you embraced not Antony
As you did love, but as you feared him.

CLEOPATRA O!

THIDIAS The scars upon your honour therefore he
Does pity, as constrainèd blemishes,
Not as deserved.

CLEOPATRA He is god, and knows 60
What is most right. Mine honour was not yielded,
But conquered merely.

ENOBARBUS [*Aside*] To be sure of that,
I will ask Antony. Sir, sir, thou art so leaky
That we must leave thee to thy sinking, for
Thy dearest quit thee.

[*Exit*

133

67   *desired* asked

71   *shroud* protection

74   *in deputation* as my representative

75   *prompt* ready

77   *all-obeying breath* commands that all obey

78   *doom of Egypt* his judgement on my country and me

79–81   *Wisdom … shake it* when it's a choice between being wise and taking a risk, choosing wisdom will ensure all will be well, no matter what

81–2   *Give me … hand* i.e. give me permission to kiss your hand

83   *mused* thought about   *taking* occupying

85   *As* as if

Antony, swearing, bursts in to find Thidias kissing Cleopatra's hand as she fondly remembers Caesar's father (her lover before Antony). Has Enobarbus fetched Antony deliberately to hear Cleopatra betray him? Cleopatra is speechless and perhaps moves away from Antony. This part of the scene requires quick and aggressive action by Antony, while the others look on with different emotions.

85   *Favours* i.e. her hand being offered to be kissed

87   *fullest* most fortunate

89   *kite* slang word for whore

90   *Authority melts from me* I am losing any authority

Compare Antony's description of his loss of power and authority (lines 90–2) with Cleopatra's 'blown rose' image earlier in this scene.

91   *muss* game in which children scramble for objects thrown on the ground   *start forth* rush forward

93   *Jack* knave or fellow

94   *better* safer   *whelp* cub

96   *tributaries* minor rulers who paid tribute to Caesar

THIDIAS	Shall I say to Caesar	65

What you require of him? – for he partly begs
To be desired to give. It much would please him,
That of his fortunes you should make a staff
To lean upon. But it would warm his spirits
To hear from me you had left Antony,   70
And put yourself under his shroud,
The universal landlord.

CLEOPATRA   What's your name?

THIDIAS   My name is Thidias.

CLEOPATRA   Most kind messenger,
Say to great Caesar this in deputation:
I kiss his conquering hand. Tell him I am prompt   75
To lay my crown at's feet, and there to kneel;
Tell him, from his all-obeying breath I hear
The doom of Egypt.

THIDIAS   'Tis your noblest course.
Wisdom and fortune combating together,
If that the former dare but what it can,   80
No chance may shake it. Give me grace to lay
My duty on your hand.

CLEOPATRA   Your Caesar's father oft –
When he hath mused of taking kingdoms in –
Bestowed his lips on that unworthy place,
As it rained kisses.

Enter **ANTONY** *and* **ENOBARBUS**

ANTONY   Favours, by Jove that thunders!   85
What art thou, fellow?

THIDIAS   One that but performs
The bidding of the fullest man, and worthiest
To have command obeyed.

ENOBARBUS [*Aside*]   You will be whipped.

ANTONY   Approach there! Ah, you kite! Now, gods and devils,
Authority melts from me! Of late, when I cried 'Ho!'   90
Like boys unto a muss, kings would start forth
And cry 'Your will?' Have you no ears?
I am Antony yet.

Enter **SERVANTS**

Take hence this Jack and whip him.

ENOBARBUS [*Aside*] 'Tis better playing with a lion's whelp,
Than with an old one dying.

ANTONY   Moon and stars!   95
Whip him! Were't twenty of the greatest tributaries

135

98   *saucy* stronger than the modern meaning

> *Thidias is struggling against being taken away to be whipped. Tactfully Cleopatra remains silent in the face of Antony's fearsome rage. The violent action on stage is mirrored in the fury of Antony's words.*

100   *cringe* twist

103   *again* back here again

104   *errand* message

105   *blasted* already withered or blighted

106   *pillow* i.e. marriage bed   *unpressed* neglected, unused

107   *Forborne … race* neglected to have legitimate children

108   *gem of a woman* i.e. Octavia   *abused* deceived

109   *feeders* parasites, servants

110   *boggler* unreliable, fickle (from falconry, a hawk that was distracted)

111   *grow hard* become cruel

112   *seel* seal, stop up (from falconry, a wild hawk's eyes were sewn up)

113   *own filth* like a caged bird (continuing the falconry imagery)

115   *confusion* destruction

116   *morsel* scrap of food

117   *Dead Caesar's* Julius, the father of Octavius

        trencher wooden food plate   *fragment* scrap left after a meal

118   *Gnaeus Pompey* Pompey's brother

        besides what hotter hours alongside other sexual liaisons

119   *Unregistered in vulgar fame* not featuring in common gossip

120   *Luxuriously picked out* selected for sexual satisfaction

121   *temperance* sexual modesty

123   *fellow* one below your status   *take rewards* have sexual favours

124   *say 'God quit you'* a phrase of thanks used by beggars

125   *seal* contract, bond

126   *plighter of high hearts* pledging noble hearts

127   *Basan* Biblical reference, a place where bulls are found

128   *hornèd herd* Cuckolds were traditionally thought of as wearing horns.
        savage wild (as an animal)

129   *proclaim it civilly* speak it politely

130   *haltered neck* as a neck put in a hangman's noose

131   *yare* brisk and quick

> *Antony's rage makes him as cruel to Cleopatra as he accuses her of being to him. He charges her with sexual promiscuity, claiming he found her after her previous lovers had discarded her. She tries to stop him, but he is unswerving in his demolition of her character. Think of the possibilities for the actors as they play this tirade of abuse. It comes to a halt when Antony turns his anger on the whipped and broken Thidias.*

That do acknowledge Caesar, should I find them
So saucy with the hand of she here – what's her name
Since she was Cleopatra? Whip him, fellows,
Till like a boy you see him cringe his face   100
And whine aloud for mercy. Take him hence.

THIDIAS   Mark Antony –

ANTONY   Tug him away. Being whipped,
Bring him again – this Jack of Caesar's shall
Bear us an errand to him.

                                    [*Exeunt* SERVANTS *with* THIDIAS
You were half blasted ere I knew you. Ha?   105
Have I my pillow left unpressed in Rome,
Forborne the getting of a lawful race –
And by a gem of women – to be abused
By one that looks on feeders?

CLEOPATRA   Good my lord –

ANTONY   You have been a boggler ever,   110
But when we in our viciousness grow hard –
O, misery on't! – the wise gods seel our eyes,
In our own filth drop our clear judgements, make us
Adore our errors, laugh at's while we strut
To our confusion.

CLEOPATRA   O, is't come to this?   115

ANTONY   I found you as a morsel, cold upon
Dead Caesar's trencher – nay, you were a fragment
Of Gnaeus Pompey's, besides what hotter hours
Unregistered in vulgar fame, you have
Luxuriously picked out. For I am sure,   120
Though you can guess what temperance should be,
You know not what it is.

CLEOPATRA   Wherefore is this?

ANTONY   To let a fellow that will take rewards
And say 'God quit you!' be familiar with
My playfellow, your hand, this kingly seal   125
And plighter of high hearts! O that I were
Upon the hill of Basan, to outroar
The hornèd herd! For I have savage cause –
And to proclaim it civilly were like
A haltered neck, which does the hangman thank   130
For being yare about him.

                    Enter a SERVANT *with* THIDIAS
                    Is he whipped?

SERVANT   Soundly, my lord.

ANTONY   Cried he? And begged 'a pardon?

135   *made his daughter* Thidias' crying was considered unmanly.

137   *Henceforth* from now on

138–9   *The white … look on't* even looking on a woman's white hand will make you tremble

---

Compare Antony's violent treatment of Thidias with the way Cleopatra beat the messenger in Act 2 Scene 6. They both have passionate natures that are easily provoked into violence.

---

140   *thy entertainment* how you were treated   *Look* be sure

145   *good stars* planets of my good fortune

146   *Have empty … orbs* now are empty of any good fortune for me

147   *abysm* abyss

149   *Hipparchus* one of those who deserted Antony

      enfranchèd bondman freed slave

151   *quit me* pay me back

152   *stripes* marks of whipping

Antony angrily sends Thidias back as a message to Caesar and turns back to Cleopatra. Her terse 'Have you done yet?' perhaps tells us something about her knowledge of Antony's outbursts of anger. Cleopatra waits for him to quieten and we see their gradual reconciliation. What possibilities are there for playing the final part of this scene?

---

153   *terrene moon* i.e. Cleopatra (the moon goddess Isis)

154   *portends alone* predicts nothing but

155   *stay his time* give him time to recover his senses

156   *mingle eyes* flirt

157   *one that ties his points* one who laces his clothes (i.e. Thidias)

159   *engender* create

160   *in the source* in my heart

161   *neck* throat   *determines* melts

162   *Caesarion smite* strike my son, Caesarion

163   *the memory of my womb* i.e. my children

165   *discandying* melting   *pelleted* hail

166   *graveless* unburied

167   *buried* covered then devoured

168   *sits down* is besieging

169   *oppose his fate* resist his destiny

Compare Antony's words here about Caesar and fate with the Soothsayer's advice to him in Act 2 Scene 3.

---

170   *nobly held* remained intact

SERVANT	He did ask favour.

ANTONY   If that thy father live, let him repent
Thou wast not made his daughter; and be thou sorry   **135**
To follow Caesar in his triumph, since
Thou hast been whipped for following him. Henceforth
The white hand of a lady fever thee –
Shake thou to look on't. Get thee back to Caesar,
Tell him thy entertainment. Look thou say   **140**
He makes me angry with him; for he seems
Proud and disdainful, harping on what I am,
Not what he knew I was. He makes me angry,
And at this time most easy 'tis to do't,
When my good stars that were my former guides   **145**
Have empty left their orbs, and shot their fires
Into the abysm of hell. If he mislike
My speech and what is done, tell him he has
Hipparchus, my enfranchèd bondman, whom
He may at pleasure whip, or hang, or torture,   **150**
As he shall like to quit me. Urge it thou –
Hence with thy stripes, be gone!

                                        [*Exit* THIDIAS

CLEOPATRA   Have you done yet?

ANTONY   Alack, our terrene moon
Is now eclipsed, and it portends alone
The fall of Antony!

CLEOPATRA   I must stay his time.   **155**

ANTONY   To flatter Caesar, would you mingle eyes
With one that ties his points?

CLEOPATRA   Not know me yet?

ANTONY   Cold-hearted toward me?

CLEOPATRA   Ah, dear, if I be so,
From my cold heart let heaven engender hail,
And poison it in the source, and the first stone   **160**
Drop in my neck: as it determines, so
Dissolve my life! The next Caesarion smite,
Till by degrees the memory of my womb,
Together with my brave Egyptians all,
By the discandying of this pelleted storm,   **165**
Lie graveless, till the flies and gnats of Nile
Have buried them for prey!

ANTONY   I am satisfied.
Caesar sits down in Alexandria, where
I will oppose his fate. Our force by land
Hath nobly held; our severed navy too   **170**

171   *Have knit again, and fleet* is together at sea
172   *heart* courage
173   *field* of battle
174   *in blood* (1) covered in blood, (2) with renewed strength
175   *chronicle* place in history
178   *treble-sinewed* the strength of three
179   *maliciously* fiercely

> *Antony's extreme mood swing reminds us of how Cleopatra*
> *sometimes behaves. How might his actions and movement*
> *illustrate his new optimism and vigour?*

180   *nice and lucky* pampered by good fortune
180–1   *men … jests* men bought their lives from me by telling a joke
182   *send to darkness* i.e. kill
183   *one other gaudy* one more joyous
184   *bowls* drinking cups
186   *held it poor* hardly celebrated it
192   *There's sap in't yet* there's life in me yet (for fighting, drinking and sex)
193   *contend* compete
194   *pestilent scythe* deaths during a plague

> *Enobarbus' comments serve as a chorus. Before he tells us of his*
> *intentions to defect to Caesar's side, his honest comments offer the*
> *audience another perspective on Antony's intentions.*

197   *the dove … estridge* an unnatural reversal, as a goshawk kills a dove
198–9   *A diminution … heart* Antony's renewed courage is due to his loss of reason
199–200   *When valour … with* when courage overcomes reason it destroys its own means of survival

What we have seen of Antony's behaviour reminds us of the similarities between his personality and Cleopatra's: his rage, cruelty and violence, his unpredictable mood swings, his quickly renewed optimism and conviction. Enobarbus, an honest commentator on events, thinks it is time he left the sinking ship of Antony's fortunes. He predicts failure for Antony if he takes up arms again against Caesar.
In Act 3 we have seen the break up of the alliance between Antony and Caesar, culminating in the war between them. There has been a decisive victory for Caesar's sea forces, which became a humiliating, shameful and dishonourable defeat for Antony. The balance of power is now with Caesar. He wants Antony removed and Cleopatra for himself. After coming close to committing suicide, Antony is now revitalised and wants to battle against Caesar again.

Have knit again, and fleet, threatening most sea-like.
Where hast thou been, my heart? Dost thou hear, lady?
If from the field I shall return once more
To kiss these lips, I will appear in blood.
I and my sword will earn our chronicle.   175
There's hope in't yet.

CLEOPATRA   That's my brave lord!

ANTONY   I will be treble-sinewed, hearted, breathed,
And fight maliciously. For when mine hours
Were nice and lucky, men did ransom lives   180
Of me for jests; but now I'll set my teeth
And send to darkness all that stop me. Come,
Let's have one other gaudy night; call to me
All my sad captains; fill our bowls once more –
Let's mock the midnight bell.

CLEOPATRA   It is my birthday.   185
I had thought t'have held it poor. But since my lord
Is Antony again, I will be Cleopatra.

ANTONY   We will yet do well.

CLEOPATRA   Call all his noble captains to my lord.

ANTONY   Do so, we'll speak to them, and tonight I'll force   190
The wine peep through their scars. Come on, my Queen,
There's sap in't yet! The next time I do fight,
I'll make death love me, for I will contend
Even with his pestilent scythe.

                                    [*Exeunt all but* **ENOBARBUS**

ENOBARBUS   Now he'll outstare the lightning. To be furious   195
Is to be frighted out of fear, and in that mood
The dove will peck the estridge; and I see still
A diminution in our captain's brain
Restores his heart. When valour preys on reason,
It eats the sword it fights with. I will seek   200
Some way to leave him.

                                                        [*Exit*

141

4:1

Act 4 consists of a series of short scenes during which we follow the fortunes of Antony and Caesar as they struggle for absolute control over Rome's empire. In the first of these scenes Caesar enters reading a letter from Antony that contains insults and a challenge to fight him in single combat.

1 *boy* In Act 3 Scene 13 Antony accused Caesar of immaturity. Here is an additional offence in that 'boy' is how a servant would be addressed.
chides as rebukes me as if

6 *Laugh at* I mock

Even though Caesar has been insulted by Antony, his response seems to indicate that he doesn't take Antony's threats too seriously. How could he show his contempt as he dismisses the challenge of 'the old ruffian'?

7–8 *he's hunted Even to falling* an image of an animal exhausted by being chased

8 *breath* breathing space, chance to re-group

9 *Make boot* take advantage *distraction* confused rage *Never* never did

---

Compare Maecenas' words about Antony's emotions overcoming his reason with those of Enobarbus at the end of Act 3.

---

10 *best heads* chief officers

12 *files* armies, sorted into ranks and files of men

13 *but late* lately

14 *fetch him in* capture him

15 *store* plenty

16 *the waste* the cost (of feeding them)

The short scene ends on an ambiguous note. Is there genuine sympathy in Caesar's 'Poor Antony!' or is it merely heavy sarcasm? Whatever the interpretation, one thing is clear: Caesar is preparing to finish Antony off.

4:2

The scene switches to Antony's camp. Caesar's reply has arrived.

5–7 *Or I ... live again* either I'll survive or revitalise my dying reputation by my bloody death

7 *Woo't* colloquial for 'wilt' (will)

8 *strike* (1) hit, (2) strike the colours, i.e. surrender

Antony twists the emotional strings of the audience. The first twist is unintentional as he asks Enobarbus about fighting for him in the battle. The audience knows he intends deserting Antony and going over to Caesar. How does Enobarbus play the dramatic irony of his equivocal reply?
The second twist is intentional, as Antony calls in the servants and thanks them for their loyalty and service. Is this the human touch of a once great man, or just self-indulgence? How does the actor play the scene so as to avoid sentimentality and achieve genuine sympathy?

4:1   *Enter* CAESAR *with his army,* AGRIPPA *and* MAECENAS; CAESAR *reading a letter*

CAESAR   He calls me boy, and chides as he had power
              To beat me out of Egypt. My messenger
              He hath whipped with rods; dares me to personal combat,
              Caesar to Antony. Let the old ruffian know
              I have many other ways to die; meantime   5
              Laugh at his challenge.

MAECENAS   Caesar must think,
              When one so great begins to rage, he's hunted
              Even to falling. Give him no breath, but now
              Make boot of his distraction. Never anger
              Made good guard for itself.

CAESAR   Let our best heads   10
              Know that tomorrow the last of many battles
              We mean to fight. Within our files there are,
              Of those that served Mark Antony but late,
              Enough to fetch him in. See it done,
              And feast the army – we have store to do't,   15
              And they have earned the waste. Poor Antony!

                                                        [*Exeunt*

4:2   *Enter* ANTONY, CLEOPATRA, ENOBARBUS, CHARMIAN, IRAS, ALEXAS, *with others*

ANTONY   He will not fight with me, Domitius?

ENOBARBUS   No.

ANTONY   Why should he not?

ENOBARBUS   He thinks, being twenty times of better fortune,
              He is twenty men to one.

ANTONY   Tomorrow, soldier,
              By sea and land I'll fight. Or I will live   5
              Or bathe my dying honour in the blood
              Shall make it live again. Woo't thou fight well?

ENOBARBUS   I'll strike, and cry 'Take all!'

ANTONY   Well said; come one –
              Call forth my household servants. Let's tonight
              Be bounteous at our meal.

                   Enter three or four SERVITORS

13   *kings … fellows* you are equal to kings, because they too have served me

14   *tricks* whims   *shoots* produces

16   *made so many men* divided into as many as you are

17   *clapped up* put together hastily

21   *Scant not my cups* keep my wine cup filled
make as much of me treat me

22   *fellow* equal

23   *suffered my command* was subject to my authority

> During Antony's intimate conversation with his servants, Cleopatra
> and Enobarbus stand to one side. Their asides reveal Cleopatra's
> puzzlement at Antony's behaviour and Enobarbus' views on
> Antony's emotional display. In reply to Cleopatra's question 'What
> does he mean?', the tone of Enobarbus' answer 'To make his
> followers weep' could range from sincere to heavily ironic.

24   *Tend* serve

25   *period* end

26   *Haply* perhaps

27   *mangled shadow* disfigured ghost

33   *yield* repay

> Enobarbus' ability to predict what Antony does is shown again in his
> 'To make his followers weep'. The servants weep at Antony's words
> and Enobarbus asks him to stop making them all so sad. Antony
> tries to laugh off the depressed atmosphere he has created. It is
> important that the director creates the right mood for this scene.
> Pathos (the arousal of pity or sorrow) can sometimes unintentionally
> lapse into bathos (the reduction of heightened emotions into
> something ridiculous).

35   *onion-eyed* with eyes watering

37   *the witch take me* may I be bewitched

38   *Grace grow* may God's grace grow   *drops* tears
hearty loving

39   *dolorous* mournful

41   *burn this night with torches* enjoy the night revelling

43–4   *Where … honour* to victory rather than an honourable death

45   *consideration* worrying

*Antony and his servants know that he may have spoken his final farewell.
Against this background of sorrowful loyalty we know that at least one of
Antony's followers, Enobarbus, is going to desert him. Will there be any more
before Antony and Caesar meet in battle?*

Give my thy hand.   **10**
Thou hast been rightly honest – so hast thou –
Thou – and thou – and thou. You have served me well,
And kings have been your fellows.

CLEOPATRA [*Aside to* ENOBARBUS]   What means this?

ENOBARBUS [*Aside to* CLEOPATRA] 'Tis one of those odd tricks which sorrow shoots
    Out of the mind.

ANTONY   And thou art honest too.   **15**
I wish I could be made so many men,
And all of you clapped up together in
An Antony, that I might do you service
So good as you have done.

ALL THE SERVITORS   The gods forbid!

ANTONY   Well, my good fellows, wait on me tonight.   **20**
Scant not my cups, and make as much of me
As when mine empire was your fellow too,
And suffered my command.

CLEOPATRA [*Aside to* ENOBARBUS]   What does he mean?

ENOBARBUS [*Aside to* CLEOPATRA] To make his followers weep.

ANTONY   Tend me tonight –
May be it is the period of your duty;   **25**
Haply you shall not see me more, or if,
A mangled shadow. Perchance tomorrow
You'll serve another master. I look on you
As one that takes his leave. Mine honest friends,
I turn you not away, but like a master   **30**
Married to your good service, stay till death.
Tend me tonight two hours – I ask no more –
And the gods yield you for't!

ENOBARBUS   What mean you, sir,
To give them this discomfort? Look, they weep,
And I, an ass, am onion-eyed. For shame,   **35**
Transform us not to women.

ANTONY   Ho, ho, ho!
Now the witch take me if I meant it thus!
Grace grow where those drops fall! My hearty friends,
You take me in too dolorous a sense,
For I spake to you for your comfort, did desire you   **40**
To burn this night with torches. Know, my hearts,
I hope well of tomorrow, and will lead you
Where rather I'll expect victorious life
Than death and honour. Let's to supper, come,
And drown consideration.   **45**

                                  [*Exeunt*

4:3

We see Antony's soldiers on the eve of battle, and a deeper sense of Antony's hopelessness is conveyed.

1   *day* of the decisive battle
2   *determine one way* decide the outcome of the war
5   *Belike* most likely
8   *Here we* this is our place of watch
9   *hope* conviction
10 *landmen* foot soldiers   *stand up* stand firm
11 *purpose* resolution

An eerie mood needs to be created by the lighting of the night scene and the ghostly music of the oboes under the stage. To heighten the strangeness of the scene, soldiers from different parts of the stage could step out of the dark when they meet.

13   *signs* signifies
15–16 *'Tis ... leaves him* It is symbolic that Hercules, the god associated with his ancestors and his guarding spirit, should desert Antony on the eve of battle, as does Enobarbus.
20   *have quarter* to the extent of our watch
21   *give off* stop   *Content* agreed

On the eve of battle the signs are ominous for Antony.

4:3	*Enter a company of* **SOLDIERS**

FIRST SOLDIER   Brother, good night. Tomorrow is the day.

SECOND SOLDIER   It will determine one way. Fare you well.
Heard you of nothing strange about the streets?

FIRST SOLDIER   Nothing. What news?

SECOND SOLDIER   Belike 'tis but a rumour. Good night to you.   5

FIRST SOLDIER   Well, sir, good night.

[They meet other **SOLDIERS**

THIRD SOLDIER   Soldiers, have careful watch.

FIRST SOLDIER   And you. Good night, good night.

[They place themselves in every corner of the stage

SECOND SOLDIER   Here we. And if tomorrow
Our navy thrive, I have an absolute hope
Our landmen will stand up.

FIRST SOLDIER   'Tis a brave army,   10
And full of purpose.

[Music of the hautboys is under the stage

SECOND SOLDIER   Peace! What noise?

FIRST SOLDIER   List, list!

SECOND SOLDIER   Hark!

FIRST SOLDIER   Music i'the air.

THIRD SOLDIER   Under the earth.

FOURTH SOLDIER   It signs well, does it not?

THIRD SOLDIER   No.

FIRST SOLDIER   Peace, I say!
What should this mean?

SECOND SOLDIER   'Tis the god Hercules, whom Antony loved,   15
Now leaves him.

FIRST SOLDIER   Walk – let's see if other watchmen
Do hear what we do.

SECOND SOLDIER   How now, masters?

ALL *[Speaking together]*   How now?
How now? Do you hear this?

FIRST SOLDIER   Ay. Is't not strange?

THIRD SOLDIER   Do you hear, masters? Do you hear?

FIRST SOLDIER   Follow the noise so far as we have quarter.   20
Let's see how it will give off.

ALL   Content. 'Tis strange.

[Exeunt

4:4

After the previous scene, Antony's enthusiastic and energetic battle preparations ring a little hollow.

The arming of Antony.

2 *chuck* chick, an intimate term of endearment
3 *thine iron* the armour you're carrying
5 *brave* defy

There is plenty of activity in this scene as Antony puts on his armour and Cleopatra quickly works out how to help. After at first criticising her, Antony soon approves, and even praises her efforts. Again we see how changeable Antony's mood can be. The interaction between the two gives an opportunity for the actors to use these little intimate moments to show their human qualities set against the background of war.

6–7 *Thou art … my heart* i.e. your heart defends me
7 *False* wrong (i.e. not that way, but this)
8 *Sooth, la* indeed ('la' is used for emphasis)
10 *thy defences* your armour *Briefly* in a moment
11 *Rarely* splendidly
13 *daff't* take it off
14 *a squire* a knight's personal servant
15 *tight* skilled *despatch* hurry up
16 *That* if only *knew'st* understood
17 *royal occupation* Monarchs were expected show leadership on the battlefield.
18 *workman* an expert at his trade, i.e. fighting battles
19 *him … charge* a man instructed to give a warlike message
20 *betime* early
22 *riveted trim* armour
23 *port* gate of the city *expect you* await you
25 *'Tis well blown* i.e. the flourish of trumpets, or the morning has begun well
27 *to be of note* wanting to make a name for himself (with a play on 'note' of the trumpets)

4:4   *Enter* ANTONY, CLEOPATRA *and* CHARMIAN *with others*

ANTONY   Eros! Mine armour, Eros!

CLEOPATRA   Sleep a little.

ANTONY   No, my chuck. Eros! Come, mine armour, Eros!

Enter EROS *with armour*

Come, good fellow, put thine iron on –
If fortune be not ours today, it is
Because we brave her. Come,

CLEOPATRA   Nay, I'll help too.   5
What's this for?

ANTONY   Ah, let be, let be! Thou art
The armourer of my heart. False, false; this, this.

CLEOPATRA   Sooth, la, I'll help; thus it must be.

ANTONY   Well, well,
We shall thrive now. Seest thou, my good fellow?
Go put on thy defences.

EROS   Briefly, sir.   10

CLEOPATRA   Is not this buckled well?

ANTONY   Rarely, rarely.
He that unbuckles this, till we do please
To daff't for our repose, shall hear a storm.
Thou fumblest, Eros, and my queen's a squire
More tight at this than thou – despatch. O love,   15
That thou couldst see my wars today, and knew'st
The royal occupation, thou shouldst see
A workman in't.

Enter an armed SOLDIER

                    Good morrow to thee, welcome.
Thou look'st like him that knows a warlike charge.
To business that we love, we rise betime   20
And go to't with delight.

SOLDIER   A thousand, sir,
Early though't be, have on their riveted trim,
And at the port expect you.

[*Shout. Trumpets flourish*

Enter CAPTAINS *and* SOLDIERS

CAPTAIN   The morn is fair. Good morrow, General.

ALL THE SOLDIERS Good morrow, General.

ANTONY   'Tis well blown, lads.   25
This morning, like the spirit of a youth
That means to be of note, begins betimes.

28 *well said* well done
30 *rebukeable* open to reprimand
31 *worthy shameful check* worth a shameful rebuke
31–2 *to stand … compliment* to linger on a more common farewell
32 *mechanic* working man

‖ *Antony continues to have his armour put on as he speaks to the*
newly arrived soldiers. He kisses Cleopatra with a soldier's farewell,
without any of the sentimental emotions of the previous scene.

33 *man of steel* Antony is physically and metaphorically armoured.

‖ *How might the actor playing Antony use his warlike appearance and*
confident manner as he leaves the stage? There is scope for lots of
activity as weapons, shields and flags are brandished in the bustle of
the soldiers following Antony. As the warlike sounds die away, for
contrast there might be a moment of silence before Charmian speaks.

35 *Please you* do you wish
36 *That* if only
38 *Then Antony – but now* i.e. Antony would win that contest, but of
this one I have doubts

We see a more confident and cheerful Antony, but after he leaves Cleopatra
appears less confident of his success.

4:5

‖ *On the battlefield Antony meets the soldier whose advice not to fight at sea he*
ignored (Act 3 Scene 7).

1 *happy* fortunate
2 *thy scars* the evidence of battle
4 *have revolted* did desert you
6 *Followed thy heels* i.e. like a faithful dog

‖ *Antony's answers show his shock and disbelief that Enobarbus*
should desert him. Yet immediately he displays his generosity when
he sends a friendly message to Enobarbus, along with his treasure.
The actor has to display first the impact the news has on Antony
and then the warmth of his response.

So, so. Come, give me that. This way – well said!
Fare thee well, dame. Whate'er becomes of me,
This is a soldier's kiss – rebukeable   30
And worthy shameful check it were, to stand
On more mechanic compliment. I'll leave thee
Now like a man of steel. You that will fight,
Follow me close – I'll bring you to't. Adieu.

[*Exeunt* ANTONY, EROS, CAPTAINS *and* SOLDIERS

CHARMIAN   Please you retire to your chamber?

CLEOPATRA   Lead me.   35
He goes forth gallantly. That he and Caesar might
Determine this great war in single fight!
Then Antony – but now. Well, on.

[*Exeunt*

4:5   *Trumpets sound. Enter* ANTONY *and* EROS, *a* SOLDIER *meeting them*

SOLDIER   The gods make this a happy day to Antony!

ANTONY   Would thou and those thy scars had once prevailed
To make me fight at land!

SOLDIER   Hadst thou done so,
The kings that have revolted, and the soldier
That has this morning left thee, would have still   5
Followed thy heels.

ANTONY   Who's gone this morning?

SOLDIER   Who?
One ever near thee – call for Enobarbus,
He shall not hear thee, or from Caesar's camp
Say 'I am none of thine.'

ANTONY   What sayst thou?

SOLDIER   Sir,
He is with Caesar.

EROS   Sir, his chests and treasure   10
He has not with him.

ANTONY   Is he gone?

13   *Detain no jot* don't keep back the smallest item

14   *subscribe* sign (the letter)

17   *Corrupted* ruined   *Despatch* get it over with quickly

The scene finishes with a perceptive insight from Antony. He doesn't blame Enobarbus for deserting him, but identifies the cause to be his own weakness. Can Antony recover, or is everything going wrong for him?

4:6

The last word of the previous scene was Antony's plaintive 'Enobarbus!' Immediately we see him with Caesar.

6   *Prove this* if this proves to be   *three-nooked world* the three cornered Roman world of Europe, Asia and Africa

7   *bear the olive freely* freely grow the olive (symbol of peace)

8   *charge* command

9   *Plant ... vant* put the deserters from Antony's army in the front line

12–18   *Alexas ... trust* Enobarbus goes through the fate of the other deserters.

13   *dissuade* persuade him to leave Antony

14   *incline himself* support

15   *pains* trouble that he took (in supporting Caesar)

17   *fell away* deserted   *entertainment* employment

18   *ill* wrong; this links with 'corrupted' from the previous scene

Enobarbus, who has been a perceptive commentator on events, is now alone on stage regretting his desertion of Antony. Perhaps, like Antony during his dark moments, Enobarbus may slump to the ground to show his feelings.

22   *bounty overplus* additional gifts

23   *on my guard* while I was on guard

SOLDIER	Most certain.

ANTONY   Go, Eros, send his treasure after; do it –
Detain no jot, I charge thee. Write to him –
I will subscribe – gentle adieus and greetings.
Say that I wish he never find more cause   15
To change a master. O, my fortunes have
Corrupted honest men! Despatch. Enobarbus!

                                                         [*Exeunt*

4:6   *Flourish. Enter* AGRIPPA *and* CAESAR, *with* ENOBARBUS *and* DOLABELLA

CAESAR   Go forth, Agrippa, and begin the fight.
Our will is Antony be took alive –
Make it so known.

AGRIPPA   Caesar, I shall.

                                                         [*Exit*

CAESAR   The time of universal peace is near.   5
Prove this a prosperous day, the three-nooked world
Shall bear the olive freely.

                    Enter a MESSENGER

MESSENGER   Antony
Is come into the field.

CAESAR   Go charge Agrippa
Plant those that have revolted in the vant,
That Antony may seem to spend his fury   10
Upon himself.

                              [*Exeunt all but* ENOBARBUS

ENOBARBUS   Alexas did revolt: 'a went to Jewry on
Affairs of Antony, there did dissuade
Great Herod to incline himself to Caesar
And leave his master Antony. For this pains,   15
Caesar hath hanged him. Canidius and the rest
That fell away have entertainment, but
No honourable trust. I have done ill,
Of which I do accuse myself so sorely,
That I will joy no more.

                    Enter a SOLDIER *of Caesar's*

SOLDIER   Enobarbus, Antony   20
Hath after thee sent all thy treasure, with
His bounty overplus. The messenger
Came on my guard, and at thy tent is now

26–7 *Best you … host* it is best if you ensure safe conduct for the messenger

27 *attend mine office* get on with my duties

28 *Your emperor* Antony

29 *Continues still a Jove* is still godlike (in his generosity)

30 *alone* the only, the worst

31 *feel I am so most* feel it more than anyone else

32 *mine* abundant store

33 *turpitude* crime

34 *blows my heart* makes my heart swell

35 *thought* melancholy, grief *mean* action

36 *outstrike* cancel it out

The regret Enobarbus feels at deserting Antony is intensified with news of Antony's double generosity and the praise of the soldier. Here stage lighting may be used to accentuate his oppressive guilt and despair, feelings that slowly darken and send him to his suicide.

38 *Some ditch* The unremarkable 'some' adds to the shame of dying in a ditch. *foul'st* the most foul, with stagnant water

After witnessing Caesar's cruelty in putting deserters from Antony's army in the front line, Enobarbus realises his mistake in leaving Antony. News of Antony's generosity only compounds his regret and he leaves contemplating suicide. Might Enobarbus' misfortune herald a change in Antony's fortunes?

4:7

On the battlefield and Antony is winning!

The director may choose to modernise the weaponry in the play. Smoke machines, lighting and special effects could supplement the sound of drums and trumpet calls used on Shakespeare's stage to give the impression of war.

1 *engaged* advanced

2 *has work* is having to fight hard *our oppression* the pressure on us

4 *fought indeed* well fought

5 *done so* fought like this *droven* older form of 'driven'

6 *clouts* bandages *Thou bleed'st apace* you are bleeding badly

Scarus makes light of his badly bleeding wound. He does this by saying his wound was first in the shape of the letter T, but now is shaped like the letter H. In Shakespeare's time an 'ache' was pronounced the same as the letter H – 'aitch'. This pun only works well if the actor playing Scarus makes some clear visual display of the letters T and H around his wound.

9 *bench-holes* the toilet or latrine holes

Unloading of his mules.

ENOBARBUS   I give it you.

SOLDIER   Mock not, Enobarbus –   25
I tell you true. Best you safed the bringer
Out of the host; I must attend mine office
Or would have done't myself. Your emperor
Continues still a Jove.

                                                        [*Exit*

ENOBARBUS   I am alone the villain of the earth,   30
And feel I am so most. O Antony,
Thou mine of bounty, how wouldst thou have paid
My better service, when my turpitude
Thou dost so crown with gold! This blows my heart –
If swift thought break it not, a swifter mean   35
Shall outstrike thought; but thought will do't, I feel.
I fight against thee? No, I will go seek
Some ditch wherein to die; the foul'st best fits
My latter part of life.

                                                        [*Exit*

4:7   *Alarum. Drums and trumpets. Enter* AGRIPPA *and others*

AGRIPPA   Retire! We have engaged ourselves too far –
Caesar himself has work, and our oppression
Exceeds what we expected!

                                                        [*Exeunt*

              Alarums. Enter ANTONY, *and* SCARUS *wounded*

SCARUS   O my brave Emperor, this is fought indeed!
Had we done so at first, we had droven them home   5
With clouts about their heads.

ANTONY   Thou bleed'st apace.

SCARUS   I had a wound here that was like a T,
But now 'tis made an H.

                                        [*Retreat sounded far off*

ANTONY   They do retire.

SCARUS   We'll beat 'em into bench-holes. I have yet

10	*scotches* cuts, gashes
11	*serves* ensures us
12	*score* mark, as when flogged
13–14	*And … runner* The image is of a dog chasing, then mauling, a hare.
15	*sprightly* cheerful
16	*halt after* limp after you

Antony's fortunes have changed. His army has driven Caesar's from the battlefield. But is this a decisive victory in the war?

4:8

Antony, exhilarated, enters his camp, ready to celebrate his victory.

1	*beat him to his camp* drove back Caesar's troops, fighting even in their camp
	Run one before let someone run ahead
2	*gests* deeds (in Shakespeare's time associated with medieval chivalry)
5	*doughty-handed* valiant in arms ('doughty' is another word associated with chivalry)
6–7	*Not … mine* i.e. not as if it were my cause, but your own
7	*Hectors* Hector was the heroic warrior of Troy
8	*clip* embrace, hug
10	*congealment* dried blood
10–11	*kiss … whole* with kisses heal your honourable wounds
12	*fairy* enchantress (again, with medieval associations)
13	*day* light
14	*Chain* put your arms around (with a pun on 'chain-mail')
	armed armoured *attire and all* dressed as you are
15	*proof of harness* armour that has proved to be impenetrable
16	*Ride on the pants triumphing* ride in triumph on my panting heart (as if I were a chariot)

Antony has lost the despair of earlier scenes. He now shows elation and excitement as he greets Cleopatra. He asks her to leap into his arms, describing his heart as a chariot in which Cleopatra will ride triumphantly. There is no stage direction to say whether or not Cleopatra does leap into his arms. Her dress and headgear may make this difficult, and the actor might have to do with a passionate embrace.

17	*virtue* courage
18	*snare* used to catch birds and animals
	nightingale Antony picks up the image of snare
19–20	*though grey … brown* Antony again refers to his age
20	*something* somewhat *ha'* have

Room for six scotches more.   10

Enter EROS

EROS   They are beaten, sir, and our advantage serves
              For a fair victory.

SCARUS   Let us score their backs
              And snatch 'em up, as we take hares, behind –
              'Tis sport to maul a runner.

ANTONY   I will reward thee
              Once for thy sprightly comfort, and tenfold   15
              For thy good valour. Come thee on.

SCARUS   I'll halt after.

                                                   [*Exeunt*

4:8   *Alarum. Enter* ANTONY *again, in a march;* SCARUS, *with others*

ANTONY   We have beat him to his camp. Run one before
              And let the Queen know of our gests. Tomorrow,
              Before the sun shall see's, we'll spill the blood
              That has today escaped. I thank you all,
              For doughty-handed are you, and have fought   5
              Not as you served the cause, but as't had been
              Each man's like mine; you have shown all Hectors.
              Enter the city, clip your wives, your friends,
              Tell them your feats, whilst they with joyful tears
              Wash the congealment from your wounds, and kiss   10
              The honoured gashes whole.

Enter CLEOPATRA

              [*To* SCARUS] Give me thy hand.
              To this great fairy I'll commend thy acts,
              Make her thanks bless thee. – O thou day o'the world,
              Chain mine armed neck; leap thou, attire and all,
              Through proof of harness to my heart, and there   15
              Ride on the pants triumphing!

CLEOPATRA   Lord of lords!
              O infinite virtue, com'st thou smiling from
              The world's great snare uncaught?

ANTONY   My nightingale,
              We have beat them to their beds. What, girl, though grey
              Do something mingle with our younger brown, yet ha' we 20

157

21   *nerves* muscles

22   *Get goal … youth* can match the victories of younger men

---

Compare the gracious way Antony encourages the kiss of Cleopatra's hand by Scarus (lines 22–4) with Antony's violent treatment of Thidias for doing the same thing in Act 3 Scene 13.

---

26   *Destroyed … shape* taken on the appearance of Scarus

28   *carbuncled* embossed with jewels

29   *holy Phoebus' car* the chariot of the sun god

31   *hacked targets* battered shields   *like* as becomes
      owe own

33   *camp this host* accommodate them all

34   *carouses* toasts

35   *royal peril* great danger

The actor playing Antony should deliver his instructions to the trumpeters in the most commanding voice. His voice and manner should convey triumph, celebration and confidence, and should immediately be answered by a resounding fanfare that follows them as they leave the stage.

37   *tabourines* small military drums

Antony's battlefield victory has revitalised him and we see something of the confident Antony that blazed a trail of success across the Roman Empire. Is this the turning point for him?

4:9

After the noisy fanfare ending the previous scene we have a sudden contrast – the quiet of a night scene in Caesar's camp.

2   *court of guard* guard room

3   *shiny* moonlit   *embattle* prepare for the battle

4   *second hour* Antony said in the previous scene (line 3) they would fight before sunrise.

5   *shrewd one to's* difficult for us

6   *Stand close, and list him* stay hidden and listen to him

8–9   *When … memory* deserters shall be remembered with hatred

A brain that nourishes our nerves, and can
Get goal for goal of youth. Behold this man,
Commend unto his lips thy favouring hand. –
Kiss it, my warrior. – He hath fought today
As if a god in hate of mankind had   25
Destroyed in such a shape.

CLEOPATRA   I'll give thee, friend,
An armour all of gold; it was a king's.

ANTONY   He has deserved it, were it carbuncled
Like holy Phoebus' car. Give my thy hand –
Through Alexandria make a jolly march,   30
Bear our hacked targets like the men that owe them.
Had our great palace the capacity
To camp this host, we all would sup together
And drink carouses to the next day's fate,
Which promises royal peril. Trumpeters,   35
With brazen din blast you the city's ear;
Make mingle with our rattling tabourines,
That heaven and earth may strike their sounds together,
Applauding our approach.

[*Exeunt*

4:9   *Enter a* SENTRY *and his company.* ENOBARBUS *follows*

SENTRY   If we be not relieved within this hour,
We must return to the court of guard. The night
Is shiny, and they say we shall embattle
By the second hour i'the morn.

FIRST WATCH   This last day was
A shrewd one to's.

ENOBARBUS   O bear me witness, night –   5

SECOND WATCH What man is this?

FIRST WATCH   Stand close, and list him.

ENOBARBUS   Be witness to me, O thou blessèd moon,
When men revolted shall upon record
Bear hateful memory, poor Enobarbus did
Before thy face repent.

11 *Hark* listen

12 *O sovereign … melancholy* The moon was thought to influence forms of madness and melancholy.

13 *poisonous damp of night* Night dew was believed unhealthy in Shakespeare's time. *disponge* drop, as squeezed from a sponge

14 *a very … will* contrary to my wishes

17 *Which* i.e. his heart

19 *Nobler … infamous* your nobility is greater than my desertion

20 *in thine own particular* for the personal wrongs I have done

21 *rank me in register* list me in the records

22 *master-leaver* a servant who leaves his master

The actor falls to the ground on 'O Antony!' but there are no stage directions to indicate clearly the moment of Enobarbus' death. Melancholy grief seems to be the cause of his death, as his heart was 'dried with grief'. The director may decide that more theatricality is needed and use a knife or poison to hasten his breaking heart. As it is happening at night, the soldiers are not immediately aware that he is dead.

26 *Swoons* faints

26–7 *for … sleep* he could not sleep after the prayers he spoke

29 *raught* grasped

30 *Demurely* quietly

31 *of note* high-ranking *hour* period of watch

32 *out* over

On the eve of battle Enobarbus asks forgiveness and commits suicide. The drums of war are already sounding out.

4:10

This is the first of two very short scenes. In some productions the two scenes are run together with the two sides on stage throughout. In this scene Antony decides to risk again engaging Caesar by sea and not land.

3 *fight … the air* he's fought in two of the four elements, land and sea; fire and air are the others

4 *foot* infantry

SENTRY	Enobarbus?	
SECOND WATCH	Peace!	**10**

      Hark further.

ENOBARBUS   O sovereign mistress of true melancholy,
      The poisonous damp of night disponge upon me,
      That life, a very rebel to my will,
      May hang no longer on me. Throw my heart   **15**
      Against the flint and hardness of my fault,
      Which being dried with grief, will break to powder,
      And finish all foul thoughts. O Antony,
      Nobler than my revolt is infamous,
      Forgive me in thine own particular,   **20**
      But let the world rank me in register
      A master-leaver and a fugitive.
      O Antony! O Antony!

FIRST WATCH   Let's speak to him.

SENTRY   Let's hear him, for the things he speaks
      May concern Caesar.

SECOND WATCH   Let's do so – but he sleeps.   **25**

SENTRY   Swoons rather, for so bad a prayer as his
      Was never yet for sleep.

FIRST WATCH   Go we to him.

SECOND WATCH   Awake, sir, awake – speak to us.

FIRST WATCH   Hear you, sir?

SENTRY   The hand of death hath raught him. [*Drums afar off*] Hark! The drums
      Demurely wake the sleepers. Let us bear him   **30**
      To the court of guard; he is of note. Our hour
      Is fully out.

SECOND WATCH   Come on then; he may recover yet.

[Exeunt with the body

4:10   *Enter* **ANTONY** *and* **SCARUS**, *with their army*

ANTONY   Their preparation is today by sea –
      We please them not by land.

SCARUS   For both, my lord.

ANTONY   I would they'd fight i'the fire or i'the air;
      We'd fight there too. But this it is: our foot
      Upon the hills adjoining to the city   **5**

6 *for sea* to put to sea

7 *put forth the haven* left the harbour

8 *appointment* purpose

9 *look on* From Antony's vantage point he could look out on how well his ships were doing in the battle.

Antony has made his plans, but what of Caesar's?

4:11

Caesar gives his orders.

1 *But being charged* unless we are attacked
be still by land remain in a defensive position by land

2 *Which ... shall* which I believe will happen
best force strongest forces

3 *Is forth* has set out

4 *hold our best advantage* take up the best possible positions

Caesar wants to avoid fighting on land, as he knows that is where Antony's strength lies. Why does Antony want to fight by sea again after the last disaster?

4:12

Off stage there is the sound of alarums indicating the sea battle is about to take place. Antony wants to see how his forces are doing.

1 *not joined* i.e. in battle *straight* immediately

3 *'tis like to go* how it's going

3–4 *Swallows ... nests* a bad omen, which indicates inactivity on board Cleopatra's ships

4 *augurers* soothsayers, who predicted the future

7 *starts* sudden impulses

8 *fretted* chequered

Scarus gives us a very different picture of Antony from the confident one we saw recently celebrating his victory. His account of Antony's mood swings is interrupted by the real thing as Antony enters with a dramatic 'All is lost!' The change of mood from that of Scene 8 is most striking in the description of Cleopatra as 'This foul Egyptian'. The actor needs to show the startling contrast between the Antony we see now and the one we saw in Scene 8 in order to make the audience wonder, as Enobarbus did, about Antony's instability.

Shall stay with us – order for sea is given,
They have put forth the haven –
Where their appointment we may best discover
And look on their endeavour.

[*Exeunt*

4:11   *Enter* **CAESAR** *and his army*

CAESAR   But being charged, we will be still by land –
Which, as I take it, we shall, for his best force
Is forth to man his galleys. To the vales,
And hold our best advantage!

[*Exeunt*

4:12   *Alarum afar off, as at a sea fight. Enter* **ANTONY** *and* **SCARUS**

ANTONY   Yet they are not joined. Where yond pine does stand
I shall discover all. I'll bring thee word
Straight how 'tis like to go.   [*Exit*

SCARUS   Swallows have built
In Cleopatra's sails their nests. The augurers
Say they know not, they cannot tell, look grimly,   5
And dare not speak their knowledge. Antony
Is valiant, and dejected, and by starts
His fretted fortunes give him hope and fear
Of what he has and has not.

Enter **ANTONY**

ANTONY   All is lost!
This foul Egyptian hath betrayèd me –   10
My fleet hath yielded to the foe, and yonder
They cast their caps up and carouse together

163

13 *Triple-turned whore* presumably with Julius Caesar, Pompey and himself

14 *novice* beginner, another contemptuous reference to Caesar's youth

16 *my charm* the one who has put a spell on me, i.e. Cleopatra

17 *all* i.e. all there is to do *Bid them all fly* tell everyone to leave

18 *uprise* rising, i.e. dawn

20 *hearts* soldiers

21 *spanieled me at heels* followed at my heels (like a spaniel)

22 *discandy* become liquid

23 *this pine is barked* Antony is like a pine tree stripped bare (compared with Caesar's blossoming)

> *Antony speaks to the audience, looking for the same sympathetic response he received from his servants in Act 4 Scene 2. What gestures might accompany his references to Caesar and Cleopatra?*

24 *overtopped* was taller than, i.e. greater than

25 *grave* deadly

26 *Whose eye … home* whose glance was enough to send me to war and bring me back home

27 *bosom* heart *crownet* crown *chief end* main reason

28 *right* true *fast and loose* Gypsies at fairs played this cheating game of trick rope knots.

29 *Beguiled* cheated *heart of loss* utter ruin

30 *spell* witch *Avaunt* get away

32 *thy deserving* what you deserve (i.e. death)

33 *blemish Caesar's triumph* spoil Caesar's chance to parade you through Rome

34 *hoist thee up* i.e. as an object of public curiosity (perhaps in a cage) *plebeians* commoners

35 *spot* stain, blemish

36 *most monster-like be shown* exhibited like a freak

37 *diminutives* undersized weaklings

38 *plough thy visage* claw your face

39 *preparèd* grown long for the purpose

43–7 *The shirt … self* Antony recalls the death of his supposed ancestor Hercules (also known as Alcides) who died from wearing a shirt soaked in the poisoned blood of Nessus. In his agony Hercules threw the servant who brought him the shirt, Lichias, into the sea.

46 *heaviest club* for which Hercules was famous

49 *Under this plot* a victim of the plot he thinks Cleopatra has hatched with Caesar

> *Antony has seen his sea forces lose again, but this time the defeat is decisive and all his forces have fled. He blames Cleopatra for the defeat and irrationally thinks she has plotted with Caesar. He now contemplates his own death.*

Like friends long lost. Triple-turned whore! 'Tis thou
Hast sold me to this novice, and my heart
Makes only wars on thee. Bid them all fly –   15
For when I am revenged upon my charm,
I have done all. Bid them all fly, begone!   [*Exit* SCARUS
O sun, thy uprise shall I see no more –
Fortune and Antony part here, even here
Do we shake hands. All come to this? The hearts   20
That spanieled me at heels, to whom I gave
Their wishes, do discandy, melt their sweets
On blossoming Caesar; and this pine is barked
That overtopped them all. Betrayed I am.
O this false soul of Egypt! This grave charm –   25
Whose eye becked forth my wars, and called them home,
Whose bosom was my crownet, my chief end –
Like a right gypsy, hath at fast and loose
Beguiled me, to the very heart of loss.
What, Eros, Eros!

Enter CLEOPATRA

Ah, thou spell! Avaunt!   30

CLEOPATRA   Why is my lord enraged against his love?

ANTONY   Vanish, or I shall give thee thy deserving,
And blemish Caesar's triumph. Let him take thee,
And hoist thee up to the shouting plebeians;
Follow his chariot, like the greatest spot   35
Of all thy sex; most monster-like be shown
For poor'st diminutives, for dolts, and let
Patient Octavia plough thy visage up
With her preparèd nails.   [*Exit* CLEOPATRA
'Tis well th'art gone,
If it be well to live. But better 'twere   40
Thou fell'st into my fury, for one death
Might have prevented many. Eros, ho!
The shirt of Nessus is upon me – teach me
Alcides, thou mine ancestor, thy rage;
Let me lodge Lichas on the horns o'the moon,   45
And with those hands that grasped the heaviest club
Subdue my worthiest self. The witch shall die.
To the young Roman boy she hath sold me, and I fall
Under this plot; she dies for't. Eros, ho!

[*Exit*

4:13

Cleopatra seeks refuge after leaving an enraged Antony.

2   *Telamon* a hero (also known as Ajax) who went mad and killed
    himself after a defeat   *boar of Thessaly* a wild boar sent because
    of dishonour to destroy a kingdom

3   *embossed* foaming at the mouth
    monument the tomb Cleopatra had already built for herself

5   *rive* split

6   *greatness going off* destruction of a great person

9   *word it … piteously* say it pathetically

10 *bring me* tell me

*In fear of Antony's rage Cleopatra has gone to hide in her own tomb and sends
false news of her death.*

4:14

We now see another side of Antony's character as he reflects on life.

1   *thou yet behold'st me?* can you still see me?

2   *dragonish* in the shape of a dragon

3   *vapour* cloud or mist

4   *pendent* overhanging

6   *nod unto the world* bend in the wind

7   *mock our eyes with air* fool us with what seems real

8   *black vesper's pageants* spectacular sunsets

10 *rack dislimns* the cloud wipes out

12 *knave* a servant (used affectionately)

13 *Even such a body* Antony compares himself to the clouds.

17 *annexed unto't* included in it

4:13　　　　　　*Enter* CLEOPATRA, CHARMIAN, IRAS, MARDIAN

CLEOPATRA　Help me, my women! O, he's more mad
　　　　Than Telamon for his shield; the boar of Thessaly
　　　　Was never so embossed.

CHARMIAN　　　　　　　To the monument!
　　　　There lock yourself, and send him word you are dead.
　　　　The soul and body rive not more in parting　　　　　　5
　　　　Than greatness going off.

CLEOPATRA　　　　　　　To the monument!
　　　　Mardian, go tell him I have slain myself –
　　　　Say that the last I spoke was 'Antony',
　　　　And word it, prithee, piteously. Hence, Mardian,
　　　　And bring me how he takes my death. To the monument!　　10

　　　　　　　　　　　　　　　　　[*Exeunt*

4:14　　　　　　　　*Enter* ANTONY *and* EROS

ANTONY　　Eros, thou yet behold'st me?

EROS　　　　　　　　　　　Ay, noble lord.

ANTONY　　Sometime we see a cloud that's dragonish,
　　　　A vapour sometime like a bear or lion,
　　　　A towered citadel, a pendent rock,
　　　　A forkèd mountain, or blue promontory　　　　　　5
　　　　With trees upon't that nod unto the world
　　　　And mock our eyes with air. Thou hast seen these signs,
　　　　They are black vesper's pageants.

EROS　　　　　　　　　　　Ay, my lord.

ANTONY　　That which is now a horse, even with a thought
　　　　The rack dislimns, and makes it indistinct　　　　　　10
　　　　As water is in water.

EROS　　　　　　　　　It does, my lord.

ANTONY　　My good knave Eros, now thy captain is
　　　　Even such a body. Here I am Antony,
　　　　Yet cannot hold this visible shape, my knave.
　　　　I made these wars for Egypt, and the Queen –　　　　　　15
　　　　Whose heart I thought I had, for she had mine,
　　　　Which, whilst it was mine, had annexed unto't

18 *A million moe* the hearts of his followers
19 *Packed cards* made an underhand deal
20 *triumph* also a trump card
23 *my sword* has military and sexual connotations
25 *saucy* insolent
28 *discharged* paid, as a debt
33 *rendered* surrendered

> *Cleopatra asks Mardian to speak of her death 'piteously'. How might Mardian achieve this effect in his imaginary report of her death? No matter how sorrowful his account, the audience knows this is another of Cleopatra's tricks. In the light of this, what do you think of Antony's desolate response?*

35 *Unarm* take off my armour (a symbolic gesture of giving up)
35–6 *The long … sleep* Antony's long life is over and only death awaits
36–7 *That thou … richly* your safe departure (after giving such news) is reward enough
38 *seven fold shield of Ajax* Ajax was protected by a shield of seven layers that could not be pierced.
38–9 *keep the battery from* protect me from the attack on
39 *cleave* split
40 *continent* the body
41 *frail case* the body *Apace* quickly
42 *Bruisèd pieces* his battle-worn armour
43 *From me* leave me

Compare the slow movement of Antony removing his armour with the excitement being dressed in it by Cleopatra in Scene 4. Here, the discarding of his armour symbolises the loss of his will to live. He speaks of the armour as though it were his own limbs.

---

44 *o'ertake thee* overtake you in death
46 *length* i.e. of life
47–8 *all labour … does* anything I do fails
48–9 *very force … strength* i.e. the fiercer (an animal) struggles the more it is trapped
49 *Seal* finish
51 *couch* lie
52 *sprightly port* lively (also ghostly) manner
53 *Dido and her Aeneas* tragic lovers
54 *all the haunt be ours* they will all accompany us (with a pun on ghosts)

A million moe, now lost – she, Eros, has
Packed cards with Caesar, and false-played my glory
Unto an enemy's triumph.   **20**
Nay, weep not, gentle Eros, there is left us
Ourselves to end ourselves.

Enter MARDIAN

          O, thy vile lady! –
She has robbed me of my sword.

MARDIAN   No, Antony.
  My mistress loved thee, and her fortunes mingled
  With thine entirely.

ANTONY   Hence, saucy eunuch, peace!   **25**
  She hath betrayed me and shall die the death.

MARDIAN   Death of one person can be paid but once,
  And that she has discharged. What thou wouldst do
  Is done unto thy hand. The last she spake
  Was 'Antony! Most noble Antony!'   **30**
  Then in the midst a tearing groan did break
  The name of Antony; it was divided
  Between her heart and lips. She rendered life,
  Thy name so buried in her.

ANTONY   Dead, then?

MARDIAN   Dead.

ANTONY   Unarm, Eros. The long day's task is done,   **35**
  And we must sleep. [*To* MARDIAN] That thou depart'st hence safe
  Does pay thy labour richly. Go.   [*Exit* MARDIAN
          Off, pluck off!
  The sevenfold shield of Ajax cannot keep
  The battery from my heart. O, cleave, my sides!
  Heart, once be stronger than thy continent,   **40**
  Crack thy frail case! Apace, Eros, apace!
  No more a soldier. Bruisèd pieces, go;
  You have been nobly borne. – From me awhile.   [*Exit* EROS
  I will o'ertake thee, Cleopatra, and
  Weep for my pardon. So it must be, for now   **45**
  All length is torture; since the torch is out,
  Lie down and stray no farther. Now all labour
  Mars what it does; yea, very force entangles
  Itself with strength. Seal then, and all is done.
  Eros! – I come, my queen – Eros! – Stay for me.   **50**
  Where souls do couch on flowers, we'll hand in hand,
  And with our sprightly port make the ghosts gaze;
  Dido and her Aeneas shall want troops,
  And all the haunt be ours. – Come, Eros, Eros!

58 *Quartered* divided up

o'er green … back i.e. on the sea

59 *With ships made cities* i.e. the fleets were large

to lack for lacking

60 *less noble mind* I, less noble

61 *our Caesar tells* she tells Caesar

63 *exigent* final emergency

65 *inevitable prosecution* inescapable pursuit

> *Eros, it seems, is shocked and goes ashen when Antony asks him to take Antony's life. Does Antony draw a knife as he says this or point to his sword? Antony then tries to persuade him by demonstrating the humiliation he would suffer when captured and sent to Rome.*

72 *windowed* placed in a window

73 *pleached arms* arms bound as a captive

74 *corrigible* submissive

75 *penetrative* piercing   *wheeled seat* chariot seat

76 *branded* brutally exposed

77 *His baseness that ensued* the humiliation of the man that followed

79 *honest* honourable

80 *useful* usefully   *pardon me* excuse me from this task

81 *free* i.e. from slavery

83 *precedent services* previous duties

84 *But accidents unpurposed* just accidental, without any purpose

87 *Lo thee!* see! (you have done what I asked)

Enter **EROS**

EROS   What would my lord?

ANTONY   Since Cleopatra died,   55
I have lived in such dishonour that the gods
Detest my baseness. I, that with my sword
Quartered the world, and o'er green Neptune's back
With ships made cities, condemn myself to lack
The courage of a woman; less noble mind   60
Than she which by her death our Caesar tells
'I am conqueror of myself'. Thou art sworn, Eros,
That when the exigent should come – which now
Is come indeed – when I should see behind me
The inevitable prosecution of   65
Disgrace and horror, that on my command
Thou then wouldst kill me. Do't – the time is come.
Thou strik'st not me; 'tis Caesar thou defeat'st.
Put colour in thy cheek.

EROS   The gods withhold me!
Shall I do that which all the Parthian darts   70
Though enemy, lost aim and could not?

ANTONY   Eros,
Wouldst thou be windowed in great Rome and see
Thy master thus – with pleached arms, bending down
His corrigible neck, his face subdued
To penetrative shame; whilst the wheeled seat   75
Of fortunate Caesar, drawn before him, branded
His baseness that ensued?

EROS   I would not see't.

ANTONY   Come then – for with a wound I must be cured.
Draw that thy honest sword, which thou hast worn
Most useful for thy country.

EROS   O, sir, pardon me!   80

ANTONY   When I did make thee free, swor'st thou not then
To do this when I bade thee? Do it at once,
Or thy precedent services are all
But accidents unpurposed. Draw, and come.

EROS   Turn from me then that noble countenance   85
Wherein the worship of the whole world lies.

ANTONY   Lo thee!

EROS   My sword is drawn.

ANTONY   Then let it do at once
The thing why thou hast drawn it.

EROS   My dear master,

171

Antony and Cleopatra

> *Antony prepares to take the blade of Eros' sword, but the farewells of Eros prove to be ambiguous as he kills himself. This dramatic moment makes Antony realise he should not have asked a servant, but performed it himself. Then, in the manner characteristic of Roman suicides, Antony falls on his sword. When he does not die, this anticlimax can end up unintentionally comic or embarrassing!*

98	*got upon me*	gained advantage over me
99	*nobleness in record*	(with) a noble place in history
102	*thy scholar*	following your instructions (on how to die)
104	*despatch me!*	finish me off
105	*ill*	wrong
107	*period*	end
112	*but* only	*tidings* news of your death
113	*enter me with him*	put me in his favour

> *How might the guards and Decretas react to the pleas of the fatally wounded Antony? The audience sees how far Antony's star has fallen by the refusal of the guards to finish him off and by Decretas seizing the opportunity to win favour with Caesar by taking Antony's sword from his body.*

114	*Diomed*	Diomedes

My captain, and my emperor; let me say,   **90**
Before I strike this bloody stroke, farewell.

ANTONY   'Tis said, man, and farewell.

EROS   Farewell, great chief. Shall I strike now?

ANTONY   Now, Eros.

EROS   Why, there then! Thus I do escape the sorrow
Of Antony's death.

[Kills himself

ANTONY   Thrice nobler than myself,   **95**
Thou teachest me, O valiant Eros, what
I should, and thou couldst not. My queen and Eros
Have by their brave instruction got upon me
A nobleness in record. But I will be
A bridegroom in my death, and run into't   **100**
As to a lover's bed. Come then; and, Eros,
Thy master dies thy scholar. To do thus

[Falling on his sword

I learn of thee. How, not dead? Not dead?
The guard, ho! O, despatch me!

Enter a GUARD, DECRETAS *following them*

FIRST GUARD   What's the noise?

ANTONY   I have done my work ill, friends. O make an end   **105**
Of what I have begun.

SECOND GUARD   The star is fallen.

FIRST GUARD   And time is at his period.

ALL THE GUARDS   Alas, and woe!

ANTONY   Let him that loves me strike me dead.

FIRST GUARD   Not I.

SECOND GUARD Nor I.

THIRD GUARD   Nor anyone.   **110**

[Exeunt GUARD

DECRETAS   Thy death and fortunes bid thy followers fly.
This sword but shown to Caesar, with this tidings,
Shall enter me with him.

Enter DIOMEDES

DIOMEDES   Where's Antony?

DECRETAS   There, Diomed, there.

DIOMEDES   Lives he?
Wilt thou not answer, man?   **115**

[Exit DECRETAS

ANTONY   Art thou there, Diomed? Draw thy sword, and give me

173

117 *Sufficing strokes* sufficient blows

| There is a very intense moment on stage when Antony realises that Cleopatra is alive and that he is dying because he believed she was dead. The frantic activity that goes before this moment gives it added poignancy.

122 *Which never shall be found* for which there is no evidence
123 *disposed* agreed terms
124 *purged* cured
125 *since ... work* its effect
133–4 *to wear ... out* to use up all the service we could perform for you
135 *fate* harsh
136 *To grace ... sorrows* by honouring it with your sorrow
136–8 *Bid ... lightly* if we welcome the thing that comes to punish us, it makes it easier to bear

| Antony is taken out, borne by his guards. They might carry him in the same ceremonious way they would carry a dead hero. Lighting, drums and draped banners might all add to the effect of this exit.

Antony's raging against Cleopatra went too far on this occasion. His belief that she conspired with Caesar to overthrow him led to Cleopatra's deception. That in turn led to Antony's suicide attempt. Will Antony survive long enough to make his peace with Cleopatra? What will happen to Cleopatra after his death?

4:15

| Sheltering in her own monumental tomb, Cleopatra awaits news of Antony.

5 *Proportioned to our cause* if of the same proportions as its cause

| Diomedes' instruction to Cleopatra to 'Look out o' the other side your monument' indicates the first problem that a director has when staging this scene: what kind of structure is Cleopatra's monument going to be? Some directors create a large structure with some kind of balcony at the front; others call on the audience's imagination and employ symbolic rather than literal monuments, such as a large ornate carpet.

Sufficing strokes for death.

DIOMEDES   Most absolute lord,
My mistress Cleopatra sent me to thee.

ANTONY   When did she send thee?

DIOMEDES   Now, my lord.

ANTONY   Where is she?

DIOMEDES   Locked in her monument. She had a prophesying fear   120
Of what hath come to pass; for when she saw –
Which never shall be found – you did suspect
She had disposed with Caesar, and that your rage
Would not be purged, she sent you word she was dead;
But, fearing since how it might work, hath sent   125
Me to proclaim the truth, and I am come,
I dread, too late.

ANTONY   Too late, good Diomed. Call my guard, I prithee.

DIOMEDES   What ho! The Emperor's guard! The guard, what ho!
Come, your lord calls!   130

Enter four or five of the **GUARD** *of Antony*

ANTONY   Bear me, good friends, where Cleopatra bides –
'Tis the last service that I shall command you.

FIRST GUARD Woe, woe are we, sir, you may not live to wear
All your true followers out.

ALL THE GUARDS   Most heavy day!

ANTONY   Nay, good my fellows, do not please sharp fate   135
To grace it with your sorrows. Bid that welcome
Which comes to punish us, and we punish it
Seeming to bear it lightly. Take me up.
I have led you oft; carry me now, good friends,
And have my thanks for all.   140

[Exeunt, bearing **ANTONY**

`4:15`   *Enter* **CLEOPATRA** *and her maids aloft, with* **CHARMIAN** *and* **IRAS**

CLEOPATRA   O Charmian, I will never go from hence.

CHARMIAN   Be comforted, dear madam.

CLEOPATRA   No, I will not –
All strange and terrible events are welcome,
But comforts we despise. Our size of sorrow,
Proportioned to our cause, must be as great   5
As that which makes it.

10   *darkling*   in darkness

11   *varying*   changing

19   *importune death awhile*   ask death to delay for a short time

> '*I dare not, Lest I be taken*' (lines 22–3) tells us that Cleopatra is
> afraid to leave the safety of her monument, even to go to Antony as
> he awaits a dying kiss. Directors should think about the implication
> of this line when designing the monument.

23   *imperious show*   triumphant display

25   *brooched*   adorned

26   *operation*   their effect (refers back to drugs, i.e. being poisoned)

Compare Cleopatra's reference to Octavia's 'modest eyes' looking on her if
put on display by Caesar, with Antony's threat that Octavia would 'plough thy
visage up' with her nails (4.12.38).

---

28   *still conclusion*   silent judgement

29   *Demuring upon me*   looking at me demurely, complacently

32   *sport*   ironic reference to their past activities

33   *heaviness*   both weight and sadness

34   *Juno*   wife of the god Jupiter

35   *Mercury*   winged messenger of the gods

37   *Wishers were ever fools*   i.e. it is foolish to just wish for things

> The stage direction '*They heave Antony aloft to Cleopatra*' is the
> major staging problem of the play. In Shakespeare's time they might
> have hauled him up to the balcony above the stage. The women
> who haul Antony aloft may need some additional support. In both
> Shakespeare's and the modern theatre some kind of rope and
> pulley might be rigged up to help them carry out this stage
> direction. But this solution creates another problem: if hauling him
> up puts Antony too high above the stage, much of the audience will
> not be able to see his last moments with Cleopatra.

38   *Die*   Cleopatra puns on 'die', the Elizabethan euphemism for sexual
       climax

39   *Quicken*   come alive, with perhaps a bawdy connotation

> When she has Antony in her arms, Cleopatra shows her passionate
> nature as she plays with sexual associations before kissing him.

Enter DIOMEDES

How now? Is he dead?

DIOMEDES   His death's upon him, but not dead.
Look out o'the other side your monument –
His guard have brought him thither.

Enter, below, ANTONY, *borne by the* GUARD

CLEOPATRA   O sun,
Burn the great sphere thou mov'st in; darkling stand   10
The varying shore o'the world! O Antony,
Antony, Antony! Help, Charmian, help, Iras, help!
Help, friends below! Let's draw him hither.

ANTONY   Peace!
Not Caesar's valour hath o'erthrown Antony,
But Antony's hath triumphed on itself.   15

CLEOPATRA   So it should be, that none but Antony
Should conquer Antony, but woe 'tis so!

ANTONY   I am dying, Egypt, dying; only
I here importune death awhile, until
Of many thousand kisses the poor last   20
I lay upon thy lips.

CLEOPATRA   I dare not, dear;
Dear my lord – pardon. I dare not,
Lest I be taken. Not he imperious show
Of the full-fortuned Caesar ever shall
Be brooched with me. If knife, drugs, serpents, have   25
Edge, sting, or operation, I am safe.
Your wife Octavia, with her modest eyes
And still conclusion, shall acquire no honour
Demuring upon me. But come, come, Antony –
Help me, my women – we must draw thee up.   30
Assist, good friends.

ANTONY   O quick, or I am gone.

CLEOPATRA   Here's sport indeed! How heavy weighs my lord!
Our strength is all gone into heaviness,
That makes the weight. Had I great Juno's power,
The strong-winged Mercury should fetch thee up   35
And set thee by Jove's side. Yet come a little –
Wishers were ever fools. O, come, come, come.

[*They heave* ANTONY *aloft to* CLEOPATRA

And welcome, welcome! Die when thou hast lived;
Quicken with kissing. Had my lips that power,
Thus would I wear them out.

ALL THE GUARDS   A heavy sight!   40

43 *rail so high* curse so strongly

44 *false huswife Fortune* Fortune is personified as a treacherous hussy.
wheel i.e the wheel of Fortune

45 *offence* insults

48 *None about* nobody around

49–50 *My resolution … Caesar* Cleopatra rejects Proculeius; she will trust
nobody but herself

49 *my hands* i.e. kill myself

51–4 *The miserable … I lived* don't lament my change of fortune now I
am dying, but enjoy remembering the honourable reputation I
once had

55 *basely* ignobly

56 *Not … helmet* surrender like a coward

57 *a Roman, by a Roman* i.e (1) Antony, killed by Antony, or (2)
Antony, defeated by Caesar

59 *woo't* wilt, will you

The death of Antony, as with all stage deaths, has to be carefully
staged to ensure the required response from the audience. Antony
might be cradled in Cleopatra's arms, but the delivery of their final
words to each other has to be seen and heard by the audience.
Slowly subdued lighting effects could enhance the images of
disintegration spoken by Cleopatra after the moment of Antony's
death.

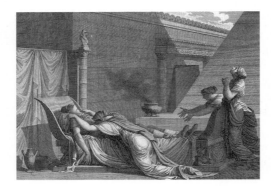

The death of Antony.

64 *garland* a crown of oak leaves awarded to successful generals, i.e.
hero

65 *pole* several disputed meanings, including: (1) a rod that a soldier
was measured by, (2) a standard carried in battle, (3) the pole star
that guided soldiers

66 *The odds is gone* everything is of the same value

67 *remarkable* wonderful, exceptional

73 *No more but e'en a woman* nothing more than a mere woman

74 *poor passion* refers not only to grief, but her fainting

ANTONY   I am dying, Egypt, dying.
            Give me some wine, and let me speak a little.

CLEOPATRA   No, let me speak, and let me rail so high
            That the false huswife Fortune break her wheel,
            Provoked by my offence.

ANTONY   One word, sweet queen;   45
            Of Caesar seek your honour, with your safety. O!

CLEOPATRA   They do not go together.

ANTONY   Gentle, hear me:
            None about Caesar trust but Proculeius.

CLEOPATRA   My resolution and my hands I'll trust –
            None about Caesar.   50

ANTONY   The miserable change now at my end
            Lament nor sorrow at, but please your thoughts
            In feeding them with those my former fortunes,
            Wherein I lived; the greatest prince o'the world,
            The noblest; and do now not basely die,   55
            Not cowardly put off my helmet to
            My countryman; a Roman, by a Roman
            Valiantly vanquished. Now my spirit is going –
            I can no more.

CLEOPATRA   Noblest of men, woo't die?
            Hast thou no care of me? Shall I abide   60
            In this dull world, which in thy absence is
            No better than a sty? O, see, my women,   [ANTONY dies
            The crown o'the earth doth melt. My lord?
            O, withered is the garland of the war,
            The soldier's pole is fall'n; young boys and girls   65
            Are level now with men. The odds is gone,
            And there is nothing left remarkable
            Beneath the visiting moon.

                                                              [*Faints*

CHARMIAN   O quietness, lady!

IRAS   She's dead too, our sovereign.

CHARMIAN   Lady!

IRAS   Madam!

CHARMIAN   O madam, madam, madam!

IRAS   Royal Egypt!   70
            Empress!

                                                    [CLEOPATRA *stirs*

CHARMIAN   Peace, peace, Iras!

CLEOPATRA   No more but e'en a woman, and commanded
            By such poor passion as the maid that milks

75   *chares* chores, household tasks, as in 'char lady'

78   *All's but naught* everything is worthless

79   *sottish* stupid

79–80   *does Become* befits

> As Cleopatra falls to the ground, her followers think she has died. As she stirs, they gather round and help her to her feet. As she is recovering, she seems to regain control of herself and calmly contemplates committing suicide. This dismays her followers, but she tells them to cheer up! They then carry out Antony's body, but not the way he came in! There is a lot of activity to end this scene.

80–2   *Then is it ... us?* Cleopatra asks about the morality of committing suicide.

83   *good cheer!* cheer up!

85   *is spent* used up   *sirs* used to address men and women

87   *after ... fashion* in the Roman style, as suicide was considered an honourable death

89   *case* body

91   *resolution* determination   *briefest* quickest

Antony dies in Cleopatra's arms, and now she wishes to die too. But Caesar wants her to live, so he can ride through Rome with her in triumphant victory. Cleopatra views this as an exhibition of her as a trophy of war and will not allow herself to be so humiliated. Who will achieve their goal?

In Act 4 we have seen rapid changes in Antony's fortunes. In war, he eventually loses to Caesar because of his own failings; he also loses many allies, including the friendship of Enobarbus, who regrets his desertion and commits suicide. His relationship with Cleopatra was passionate and volatile, but eventually the two great lovers are reunited before his death.

And does the meanest chares. It were for me 75
To throw my sceptre at the injurious gods,
To tell them that this world did equal theirs
Till they had stolen our jewel. All's but naught –
Patience is sottish, and impatience does
Become a dog that's mad. Then is it sin 80
To rush into the secret house of death
Ere death dare come to us? How do you, women?
What, what, good cheer! Why, how now, Charmian?
My noble girls! Ah, women, women – look,
Our lamp is spent, it's out. Good sirs, take heart, 85
We'll bury him; and then, what's brave, what's noble,
Let's do it after the high Roman fashion,
And make death proud to take us. Come, away.
This case of that huge spirit now is cold.
Ah, women, women! Come, we have no friend 90
But resolution, and the briefest end.

[*Exeunt, bearing off* ANTONY's *body*

5:1

The final act opens in Caesar's camp which has not yet received news of Antony's death.

1	*him*	Antony
2	*frustrate*	ineffectual
2–3	*he mocks … makes*	his delays in surrendering are a mockery

When Decretas enters carrying Antony's sword Caesar is startled, perhaps thinking that it is an assassination attempt. The actor can show Caesar lacking or having courage in these moments before he understands Decretas' intentions with his news in line 13.

8–9	*I wore … haters*	I lived to fight his enemies
14	*breaking*	(1) destruction, (2) telling (of news)
15	*crack*	(1) loud noise, (2) rift, damage
16	*civil*	city
17	*their dens*	i.e. of the lions
18	*not a single doom*	not just the fate of one
19	*moiety*	half
21	*self*	same
25	*robbed*	an appropriate word considering Decretas left Antony mortally wounded

Caesar weeps at news of Antony's death. This public display of emotion might make the audience think favourably of him, or they might think back to Enobarbus speaking about the kind of tears that are shed by a victor when a rival is defeated (3.2.57–9).

29–30	*nature … deeds*	our humanity makes us mourn the death we wished for
30–1	*His taints … him*	Antony's faults and strengths were in equal measure
31–2	*A rarer … humanity*	no man was ever governed by a better spirit

5:1

Enter CAESAR, AGRIPPA, DOLABELLA, MAECENAS, GALLUS,
PROCULEIUS, *and others, his council of war*

CAESAR	Go to him, Dolabella, bid him yield.
	Being so frustrate, tell him, he mocks
	The pauses that he makes.
DOLABELLA	Caesar, I shall. [*Exit*

Enter DECRETAS, *with the sword of Antony*

CAESAR   Wherefore is that? And what art thou that dar'st
Appear thus to us?

DECRETAS   I am called Decretas.   5
Mark Antony I served, who best was worthy
Best to be served. Whilst he stood up and spoke,
He was my master, and I wore my life
To spend upon his haters. If thou please
To take me to thee, as I was to him   10
I'll be to Caesar – if thou pleasest not,
I yield thee up my life.

CAESAR   What is't thou sayst?

DECRETAS   I say, O Caesar, Antony is dead.

CAESAR   The breaking of so great a thing should make
A greater crack. The round world   15
Should have shook lions into civil streets,
And citizens to their dens. The death of Antony
Is not a single doom – in the name lay
A moiety of the world.

DECRETAS   He is dead, Caesar,
Not by a public minister of justice,   20
Nor by a hirèd knife; but that self hand
Which writ his honour in the acts it did,
Hath, with the courage which the heart did lend it,
Splitted the heart. This is his sword –
I robbed his wound of it. Behold it stained   25
With his most noble blood.

CAESAR   Look you sad, friends?
The gods rebuke me, but it is a tidings
To wash the eyes of kings.

AGRIPPA   And strange it is,
That nature must compel us to lament
Our most persisted deeds.

MAECENAS   His taints and honours   30
Waged equal with him.

AGRIPPA   A rarer spirit never

32 *will give us* insist on giving us

34 *spacious mirror* an image of Antony showing Caesar what he was like

36 *followed* pursued *launch* lance, cut out

37–9 *I must … thine* either I caused your downfall or you would have caused mine

39 *stall* inhabit the same space

41 *sovereign* strong

42 *competitor* partner (and rival)

43 *top of all design* great enterprises

44 *front of war* at the forefront of fighting

45–6 *the heart … kindle* his heart inspired courage in mine

46 *his* its

46–8 *that our stars … to this* it is a shame that our incompatible ambitions drove a wedge between our equal natures

49 *meeter season* more suitable time

50 *The business … man* the urgent business of this man is obvious in his looks

53 *all she has* in her only possession

54 *Of thy … instruction* ask what you intend to do (with her)

55–6 *That she … forced to* so she may arrange her affairs according to what you want

57 *ours* my followers

63 *quality of her passion* intensity of her grief

64 *greatness* lofty spirit *mortal stroke* fatal blow (suicide)

65–6 *For her … triumph* to bring her to Rome would make me eternally famous

67 *with your speediest* as quickly as possible

68 *of her* her condition

The audience might think favourably of Caesar as he sends a message to Cleopatra assuring her of his honourable and kind intentions towards her. However, he shows his political skill by sending Proculeius to ensure she does not commit suicide, as he wants to bring her back to Rome as a trophy of victory.

Did steer humanity. But you gods will give us
Some faults to make us men. Caesar is touched.

MAECENAS   When such a spacious mirror's set before him,
He needs must see himself.

CAESAR   O Antony,   35
I have followed thee to this, but we do launch
Diseases in our bodies. I must perforce
Have shown to thee such a declining day,
Or look on thine – we could not stall together
In the whole world. But yet let me lament   40
With tears as sovereign as the blood of hearts,
That thou my brother, my competitor
In top of all design, my mate in empire,
Friend and companion in the front of war,
The arm of mine own body, and the heart   45
Where mine his thoughts did kindle – that our stars,
Unreconciliable, should divide
Our equalness to this. Hear me, good friends –

                    Enter an EGYPTIAN

But I will tell you at some meeter season.
The business of this man looks out of him,   50
We'll hear him what he says. Whence are you?

EGYPTIAN   A poor Egyptian yet. The Queen my mistress,
Confined in all she has, her monument,
Of thy intents desires instruction,
That she preparèdly may frame herself   55
To the way she's forced to.

CAESAR   Bid her have good heart –
She soon shall know of us, by some of ours,
How honourable and how kindly we
Determine for her. For Caesar cannot live
To be ungentle.

EGYPTIAN   So the gods preserve thee!   [*Exit*   60

CAESAR   Come hither, Proculeius. Go and say
We purpose her no shame; give her what comforts
The quality of her passion shall require,
Lest, in her greatness, by some mortal stroke
She do defeat us. For her life in Rome   65
Would be eternal in our triumph. Go,
And with your speediest bring us what she says,
And how you find of her.

PROCULEIUS   Caesar, I shall.   [*Exit*

CAESAR   Gallus, go you along.

                                        [*Exit* GALLUS

74   *hardly* reluctantly
75   *still* constantly
77   *in this* of how I was drawn reluctantly into this (conflict with Antony)

Caesar weeps for and pays tribute to Antony, but when word comes from Cleopatra he immediately re-focuses on his intention to take her to Rome in triumph. Are the tears he shed for Antony heartfelt? Caesar invites Decretas to show him how the quarrel was not of his making. Is this merely to ease his conscience?

5:2

The play's final and longest scene takes place at Cleopatra's monument. It is divided up into short episodes, each introduced by the entrance of a character.

The problems discussed earlier about the structure of Cleopatra's monument arise also with the setting of this scene. How are the various entrances to be dealt with? Is Cleopatra still above the stage, or have we now moved inside the monument? It would seem, taking all the entrances and exits into account, that the scene would be played as normal on the level stage and the action is inside the monument.

1   *desolation* ruin
2   *A better life* i.e. me more philosophical   *'Tis paltry* it is insignificant
3   *knave* servant
4   *A minister of her will* i.e. he does what she tells him
5   *do that thing* commit suicide
6   *shackles … change* stops chance happenings and keeps things the same (notice Cleopatra's use of images of imprisonment)
7   *palates* tastes   *dung* the earth; compare with 'our dungy earth' (1.1.35)

Proculeius is the first of Cleopatra's visitors, bringing a message from Caesar. Notice the lack of ceremony in Proculeius' address to Cleopatra. After what we have just heard Cleopatra say, how will she react to Caesar terms?

10   *study on* consider
14   *to be deceived* if I am deceived or not
15   *That* because I
17   *to keep decorum* to behave suitably
18   *No less beg* ask for nothing less

186

Where's Dolabella,
  To second Proculeius?

ALL   Dolabella!   70

CAESAR Let him alone, for I remember now
  How he's employed. He shall in time be ready.
  Go with me to my tent, where you shall see
  How hardly I was drawn into this war,
  How calm and gentle I proceeded still   75
  In all my writings. Go with me, and see
  What I can show in this.

                 [*Exeunt*

5:2   *Enter* CLEOPATRA, CHARMIAN *and* IRAS

CLEOPATRA My desolation does begin to make
  A better life. 'Tis paltry to be Caesar:
  Not being Fortune, he's but Fortune's knave,
  A minister of her will. And it is great
  To do that thing that ends all other deeds,   5
  Which shackles accidents and bolts up change;
  Which sleeps, and never palates more the dung,
  The beggar's nurse, and Caesar's.

          Enter PROCULEIUS

PROCULEIUS Caesar sends greeting to the Queen of Egypt,
  And bids thee study on what fair demands   10
  Thou mean'st to have him grant thee.

CLEOPATRA   What's thy name?

PROCULEIUS My name is Proculeius.

CLEOPATRA   Antony
  Did tell me of you, bade me trust you, but
  I do not greatly care to be deceived,
  That have no use for trusting. If your master   15
  Would have a queen his beggar, you must tell him
  That majesty, to keep decorum, must
  No less beg than a kingdom. If he please
  To give me conquered Egypt for my son,
  He gives me so much of mine own as I   20
  Will kneel to him with thanks.

PROCULEIUS   Be of good cheer –

23 *your full reference* all your requests
24 *grace* gracious kindness
26 *sweet dependency* meek submission
27 *pray … kindness* ask you to help him to be kind to you
28 *he … kneeled to* when kindness is asked of him
29 *vassal* slave

Compare what Cleopatra says in line 29 about her and Fortune with what she says about Caesar and Fortune in the opening lines of this scene.

---

30 *The greatness he has got* acknowledgement of his greatness
34 *Of* by

Gallus is the next arrival. He surprises Cleopatra and seizes her. The staging of this would be difficult if the 'balcony', i.e. the external representation of the monument, were being used for this scene. Cleopatra's seizing, the struggle and her failed attempt at suicide quicken the action on stage.

39 *Hold* stop
40 *in this* i.e. being seized by the guards
41 *Relieved* rescued
42 *languish* wasting disease
44 *undoing* destruction
45 *well acted* in action, but the notion of it being an act is also present
46 *never let come forth* prevent
48 *temperance* show restraint
49 *meat* food
50 *If idle … necessary* if I have to waste time in idle talk
51 *house* body
52 *Do … can* no matter what Caesar does
53 *pinioned* arms bound, like a bird with clipped wings

Y'are fall'n into a princely hand; fear nothing,
Make your full reference freely to my lord,
Who is so full of grace that it flows over
On all that need. Let me report to him   **25**
Your sweet dependency, and you shall find
A conqueror that will pray in aid for kindness,
Where he for grace is kneeled to.

CLEOPATRA   Pray you, tell him
I am his fortune's vassal, and I send him
The greatness he has got. I hourly learn   **30**
A doctrine of obedience, and I would gladly
Look him i'the face.

PROCULEIUS   This I'll report, dear lady.
Have comfort, for I know your plight is pitied
Of him that caused it.

Enter GALLUS *and* SOLDIERS *behind*

GALLUS   You see how easily she may be surprised.   [*They seize* CLEOPATRA   **35**
Guard her till Caesar come.

                                                                    [*Exit*

IRAS   Royal queen!

CHARMIAN   O Cleopatra! Thou art taken, Queen.

CLEOPATRA   Quick, quick, good hands!   [*Drawing a dagger*

PROCULEIUS   Hold, worthy lady, hold!
                                                        [*Seizes and disarms her*
Do not yourself such wrong, who are in this   **40**
Relieved, but not betrayed.

CLEOPATRA   What, of death too,
That rids our dogs of languish?

PROCULEIUS   Cleopatra,
Do not abuse my master's bounty, by
The undoing of yourself. Let the world see
His nobleness well acted, which your death   **45**
Will never let come forth.

CLEOPATRA   Where art thou, death?
Come hither, come! Come, come, and take a queen
Worth many babes and beggars!

PROCULEIUS   O, temperance, lady!

CLEOPATRA   Sir, I will eat no meat, I'll not drink, sir –
If idle talk will once be necessary –   **50**
I'll not sleep neither. This mortal house I'll ruin,
Do Caesar what he can. Know, sir, that I
Will not wait pinioned at your master's court,
Nor once be chastised with the sober eye

56   *varletry* rabble

> Compare Cleopatra's wishes to die in a ditch in Egypt rather than go to Rome with Enobarbus' ignoble death in a ditch (Act 4 Scene 6).

60   *Blow me into abhorring* deposit their eggs in me so I become a figure of disgust. (When compared with other sexual images used by Cleopatra, this one achieves her intended sense of revulsion.)

61   *pyramides* four-syllable version of pyramids
gibbet gallows

62   *extend* exaggerate

> *Cleopatra might struggle against her bonds as she delivers her defiant speech to Proculeius. The arrival of Dolabella does nothing to ease Cleopatra's defiance, as shown by her scornful message to Caesar via Proculeius.*

67   *take her to my guard* take charge of her

71   *Empress* Is this flattery or genuine admiration?

75   *trick* way of doing things

77   *O such* O for such

79   *stuck* were set

81   *O* the globe of the earth

> *Dolabella is unable to get a word in while Cleopatra is telling him of her magnificent dreams about Antony. He makes several attempts from 'Most noble Empress' to 'Hear me good madam' before being able to interrupt her. How does the actor playing Dolabella respond to Cleopatra's eulogy?*

82   *bestrid* bestrode

82–3   *his reared … world* images from heraldry

83–4   *was propertied … spheres* sounded as musical as the spheres of heaven

85   *quail … orb* frighten and make the world tremble

86   *For his bounty* as for his generosity

87–8   *an autumn … reaping* his generosity, like autumn, grew the more he gave

88–90   *his delights … lived in* i.e. his delights rise above the world in which he lived

Of dull Octavia. Shall they hoist me up   **55**
And show me to the shouting varletry
Of censuring Rome? Rather a ditch in Egypt
Be gentle grave unto me! Rather on Nilus' mud
Lay me stark nak'd and let the waterflies
Blow me into abhorring! Rather make   **60**
My country's high pyramides my gibbet
And hang me up in chains!

PROCULEIUS   You do extend
These thoughts of horror further than you shall
Find cause in Caesar.

                        Enter **DOLABELLA**

DOLABELLA   Proculeius,
What thou hast done thy master Caesar knows,   **65**
And he hath sent for thee. For the Queen,
I'll take her to my guard.

PROCULEIUS   So, Dolabella,
It shall content me best. Be gentle to her.
[*To* **CLEOPATRA**] To Caesar I will speak what you shall please,
If you'll employ me to him.

CLEOPATRA   Say I would die.   [*Exit* **PROCULEIUS**   **70**

DOLABELLA   Most noble Empress, you have heard of me?

CLEOPATRA   I cannot tell.

DOLABELLA   Assuredly you know me.

CLEOPATRA   No matter, sir, what I have heard or known,
You laugh when boys or women tell their dreams,
Is't not your trick?

DOLABELLA   I understand not, madam.   **75**

CLEOPATRA   I dreamt there was an emperor Antony –
O such another sleep, that I might see
But such another man!

DOLABELLA   If it might please ye –

CLEOPATRA   His face was as the heavens, and therein stuck
A sun and moon, which kept their course and lighted   **80**
The little O, the earth.

DOLABELLA   Most sovereign creature –

CLEOPATRA   His legs bestrid the ocean, his reared arm
Crested the world; his voice was propertied
As all the tunèd spheres, and that to friends –
But when he meant to quail and shake the orb,   **85**
He was as rattling thunder. For his bounty,
There was no winter in't – an autumn 'twas
That grew the more by reaping; his delights

90–1	*In his livery … crownets* i.e. kings and princes served him
91	*crownets* coronets worn by princes
92	*plates* silver coins
97	*past … dreaming* beyond any dream
97–100	*Nature … shadows quite* i.e. Nature cannot compete with what the imagination can create, yet Antony was Nature's masterpiece and exceeded any flight of the imagination
102	*As answering to the weight* as greatly as yourself
102–3	*Would I … feel* i.e. may I never achieve success if I do not feel
104	*rebound* echo *smites* strikes

> The arrival of Caesar is both triumphant and humiliating. The cries of 'Make way there!' and the large train of followers that flow across the stage impress us with Caesar's power and authority. Asking 'Which is the Queen of Egypt' insults Cleopatra, as she would be obviously recognisable with her clothes and royal appearance. As it is equally obvious who Caesar is, is Dolabela ironically reversing Caesar's insult with 'It is the Emperor, madam'? Or perhaps Caesar's question is quietly spoken to Dolabella, who then introduces her?

117	*Take … hard thoughts* do not think I will treat you harshly
119	*written in our flesh* i.e. in the wounds of my soldiers
120	*but done by chance* only done accidentally

Were dolphin-like, they showed his back above
The element they lived in. In his livery   90
Walked crowns and crownets; realms and islands were
As plates dropped from his pocket.

DOLABELLA   Cleopatra –

CLEOPATRA   Think you there was, or might be such a man
As this I dreamt of?

DOLABELLA   Gentle madam, no.

CLEOPATRA   You lie, up to the hearing of the gods.   95
But if there be or ever were one such,
It's past the size of dreaming. Nature wants stuff
To vie strange forms with fancy, yet to imagine
An Antony were nature's piece 'gainst fancy,
Condemning shadows quite.

DOLABELLA   Hear me, good madam.   100
Your loss is as yourself, great; and you bear it
As answering to the weight. Would I might never
O'ertake pursued success, but I do feel –
By the rebound of yours – a grief that smites
My very heart at root.

CLEOPATRA   I thank you, sir.   105
Know you what Caesar means to do with me?

DOLABELLA   I am loath to tell you what, I would you knew.

CLEOPATRA   Nay, pray you, sir –

DOLABELLA   Though he be honourable –

CLEOPATRA   He'll lead me then in triumph?

DOLABELLA   Madam, he will – I know't.   110

Flourish. Enter **PROCULEIUS, CAESAR, GALLUS, MAECENAS,**
and others of Caesar's train

ALL   Make way there! Caesar!

CAESAR   Which is the Queen of Egypt?

DOLABELLA   It is the Emperor, madam.   *[***CLEOPATRA** *kneels*

CAESAR   Arise, you shall not kneel –
I pray you rise, rise, Egypt.

CLEOPATRA   Sir, the gods   115
Will have it thus, my master and my lord
I must obey.

CAESAR   Take to you no hard thoughts;
The record of what injuries you did us,
Though written in our flesh, we shall remember
As things but done by chance.

120   *sir* master

121   *project* put forward

122   *clear* blameless

123   *like frailties* the sort of weaknesses

125   *extenuate* excuse (your frailties)   *enforce* stress

126   *apply … intents* conform to my plans

129   *lay on me a cruelty* make me seem cruel

130   *bereave yourself* lose my (note the threat in 'bereave')

131   *purposes* intentions

133   *If thereon you rely* if you rely on my good intentions

134   *And may* i.e. take your leave anywhere

135   *scutcheons* (captured) shields often displayed as trophies

137   *in all for* in everything concerning

> *Having shown her womanly wiles in handling Caesar, Cleopatra hands him a list of her possessions. This is the start of an elaborate game to fool Caesar into thinking that because she has tried to cheat him of half her possessions she must have her mind on her future and is, therefore, not contemplating suicide. Cleopatra must play this intended 'deception' as realistically as possible, even to blushing with shame at being exposed, so as to fool Caesar (and perhaps the audience).*

138   *brief* summary

140   *Not … admitted* except trivial items

143   *Upon his peril* under threat of death   *reserved* kept back

146   *seel* sew up

148   *Enough … known* i.e. as much again as you have accounted for

151   *pomp* power (Seleucus follows Caesar rather than his own queen, it seems)

152   *shift estates* changes positions

> *In the Greek writer Plutarch's account of this incident, Cleopatra goes into a rage with Seleucus, dragging him by the hair and boxing his ears while Caesar stands by roaring with laughter before parting them. Although there are no explicit stage directions, similar actions to those Plutarch describes would suit Cleopatra's reputation for hot-headedness and her pretended rage.*

157   *Though* even if

158   *rarely* exceptionally

CLEOPATRA   Sole sir o'the world,   **120**
      I cannot project mine own cause so well
      To make it clear, but do confess I have
      Been laden with like frailties, which before
      Have often shamed our sex.

CAESAR   Cleopatra, know,
      We will extenuate rather than enforce: **125**
      If you apply yourself to our intents,
      Which towards you are most gentle, you shall find
      A benefit in this change; but if you seek
      To lay on me a cruelty by taking
      Antony's course, you shall bereave yourself   **130**
      Of my good purposes, and put your children
      To that destruction which I'll guard them from
      If thereon you rely. I'll take my leave.

CLEOPATRA   And may through all the world; 'tis yours, and we
      Your scutcheons, and your signs of conquest shall   **135**
      Hang in what place you please. Here, my good lord –

CAESAR   You shall advise me in all for Cleopatra.

CLEOPATRA [*handing a paper*] – This is the brief of money, plate, and jewels
      I am possessed of. 'Tis exactly valued,
      Not pretty things admitted. Where's Seleucus?   **140**

Enter SELEUCUS

SELEUCUS   Here, madam.

CLEOPATRA   This is my treasurer – let him speak, my lord,
      Upon his peril, that I have reserved
      To myself nothing. Speak the truth, Seleucus.

SELEUCUS   Madam,   **145**
      I had rather seel my lips than to my peril
      Speak that which is not.

CLEOPATRA   What have I kept back?

SELEUCUS   Enough to purchase what you have made known.

CAESAR   Nay, blush not, Cleopatra. I approve
      Your wisdom in the deed.

CLEOPATRA   See, Caesar! O behold,   **150**
      How pomp is followed! Mine will now be yours,
      And should we shift estates, yours would be mine.
      The ingratitude of this Seleucus does
      Even make me wild. O slave, of no more trust
      Then love that's hired! What, goest thou back? Thou shalt   **155**
      Go back, I warrant thee; but I'll catch thine eyes
      Though they had wings. Slave, soulless villain, dog!
      O rarely base!

160 *vouchsafing* condescending

162 *so meek* This is heavily ironic in the light of any violence done to Seleucus.

163 *Parcel the sum* enumerate

164 *Say* suppose

165 *lady* lady's

166 *Immoment* trivial

167 *modern* ordinary *withal* with

168 *token* gifts (signs of my respect)

169 *Livia* Caesar's wife

169–70 *to induce their mediation* to persuade them to intercede on my behalf

170 *unfolded* exposed

171 *With ... bred* by one brought up in my household

171–2 *It smites ... have* i.e. it knocks me lower than I was

173 *cinders* smouldering coals

174 *chance* misfortune
a man addressed to Seleucus, indicating perhaps he is a eunuch

175 *Forbear* withdraw

176 *we, the greatest* Cleopatra, reasserting the royal 'we', reminds Caesar of similarities between them. *misthought* misjudged

178 *We answer ... name* i.e. we are blamed for the others' misdeeds performed in our names
merits what is deserved (either good or bad)

181 *roll of conquest* i.e. (I won't include these items) in my entitlement

183 *make prize* bargain

184 *Of* over

185 *Make ... prisons* don't be imprisoned by your fears (for you are free)

186 *dispose you* deal with you

How might Cleopatra's manner change as Caesar leaves? After playing the humble defeated queen, she might show her true feelings.

191 *words me* softens me with words

192 *noble* honourable

As Cleopatra whispers her plans to Charmian, the stage lighting perhaps begins to dim, as indicated by Iras' words about bright and dark.

194 *Hie thee* hurry back

Caesar	Good queen, let us entreat you.	
Cleopatra	O Caesar, what a wounding shame is this,	
	That thou vouchsafing here to visit me,	160
	Doing the honour of thy lordliness	
	To one so meek, that mine own servant should	
	Parcel the sum of my disgraces by	
	Addition of his envy. Say, good Caesar,	
	That I some lady trifles have reserved,	165
	Immoment toys, things of such dignity	
	As we greet modern friends withal; and say	
	Some nobler token I have kept apart	
	For Livia and Octavia, to induce	
	Their mediation – must I be unfolded	170
	With one that I have bred? The gods! It smites me	
	Beneath the fall I have. [*To* **Seleucus**] Prithee go hence,	
	Or I shall show the cinders of my spirits	
	Through the ashes of my chance. Wert thou a man,	
	Thou wouldst have mercy on me.	
Caesar	Forbear, Seleucus.	175

[*Exit* **Seleucus**

Cleopatra	Be it known that we, the greatest, are misthought	
	For things that others do; and when we fall,	
	We answer others' merits in our name,	
	Are therefore to be pitied.	
Caesar	Cleopatra,	
	Not what you have reserved, nor what acknowledged,	180
	Put we i'the roll of conquest. Still be't yours –	
	Bestow it at your pleasure, and believe	
	Caesar's no merchant, to make prize with you	
	Of things that merchants sold. Therefore be cheered,	
	Make not your thoughts your prisons. No, dear queen,	185
	For we intend so to dispose you as	
	Yourself shall give us counsel. Feed and sleep.	
	Our care and pity is so much upon you	
	That we remain your friend; and so adieu.	
Cleopatra	My master, and my lord!	
Caesar	No so – adieu.	190

[*Flourish. Exeunt* **Caesar** *and his train*

Cleopatra	He words me, girls, he words me, that I should not	
	Be noble to myself. But hark thee, Charmian.	

[*Whispers to* **Charmian**

Iras	Finish, good lady, the bright day is done,
	And we are for the dark.
Cleopatra	Hie thee again,

195 *provided* arranged
196 *to the haste* quickly into action
202 *before* ahead of him
203 *this* i.e. this information
204 *Your pleasure* what you requested
208 *puppet* pantomime actor
209 *Mechanic slaves* common labourers
211 *thick* foul
212 *Rank of gross diet* reeking of coarse food
     enclouded enveloped
213 *drink their vapour* inhale what they breathe out
214 *Saucy lictors* insolent officers (similar to the English beadles who
     among other duties disciplined prostitutes)
215 *catch at us like strumpets* treat us badly as if we were prostitutes
215–16 *scald … tune* crude writers will make up tuneless stories about us
216 *quick* clever, quick-witted
217 *Extemporally will stage us* will stage improvised plays about us
217–18 *present … revels* display our times in Alexandria

When Cleopatra speaks of a squeaking boy actor playing her on
stage it is Shakespeare's joke for his audience, as on the Elizabethan
stage Cleopatra would be played by a boy actor. A director might
want Cleopatra to provide a lighter moment in this episode,
perhaps by exaggerating the squeaking of her lines.

220 *boy* (1) boy actor, (2) being parodied
221 *posture* manner

	I have spoke already, and it is provided –	195
	Go put it to the haste.	

CHARMIAN   Madam, I will.

Enter DOLABELLA

DOLABELLA   Where's the Queen?

CHARMIAN   Behold, sir.   [*Exit*

CLEOPATRA   Dolabella!

DOLABELLA   Madam, as thereto sworn, by your command –
Which my love makes religion to obey –
I tell you this: Caesar through Syria   200
Intends his journey, and within three days
You with your children will be send before.
Make your best use of this. I have performed
Your pleasure and my promise.

CLEOPATRA   Dolabella,
I shall remain your debtor.

DOLABELLA   I, your servant.   205
Adieu, good Queen, I must attend on Caesar.

CLEOPATRA   Farewell, and thanks.

                                  [*Exit* DOLABELLA
                  Now, Iras, what think'st thou?
Thou, an Egyptian puppet, shall be shown
In Rome as well as I. Mechanic slaves
With greasy aprons, rules, and hammers shall   210
Uplift us to the view. In their thick breaths,
Rank of gross diet, shall we be enclouded,
And forced to drink their vapour.

IRAS   The gods forbid!

CLEOPATRA   Nay, 'tis most certain, Iras. Saucy lictors
Will catch at us like strumpets, and scald rhymers   215
Ballad us out o'tune. The quick comedians
Extemporally will stage us, and present
Our Alexandrian revels: Antony
Shall be brought drunken forth, and I shall see
Some squeaking Cleopatra boy my greatness   220
I'the posture of a whore.

IRAS   O the good gods!

CLEOPATRA   Nay, that's certain.

IRAS   I'll never see't! For I am sure my nails
Are stronger than mine eyes.

CLEOPATRA   Why, that's the way
To fool their preparation, and to conquer   225
Their most absurd intents.

228 *Cydnus* the river where Antony first saw Cleopatra on her barge, as magnificently described by Enobarbus (2.2.186–227)

229 *Sirrah* address to servants, male or female

230 *despatch* various meanings: (1) hasten, (2) finish, (3) send off, echoing Antony's 'O, despatch me' (4.14.104)

231 *chare* chore, task

232 *play till doomsday* be forever idle

234 *not be denied* refuses to be

236 *What* how

238 *placed* fixed

240 *marble-constant* as hard and unchanging as marble
fleeting changeable, inconstant

The stage direction is 'Clown with a basket'. On Shakespeare's stage the Clown roles were usually played by the same actor, who was very popular with the audiences (often too popular for the writer's liking, as he made up extra material for himself). The Clown was often a rustic or country yokel figure laughed at by the city audience for his lack of sophistication and verbal fumbling, yet could dispense home-spun wisdom. In this episode the Clown plays on the sexual associations of words.

242 *Avoid* go

243 *worm of Nilus* small poisonous snake from the Nile valley

246 *immortal* the Clown's mistake: he means mortal = deadly, as shown by his next sentence

250 *honest* (1) truthful, (2) virtuous (sexually)
something given to lie prone to (1) dishonesty, (2) having frequent sex

251 *died* (1) physical death, (2) euphemism for sexual climax

253 *worm* (1) snake, (2) euphemism for penis
be saved i.e. from (1) death, (2) damnation

254 *falliable* the Clown's mistake: he means infallible = unfailing

Having obtained the asp from the Clown, Cleopatra now wants to be rid of him. He is unwilling to go quietly with his rustic 'Look you', but within his words about the worm (lines 260–70) are implicit comments about the power, for good or evil, of sexuality.

258 *his kind* what is in his nature

Enter CHARMIAN

Now, Charmian!
Show me, my women, like a queen. Go fetch
My best attires. I am again for Cydnus,
To meet Mark Antony. Sirrah Iras, go
(Now, noble Charmian, we'll despatch indeed)   230
And when thou hast done this chare, I'll give thee leave
To play till doomsday. Bring our crown and all.

> [*Exit* IRAS. *A noise within*

Wherefore's this noise?

Enter a GUARDSMAN

GUARDSMAN   Here is a rural fellow
That will not be denied your highness' presence.
He brings you figs.   235

CLEOPATRA   Let him come in.   [*Exit* GUARDSMAN
                      What poor an instrument
May do a noble deed! He brings me liberty.
My resolution's placed, and I have nothing
Of woman in me. Now from head to foot
I am marble-constant; now the fleeting moon   240
No planet is of mine.

Enter GUARDSMAN *and* CLOWN *with a basket*

GUARDSMAN   This is the man.

CLEOPATRA   Avoid, and leave him.   [*Exit* GUARDSMAN
Hast thou the pretty worm of Nilus there,
That kills and pains not?

CLOWN   Truly I have him; but I would not be the party that should desire   245
             you to touch him, for his biting is immortal. Those that do die of it do
             seldom or never recover.

CLEOPATRA   Remember'st thou any that have died on't?

CLOWN   Very many, men and women too. I heard of one of them no longer
             than yesterday – a very honest woman, but something given to lie, as a   250
             woman should not do but in the way of honesty; how she died of the
             biting of it, what pain she felt; truly, she makes a very good report o'the
             worm. But he that will believe all that they say shall never be saved by
             half that they do. But this is most falliable, the worm's an odd worm.

CLEOPATRA   Get thee hence, farewell.   255

CLOWN   I wish you all joy of the worm.   [*Setting down his basket*

CLEOPATRA   Farewell.

CLOWN   You must think this, look you, that the worm will do his kind.

CLEOPATRA   Ay, ay, farewell.

262   *Take thou no care*   don't worry

266   *simple* foolish   *but I know* that I'm not aware that

267   *dish* food (but with sexual associations)

268   *dress* (1) prepare for cooking, (2) put on her clothes
        whoreson damned (an Elizabethan oath – literally 'son of a whore')

269   *in* regarding

270   *mar* spoil

We presume that so as to ensure her death will have the most impact Cleopatra dresses in her finest regal robes and crown. As Iras helps Cleopatra into her robes she jokingly recalls the Clown's words with 'Immortal longings'.

276   *Yare* quickly

279–80   *which … wrath* which the gods give, so they can afterwards punish for having it

282   *fire and air* a metaphor for the separation of the soul from the body. Cleopatra identifies herself with these two higher elements, leaving the baser elements, earth and water, behind.

Iras dies before Cleopatra, yet there is no stage direction to indicate how she dies. Cleopatra's comment 'So, have you done?' (line 283) might indicate that Iras has taken the asp to her breast already. Cleopatra kisses her as the asp's bite takes effect; this might explain her comment: 'Have I the aspic in my lips?' (line 286).

286   *aspic* asp

287   *nature* life

288–9   *The stroke … still?* At the point of death Cleopatra's images are sexual, echoing the Clown's sexual euphemisms of 'die' and 'lie'. 'Stroke' suggests (1) death's blow, and (2) a lover's gentle caress.

293   *This* i.e. Iras' death

294   *curlèd* with curly hair

295   *spend that kiss* expend his passion on her

296   *mortal wretch* deadly little thing (here 'wretch' is used affectionately)

297   *intrinsicate* intricate

CLOWN	Look you, the worm is not to be trusted but in the keeping of wise people; for indeed there is no goodness in the worm.	260
CLEOPATRA	Take thou no care – it shall be heeded.	
CLOWN	Very good. Give it nothing, I pray you, for it is not worth the feeding.	
CLEOPATRA	Will it eat me?	265
CLOWN	You must not think I am so simple but I know the devil himself will not eat a woman. I know that a woman is a dish for the gods, if the devil dress her not. But truly, these same whoreson devils do the gods great harm in their women; for in every ten that they make, the devils mar five.	270
CLEOPATRA	Well, get thee gone, farewell.	
CLOWN	Yes, forsooth. I wish you joy o'the worm.	

[*Exit*

Enter **IRAS** *with a robe, crown, etc.*

CLEOPATRA   Give me my robe, put on my crown, I have
Immortal longings in me. Now no more
The juice of Egypt's grape shall moist this lip.   275
Yare, yare, good Iras; quick – methinks I hear
Antony call. I see him rouse himself
To praise my noble act. I hear him mock
The luck of Caesar, which the gods give men
To excuse their after wrath. Husband, I come.   280
Now to that name, my courage prove my title!
I am fire and air – my other elements
I give to baser life. So, have you done?
Come then, and take the last warmth of my lips.
Farewell, kind Charmian, Iras, long farewell.   285

[*Kisses them.* **IRAS** *falls and dies*

Have I the aspic in my lips? Dost fall?
If thou and nature can so gently part,
The stroke of death is as a lover's pinch,
Which hurts, and is desired. Dost thou lie still?
If thus thou vanishest, thou tell'st the world   290
It is not worth leave-taking.

CHARMIAN   Dissolve, thick cloud, and rain, that I may say
The gods themselves do weep!

CLEOPATRA   This proves me base;
If she first meet the curlèd Antony,
He'll make demand of her, and spend that kiss   295
Which is my heaven to have.

[*To an asp, which she applies to her breast*]
Come thou mortal wretch,
With thy sharp teeth this knot intrinsicate

> According to Plutarch, Cleopatra had to arouse the asp's anger so as to make it bite her more firmly. The text here (lines 298–9) seems to indicate that implicit stage direction.

The death of Cleopatra

298	*fool* here used affectionately
299	*despatch* as used earlier: (1) hasten, (2) finish, (3) send off
300–1	*ass, Unpolicied* outwitted fool
301	*O eastern star* Venus, the morning star
302–3	*Dost … asleep?* Cleopatra refers to the snake as a suckling infant.

> Cleopatra's death is as gentle as the text indicates. She should be seated on a couch so the image of the asp being a child sucking at her breast is visually effective, before she puts the second asp to her arm.

303	*break!* Perhaps Charmian is referring to her own heart , or urging Cleopatra's quick death.
306	*What* why
309	*windows* eyelids
310	*Phoebus* the sun god
311	*Of* by
312	*mend it* straighten it *then play* i.e. with the asp, for death

> The stage direction 'rustling in' indicates that the guards enter noisily, disturbing the peaceful calm of the death scene. Charmian ironically comments on how the messenger is too slow, before asking the snake to give her a speedy death.

316	*beguiled* deceived
322–3	*thy thoughts … this* your fears (of Cleopatra's suicide) are realised
326	*too sure an augurer* too accurate a predictor
327	*That* that which

Of life at once untie. Poor venomous fool,
Be angry, and despatch. O, couldst thou speak,
That I might hear thee call great Caesar ass,   **300**
Unpolicied!

CHARMIAN   O eastern star!

CLEOPATRA   Peace, peace!
Dost thou not see my baby at my breast,
That sucks the nurse asleep?

CHARMIAN   O, break! O, break!

CLEOPATRA   As sweet as balm, as soft as air, as gentle –
O, Antony! Nay, I will take thee too.   **305**

[Applying another asp to her arm

What should I stay –

[Dies

CHARMIAN   In this vile world? So fare thee well.
Now boast thee, death, in thy possession lies
A lass unparalleled. Downy windows, close,
And golden Phoebus never be beheld   **310**
Of eyes again so royal! Your crown's awry;
I'll mend it, and then play –

Enter the GUARD, *rustling in, and* DOLABELLA

FIRST GUARD   Where's the Queen?

CHARMIAN   Speak softly, wake her not.

FIRST GUARD   Caesar hath sent –

CHARMIAN   Too slow a messenger.   *[Applies an asp*
O, come apace, despatch. I partly feel thee.   **315**

FIRST GUARD   Approach ho, all's not well – Caesar's beguiled!

SECOND GUARD There's Dolabella sent from Caesar; call him.

FIRST GUARD   What work is here, Charmian? Is this well done?

CHARMIAN   It is well done, and fitting for a princess
Descended of so many royal kings.   **320**
Ah, soldier!   *[Dies*

DOLABELLA   How goes it here?

SECOND GUARD   All dead.

DOLABELLA   Caesar, thy thoughts
Touch their effects in this. Thyself art coming
To see performed the dreaded act which thou
So sought'st to hinder.

Enter CAESAR, *and all his train, marching*

ALL   A way there, a way for Caesar!   **325**

DOLABELLA   O, sir, you are too sure an augurer –
That you did fear is done.

328	*levelled* guessed
331	*simple* humble
333	*now* a moment ago
334	*trimming up the diadem* straightening the crown
337	*'twould appear* it would be shown
338	*like sleep* as if she were asleep
340	*strong toil of grace* snare of beauty
341	*vent* discharge *blown* deposited, left on (the guard in the next speech explains what this is)
342	*like* same
347	*conclusions infinite* innumerable experiments
351	*clip* clasp, embrace
352	*High events* tragic outcomes
353	*Strike … them* are deeply felt by those who cause them
353–5	*their story … lamented* the pity that accompanies the sad story of Antony and Cleopatra is no less than the glory of the man (i.e. Caesar) who made them lamentable
358	*High … solemnity* i.e. all ceremonial rites

Although Cleopatra's death cheats Caesar of the opportunity to display her triumphantly in Rome, he shows noble qualities in offering gracious tributes to her and Antony. Antony and Cleopatra achieved their place in history, but it was Octavius Caesar who went on, as Caesar Augustus, to bring peace to the Roman world.

CAESAR   Bravest at the last,
She levelled at our purposes and, being royal,
Took her own way. The manner of their deaths?
I do not see them bleed.

DOLABELLA   Who was last with them?   330

FIRST GUARD   A simple countryman, that brought her figs.
This was his basket.

CAESAR   Poisoned then.

FIRST GUARD   O Caesar,
This Charmian lived but now – she stood and spake.
I found her trimming up the diadem
On her dead mistress. Tremblingly she stood,   335
And on the sudden dropped.

CAESAR   O noble weakness!
If they had swallowed poison, 'twould appear
By external swelling; but she looks like sleep,
As she would catch another Antony
In her strong toil of grace.

DOLABELLA   Here, on her breast,   340
There is a vent of blood, and something blown;
The like is on her arm.

FIRST GUARD   This is an aspic's trail; and these fig leaves
Have slime upon them, such as the aspic leaves
Upon the caves of Nile.

CAESAR   Most probable   345
That so she died; for her physician tells me
She hath pursued conclusions infinite
Of easy ways to die. Take up her bed,
And bear her women from the monument;
She shall be buried by her Antony.   350
No grave upon the earth shall clip in it
A pair so famous. High events as these
Strike those that make them; and their story is
No less in pity than his glory which
Brought them to be lamented. Our army shall   355
In solemn show attend this funeral,
And then to Rome. Come, Dolabella, see
High order in this great solemnity.

                             [*Exeunt*

List of other titles in this series:

2003 titles:

Henry IV Part One
Lawrence Green
0-7487-6960-9

Henry IV Part One Teacher Resource Book
Lawrence Green
0-7487-6968-4

Julius Caesar
Mark Morris
0-7487-6959-5

Julius Caesar Teacher Resource Book
Mark Morris
0-7487-6967-6

Macbeth
Dinah Jurksaitis
0-7487-6955-2

Macbeth Teacher Resource Book
Dinah Jurksaitis
0-7487-6961-7

The Merchant of Venice
Tony Farrell
0-7487-6957-9

The Merchant of Venice Teacher Resource book
Tony Farrell
0-7487-6963-3

Romeo and Juliet
Duncan Beal
0-7487-6956-0

Romeo and Juliet Teacher Resource Book
Duncan Beal
0-7487-6962-5

The Tempest
David Stone
0-7487-6958-7

The Tempest Teacher Resource Book
David Stone
0-7487-6965-X

2004 titles:

Antony and Cleopatra
Tony Farrell
0-7487-8602-3

Antony and Cleopatra Teacher Resource Book
Tony Farrell
0-7487-8606-6

A Midsummer Night's Dream
Dinah Jurksaitis
0-7487-8604-X

A Midsummer Night's Dream Teacher Resource Book
Dinah Jurksaitis
0-7487-8608-2

Much Ado About Nothing
Lawrence Green
0-7487-8607-4

Much Ado About Nothing Teacher Resource Book
Lawrence Green
0-7487-8603-1

Othello
Steven Croft
0-7487-8601-5

Othello Teacher Resource Book
Steven Croft
0-7487-8605-8